THE BEST OF LAKEWOOD PUBLISHING
STRATEGIES & TECHNIQUES FOR MANAGERS & TRAINERS

MANAGING TRAINING IN THE ORGANIZATION

BOOK I

The Influential Training Leader

Third Edition

*Compiled By DAVE ZIELINSKI
from articles that have been published in*

TRAINING
The Magazine Covering the Human Side of Business

and

Training Directors' Forum Newsletter

Lakewood Publications

The Complete New Training Library:

Book 1 *Basic Training: The Language of Corporate Education*
Book 2 *Adult Learning in Your Classroom*
Book 3 *The Best of Creative Training Techniques*
Book 4 *Designing Training for Results*
Book 5 *The Training Mix: Choosing and Using Media and Methods*
Book 6 *Managing Training in the Organization, Book I*
Book 7 *Managing Training in the Organization, Book II*
Book 8 *Delivering Training: Mastery in the Classroom*
Book 9 *Evaluating Training's Impact*
Book 10 *Using Technology-Delivered Learning*
Book 11 *The Effective Performance Consultant*
Book 12 *Making Training Pay Off On the Job*

Bulk reprints of individual articles may be quoted and purchased through:

Reprint Services
315 Fifth Avenue N.W.
St. Paul, MN 55112
(800) 707-7798 or (612) 633-0578

LAKEWOOD BOOKS
50 South Ninth Street
Minneapolis, MN 55402
(800) 707-7769 or (612) 333-0471
Fax: (612) 333-6526
Web Page Address: http://www.lakewoodpub.com

Editorial Director: Linda Klemstein
Editor: Dave Zielinski
Production Editor: Susan Abbott
Production Manager: Pat Grawert
Cover Design: Julie Tilka
Proofreaders: Becky Wilkinson and Julie Maas

Contents of this book copyrighted ©1996 by Lakewood Publications, Minneapolis, MN 55402. All rights reserved. No part of this publication may be reproduced, stored in a retrieval system, or transmitted in any form or by any means, electronic, mechanical, photocopying, recording, or otherwise, without the prior written permission of the publisher. Printed in the United States of America.

Lakewood Publications, Inc. is a subsidiary of VNU/USA. Lakewood Publications, Inc. publishes TRAINING Magazine, Presentations magazine, Training Directors' Forum Newsletter, Creative Training Techniques Newsletter, The Lakewood Report On Technology for Learning Newsletter, Potentials In Marketing magazine, and other business periodicals, books, research, and conducts conferences.

ISBN 0-943210-54-2

10 9 8 7 6 5 4 3 2 1

PREFACE

THE NEW TRAINING LIBRARY

Contemporary training and performance improvement ideas, strategies and techniques for managers and HRD professionals

Welcome to *The New Training Library*. Before you read on, there are a few things you should know about this series of books and how it came into existence.

Each book in *The New Training Library* contains articles originally published in *TRAINING Magazine*, *The Training Directors' Forum Newsletter*, *Creative Training Techniques Newsletter*, or *The Lakewood Report On Technology for Learning Newsletter*, all Lakewood publications that explore contemporary human resources development issues, trends and ideas from different angles and perspectives. While there is some overlap among the books in the series, each of them stands on its own.

Our editors selected articles to illuminate a particular theme or subject area — from the dynamics of adult occupational learning, to designing cost-effective training programs, to powerful performance consulting, to measuring training's ROI. And more.

The pervasive style of the selected articles is that of magazine and newsletter journalism, opinion and commentary. In this accessible, nonacademic style, the authors address the real and immediate challenges you face as practicing HRD professionals or as managers and motivators of people.

The edited articles are contained between the covers of the books in *The New Training Library*. Not, to repeat, as the definitive texts or final words on any one subject area, but as books that serve a different and (depending upon who you are) maybe even more useful purpose.

As the training profession evolves, it demands a solid understanding of the original ideas, theories and systems that shaped its development. Today's training professionals also must be prepared to absorb, assimilate and put into perspective an astonishing amount of new information. Like doctors, lawyers, bankers or other professionals, HRD professionals can never stop learning. Not if they want to be effective. Certainly not if they want to get ahead.

The publications that form the core of *The New Training Library* have become among the most widely read and influential in the field because their editors have never forgotten that fundamental need. In addition to featuring the best writers, theorists and practitioners in HRD, each publication also meets the HRD professional's need to understand the newest techniques, strategies and approaches to tough workplace challenges within the context of the established body of HRD knowledge.

Thus, each publication I've discussed here is carefully balanced to appeal to relative novices in HRD as well as to seasoned professionals. And so are the books in *The New Training Library*, which represents a comprehensive and systematic collection of current ideas and practical responses to meeting workplace challenges (in many cases, articulated by those who first formulated them) within the context of HRD's most enduring, time-tested fundamentals. In other words, these books manage to be both timeless and relevant to the challenges you now face in the rapidly evolving American workplace.

Plus, the books in *The New Training Library* are designed so you can find useful information fast. And with that information, you probably can meet a challenge, solve a problem or defuse a crisis right away. It's a fact that HRD changes constantly, especially today. But I think you'll find, due to the care with which the contents of these books were selected and to the editorial strengths of the publications in which this material first appeared, *The New Training Library* series will be as useful many years from now as it is today.

Philip Jones
Editorial Director
Lakewood Publications

TABLE OF CONTENTS

CHAPTER 1

Strategic Thinking and Planning

The Training Manager In the '90s 3
    By Bob Filipczak

A Trainer's Guide to Business Problems 7
    By Tom Kramlinger

Training and OD: Separated at Birth? 11
    By Allison Rossett
- Tactics to Try, Land Mines to Leap
When Moving from Training to 'Performance' Focus / *Dave Zielinski*

Reengineering the Training Department 17
    By Beverly Geber
- How the Trainer's Job Changes

10 Ways to Undermine Your HRD Effort 23
    By Ron Zemke
- 10 Ways to Blunt the HRD Effort

Is 'Just Training' Enough? 27
    By Stephen P. Becker

Decentralizing Training 29
    By Brian McDermott

Centralizing Training 33
    By Richard D. Bowser

What's Wrong With Corporate Training? 35
    By Gloria Cosgrove and Roy Speed

The Training Control Room: Creating Your Vision 39
    By Martin M. Broadwell

4 Ways You Can Make Training a Strategic Business Imperative 41
    By Dave Zielinski

Working With Top Management 43
    By Brian McDermott

Do We Still Need Formal T&D? 47
    By Dave Zielinski

2 Case Studies Show How Training
Can Play Major Role in a Restructuring 49
    By Dave Zielinski
       • 5 Ways Training Can Aid Downsizing Efforts

CHAPTER 2

Partnering With Line Management

Marketing Training to Management 53
    By Brian McDermott
       • Sprint Turns to 'Account Managers' to Help
         Market its Training Services / *Dave Zielinski*

Power Brokering in Training 57
    By Larry Winters and Jo Dimino

Added-Value Negotiating 61
    By Karl Albrecht and Steve Albrecht

What to Avoid When Shifting from Training
to Performance Consulting 65
    By Dave Zielinski
       • Performance Technology Best Sold to
         Line Managers in 'Plain Brown Wrapper'

Improving the Status of Training 67
    By Brian McDermott
       • 7 Worthwhile and Overlooked Reasons
         Your Execs Should Invest Time in Training / *Tom Brown*

Overcoming Management's Training Fears 71
    By Salvatore V. Didato
       • Trainees, Too, Fear Training

Fighting Resistance to Training 73
    By Stephen P. Becker

Gaining Power for Training 75
    By Brian McDermott

Tools and Ideas to Help You Pick and Prepare
Teams of Line Managers 77
    By Dave Zielinski

A Manager for All Seasons 79
    By Neil A. Stroul

CHAPTER 3

Tracking Business Trends and Issues

Watching the Fads for Ideas That Won't Fade 85
   By Brian McDermott

Weathering Change: Enough Already! 87
   By Bob Filipczak
     • Those Resistant (Fill in the Blank)
     • Just Say 'No?'

7 Keys to Successful Change 93
   By Clay Carr

You're On Your Own: Training, Employability,
and the New Employment Contract 97
   By Bob Filipczak

Do-It-Yourself Career Development 103
   By Robert Tucker and Milan Moravec

Why I Despair for the HR Profession 105
   By Alan Weiss

From Paternalism to Stewardship 109
   By Peter Block

Critical Mass: Putting Whole-Systems Thinking Into Practice 113
   By Bob Filipczak
     • The Triple 7: A Model for Large-Group Meetings
     • Critical Mass Models

The Case for Using Personality Tests in Training 121
   By John J. Hudy, Ronald A. Warren and Christopher W. Guest

Mentoring: The Democratic Version 125
   By Erik Gunn
     • Mentoring Do's and Don'ts

CHAPTER 1

STRATEGIC THINKING AND PLANNING

The Training Manager in the '90s

How can training directors build a new image and establish a constituency in lean, mean organizations?

BY BOB FILIPCZAK

The simple, short answer to the above question is: business savvy. According to experts and practitioners, training directors will need a head for business if they are to survive the turbulent times of the present and the future.

Does that mean knowing the business objectives already established by the executive committee? Definitely. Does it mean spending more time with rank-and-file workers and line managers, getting one's hands dirty with the business of production, marketing and sales? Probably. Does it mean lobbying and petitioning to get "top-management support" for whatever training programs one is currently running, however tenuous their connection to the organization's strategy or its key goals? Definitely not.

According to a number of experts in the training field, a solid understanding of the goals, processes and operations of the organization will be the real "core competency" of the people who run tomorrow's corporate training departments.

There may be more at stake here than simple job security. As training and human-performance issues become increasingly vital to corporate success, training directors who are focused on the right issues could become central figures in the enterprises of the '90s. In fact, the training manager's job may well become the next steppingstone to the CEO's chair, predicts Bob Mager of Mager Associates in Carefree, AZ, a charter member of the HRD (human resources development) Hall of Fame.

Now, that would be a switch. The position of training director — i.e., the manager of the training department and the people working therein — has come a long way in the last few decades. Alan Weiss, president of the Summit Consulting Group in East Greenwich, RI, contends that 20 years ago, the prevailing stereotype of a training director was often valid: He was a bothersome employee — say, a loyal but burned-out sales manager no longer making his quota—who was dumped into a department where he couldn't do much harm.

Today, Weiss observes, training departments generally are staffed by professionals who know adult-learning theory and how to deliver effective instruction. But somewhere along the way, he says, many training careerists were led astray by that professionalism. Their devotion to their own proprietary bodies of knowledge caused them to take their eyes off the ball — to forget that the point of employer-sponsored training is to make the organization more successful. In short, a lot of training professionals got sidetracked into the esoterica of whole-brain theory, egalitarian management models, and four-style personality tests. "[People] write about stewardship and servant leadership — it's all nonsense," Weiss says. "Are there germs of good ideas there? Of course there are. But do you build training programs around them? Do you equip your whole company to identify people's social styles? Of course not."

No Respect

If it is still true that training directors "can't get no respect," there may be a variety of reasons for it. David Brinkerhoff is president of Abbott Smith Associates, a Millbrook, NY, head-hunting firm that specializes in the human-resources area, finding training and personnel managers for client companies. According to Brinkerhoff, the title "training manager" is itself a handicap. The training department is unique in the business world, he says. A "training manager," especially in smaller companies, often is nothing of the kind.

"Thirty percent of the people who have the training-manager title don't manage anything other than a program they are doing at the moment," he says. They don't manage any people, and they don't manage a real budget. So, asks Brinkerhoff, how can they call themselves managers?

Another problem: training directors who are so focused on administering the training function they lose touch with the real business of the organization. Weiss says he tried to persuade one training director to become immersed in the organization's business, but the manager was more worried about processing all of his paperwork. "He's not even concerned about the trees in the forest. He's concerned about the leaves on the trees because he has no larger frame of reference," says Weiss.

Brinkerhoff adds that there's a lot of insecurity among training professionals in general. That's not surprising since, as he points out, the training department doesn't really *produce* anything. Nevertheless, other staff functions (like accounting) don't share this insecurity. Accountants don't agonize about "selling" the value of accounting services to their companies' top executives; those services are recognized as an integral part of the organization's effectiveness. Brinkerhoff declares himself fed up with going to training conferences that offer sessions about how to sell training to top management. If training isn't as essential to your organization as accounting, he argues, then your training department is probably focused on the wrong issues.

Dave Lamb, assistant vice president for information-technology education for Aetna Life & Casualty Inc., the Hartford, CT-based insurance company, opines that many training directors *should* be insecure because they don't understand the business they are in. They are the people most likely to complain that they can't get any support from top executives and to voice the often-heard claim that training is the first thing cut when

The New Training Library — *Managing Training in the Organization – Book I* 3 times get tough.

That latter claim was refuted by research conducted by TRAINING Magazine in 1987, 1991 and 1992. In all cases, the magazine found that training departments generally suffer no more than other functions when downsizings or budget cuts are under way. In fact, compared with other functions, the training department was more likely to be treated with unusual gentleness.

Claims of lopsided trimming of training people raise a red flag for Brinkerhoff. More times than not, he says, a training department that gets cut to the bone was inept at what it was supposed to be doing. He says he often gets a call within four months from a company that decimated its training department; management wants him to find a new group of people to oversee training.

A number of training veterans agree that "top-management support" is something of a red herring. The sign of an effective training department, they argue, is that it attracts the active support of line managers, not necessarily top executives. Says Mary Broad, a former training director of a federal government agency and currently a consultant in Chevy Chase, MD: "Unless we have a champion...unless there's somebody who truly cares and is an advocate, we probably shouldn't be doing [any given program]. We're probably only doing it out of habit."

If the training you're conducting is truly addressing a business need, she says, you won't need to fight for it.

It's Business, Stupid

In general, being a business-minded training director means developing a better understanding of the direction your organization is headed and aligning your training initiatives with the business goals established to get it there. In many ways, says Weiss, an astute training manager possesses the same skills as any good manager from any other department in the company.

He considers these generic management skills a beginning point for any director of training: good judgment, good strategic thinking, and the ability to cope with ambiguity, to develop the people you manage, to exemplify the values of the organization, and to deal with numbers as well as people. Brinkerhoff agrees, adding that "it's difficult to find a good training manager because if you look at the set of skills that are needed for managers — accounting, dealing with the budgets, keeping track of projects — some of [those skills are] not what makes a good stand-up trainer."

Weiss and others insist that management skills ought to be the first priority in selecting a training director. Knowledge of training and adult learning is secondary, he says, because an astute manager can pick up what she needs to know about training pretty quickly. As Lamb puts it, "This isn't rocket scientist stuff."

> "You can't be really great at HR — if that's your only frame of reference."

Another important selection criterion: As part of building a more pragmatic training department, the director has to have the ability to forge links with customers — the line managers and others who request training. According to a study by Wm. Schiemann & Associates, most training departments are still a far cry from being genuinely customer-focused. In that study, only 21 percent of 841 respondents rated their companies' training departments favorably in the area of internal customer service.

Lamb considers delivering good service to different units of the organization the best way to align training with the organization's goals. "We have to look beyond our discipline," he says. The training department must be able to speak the same language as the departments it services.

Get Out Of Dodge

The need to look beyond the sometimes narrow focus of training and development is one of the key areas of agreement among the consultants and training directors to whom we spoke. To some, that means literally leaving the training department for stints in marketing, engineering or production. To others, it means climbing down into the trenches on the front lines of the company. Still others suggest that moving "businesspeople" from other areas of the company into the training department is another way to make training more vital to the organization.

Weiss is the most ardent critic of training directors who have grown up in the HRD department. He argues that most training and human-resources departments are too insulated from the rest of the organization, which contributes to the lack of business sense he observes in training directors. "You can't be really great at HR if that's your only frame of reference," he declares.

The best alternative to sending a training director out into the real world is to bring in some managers from other units of the company. Lamb admits he was a bit concerned during a reengineering process at Aetna when managers who knew nothing about training were assigned to the department. But the managers were so sharp and picked up on things so fast that Lamb quickly reconsidered. He came to see them as important instruments for injecting some business savvy into the HRD staff.

Brinkerhoff agrees that bringing non-training people into a training department introduces fresh perspectives. When outsiders arrive, important questions about training get asked, he says.

At the same time, training careerists need to get out and build relationships with line managers and front-line workers. Direct ties with the company's operations areas expand the training department's parochial view of who needs to learn what and how. Otherwise, says Lamb, "I can go off in a corner for a year or two and come out with this great and wonderful curriculum. We shouldn't be surprised if our customer says, 'What the hell is this? How do I know it will work?'"

Training directors who get out into the operations of a company and (dare we say?) actively "partner" with line managers who have real performance problems begin to evolve into a different kind of animal. A good sign that a training director is evolving in this manner is that he begins to see a lot of problems to which training is *not* the answer, says Brad Spencer, a principal with Spencer, Shenk, Capers and Associates, a consulting firm in Gardena, CA.

When training directors start moving away from traditional HRD and toward developing performance solutions for their company, they start to become what Mager calls performance directors. A performance director has a good idea what's happening in all areas of the company because she has been involved in projects at every organizational level. And that's the future — if there is one — for training directors, says Brinkerhoff.

From HRD to CEO?

While there is general agreement that most training directors currently aren't up-to-speed as business-savvy managers, big things may be in store for those who are clearly focused on the performance goals of their organizations.

Brinkerhoff predicts that the title "training director" will be all but extinct five years from now, primarily because that role will no longer be required in the dramatically changed organizations of the future. But that is not necessarily bad news. Weiss, too, envisions a migration of training responsibility away from the centralized HRD department. Training will become the responsibility of line managers, he says, while the training director — whatever the title — will help them do the training right. "I think the training director needs to be a catalyst for all of these human-resource managers — namely every manager in the organization — so they can better educate their people." That obviously implies a very high-level person.

Bob Mager goes even further in his predictions for training directors who have shed their traditional mantles and evolved into performance directors. He ventures that they could be the next generation of CEOs in corporate America.

Mager sees the changing pedigrees of CEOs throughout the history of business as a progression of the prevailing values. In the beginning, the CEO was the entrepreneur who started the company. After the founder left the scene, the most knowledgeable line manager progressed into the position of chief executive. As the business community changed its focus, the manager in charge of finances became the next logical candidate for the corner office. When "markets" became the most important issue for companies, marketing executives stood in line to inherit the CEO position. Each step along this progression, explains Mager, occurred because the individuals chosen "knew where the bodies were buried." They had information about all aspects of the company's business and knew how to affect the most important issues.

Mager predicts that the next CEOs will be found among the people in charge of training and development, or at least among those who are actively concerned with the operations of every unit of the organization. These nontraditional training directors will have their fingers on the pulse of the most important issue in business today: human performance.

Weiss agrees that this is a strong possibility. And why not? he demands: "If your training directors can't grow to be senior managers, then what you've said is, 'This is a dead-end job and we want mediocre people.'" He cites a recent case in which Merck & Co., the pharmaceutical giant based in Rahway, NJ, promoted its senior human-resources manager to president of its Canadian operations. Lamb reports that Chrysler recently cancelled a search for a train-

---

Could the next great breeding ground for CEOs be the training department?

---

ing director on the open market, deciding instead that the position would be a two-year rotation available to senior managers who wanted to move up in the company.

How's Your Crystal Ball?

How can training directors, or performance directors, position themselves so that five years from now they look like corporate stars instead of deadwood? Let us whisper two words in your ear. The first: computers.

People have been yammering for years about the enormous significance of computers and how they will revolutionize training, but it now appears that the revolution may actually be upon us. We're finally seeing some of the payoffs that technology has promised us in the past, and training directors who want to lead their departments into the future had better keep up with technology. "If I have to start learning today, I'm dead meat," Brinkerhoff says. "If I have to start learning today, I'm five years behind...Those training managers who want to develop handbooks and workbooks or three-and-a-half-day courses might as well pack it in right now."

The best training directors today aren't just familiar with distance learning and interactive multimedia and electronic performance support, Brinkerhoff says, they are already using one or more of these technologies to leverage more training out of their departments.

The second word: precognition. Call it anticipation, call it a sixth sense of the way the wind is blowing and the next change that will sweep over the organization. In a focus group at the National Society of Performance and Instruction's April convention in San Francisco, several training directors agreed that staying ahead of this thing called "change" is the most challenging part of their jobs. At its best, a training department will not only manage the change in its own field of expertise, it will also help the entire organization adapt to constant change.

And at its worst, the training function will be caught behind the eight ball. Brinkerhoff cites the example of a company that spent $500,000 to develop a course in sales training only to realize that it wouldn't have salespeople anymore. Computers at the point of purchase in retail stores automatically forwarded orders for new stock when the bar scanners registered a certain number of sales. Consequently, the company in question, which sold merchandise to these stores, didn't need salespeople to fill orders anymore.

In the final analysis, an effective training director has to evolve into a performance consultant, no longer as concerned about training per se as about the performance of the company and its individual contributors.

Spencer adds one more competency for a successful training director that probably won't show up on most lists: energy. Good training directors, he argues, have to possess a tremendous amount of energy to juggle the balls that are continually thrown to them. Add to that, he says, a love for what they are doing — because no amount of money can compensate for the amount of work a successful training director winds up doing.

A Trainer's Guide to Business Problems

You've whipped up some lovely ROI projections but management still won't fund your course? Drop the calculator. What you need is a compass.

BY TOM KRAMLINGER

If you want training to be taken seriously in your company, stop trying to teach people things that are "nice to know," and start focusing all of your programs on key business problems.

How many times have you heard that one?

Often enough to be thunderingly bored, growls the veteran training professional — namely you.

Where is the so-called insight in this old chestnut, you demand? The vast majority of corporate training programs have always addressed business problems. Isn't it self-evident that competent workers make a business more productive? Train the sales force and sales go up; train the managers and turnover goes down; we've just solved two business problems. Most of us have always done our best to improve the bottom line. Only the naive, the overcomfortable and the knuckleheaded have *ever* championed training programs on grounds that they'd be "nice to do."

Right you are, oh, clever one. I'll bet you've even submitted a formal cost-benefit analysis for at least one of your new programs.

But the thing is...did you notice how your company's senior executives reacted? Did they fall over in amazement? Did they invite you into the inner circle? Did they bless the project and bite their nails waiting to see the return on investment? Or did they just shrug? Maybe you got a patronizing nod for the nice numbers?

Here's why: Business leaders don't care deeply about just any contribution to the bottom line. They only care about the ones that are important at the moment — the ones sometimes called critical success factors.

I knew that, you scoff. That's exactly why savvy trainers always hitch the training buggy to the theme of the year, despite all the finger-waggers telling them not to. Five years ago it was "excellence," and before that it was computerization.

Ah, now we're getting down to it. You're right again, of course. Computerization and quality represent very real business concerns — as is frequently the case with bandwagons in the corporate world. When training serves these powerful trends, it is clearly solving business problems. Jumping on a bandwagon is not necessarily the moral failing it is so often portrayed to be.

No, the real trouble is that training professionals are often too far downstream from these major trends (or crucial success factors, if you will) to do anything but react to them. "Hey," someone says, "did you hear that total quality management is in? Let's whip up (or buy) some courses in statistical process control and team problem solving."

Our friends here may be solving a business problem, all right, but do they understand *why* TQM is a business solution? Can they predict what the next bandwagon will look like and when it will rumble through?

Lost Without a Compass?

Our main difficulty as training professionals is that we generally don't know what a business problem is until some business leader tells us. We don't have a model or template to help us recognize one when we see it. Our lack of understanding about the dynamics of business prevents us from being part of the upstream dialogue and providing the right training just when it is needed. If this weren't so, we wouldn't hear so many complaints about our outmoded curricula or wonder why our business-unit customers go around us to make or buy their own training.

Before we continue, here's a little pre-test:

Consider "globalization." Is globalization a business problem? Certainly it's a problem for some companies — we read about it all the time in business and training journals — but is it a real business problem for your organization? Should you prepare some training for it? If so, for what segment of the employee population? What skills should be taught? And how will you know if this training has helped solve the problem?

That's all for the pre-test. We'll look again at globalization later. But this brings up a pesky aspect of business problems. They change a lot. We listen as our business leaders wax eloquent about some issue; they sure talk about it as if it were a business problem. So we read up and try to "get on top of this one" with some proactive training. Then — poof! — it disappears from their vocabulary. No wonder bandwagons have a bad reputation.

Why does this happen? I think it's because executives need to be both forward-thinking and business-responsive. They need to try on new ideas, but they also need to assess the impact of these ideas on the business. Executives have an inner compass that eventually tells them what the impact will be and whether real energy should be invested. (The good executive's compass works better than the poor one's, but that's beside the point.) In the meantime, they toy with the idea, "waxing eloquent" in order to build up some advance readiness so they can jump on it if necessary. If their inner compass eventually reads "no impact," they retreat and divert resources to wherever the compass shows a real need for action.

If we could get a better sense of how that compass works, maybe our requests to help with the navigation would get a friendlier hearing. We might not become "business leaders" (I certainly don't claim to be one), but we could be part of the dialogue and have a better chance of focusing our training efforts on the real business problems of our organizations.

The Business Compass

The purpose of a compass is to lead you in the direction you want to go. The purpose of the business compass is to lead the company toward profit and away from loss, toward revenue and away from expenses. A 10 percent to 20 percent tilt toward the profit side is considered good. Anything over that is considered terrific.

Every school kid knows that, you say.

Yes, but to think effectively in business terms, it's necessary to elevate your perspective to the level of the whole business. Is the *business* making or losing money? This is why it's possible to produce figures showing that some training project will generate a 20-to-1 return on investment and still not have your project taken seriously. Your $500,000 return may be only a drop in the bucket compared to some $100 million risk for the business as a whole. To address business problems on a level that truly commands top management's attention, your project can't just be about making money. It has to be about solving the problems that challenge the health of the business as a whole: problems that affect the overall balance of revenues over expenses.

The four points on the business compass derive from the fundamental nature of a free-enterprise business. A business is an organization that acquires resources at a cost and offers them as a value in the market such that customers are willing to part with revenue to obtain that value. A friend of mine owns an ice cream shop, part of a national franchise operation. His business depends on acquiring resources (the franchise, the shop, ice cream, employees, etc.) and presenting them in the market (coupons, displays, hours, location, etc.) so that customers will come in and pay money (revenue) to enjoy his tasty confections (value).

To get the full picture, we need to remember that free-market customers are fickle and will go elsewhere if they don't like their experience with the product. Thus the revenue side depends as much on satisfying customers as it does on attracting them in the first place. As Peter Drucker puts it, "The purpose of a business is to get and keep customers."

From this understanding we can plot the four cardinal points on the business compass:
- Acquiring customers.
- Satisfying customers.
- Capacity (maintaining adequate resources).
- Productivity (controlling costs).

These are the north, south, east and west of a business. There are, of course, many other factors to consider (raising capital, exercising leadership, serving the community), but the four-point model is fundamental and robust enough to give us our bearings in the big bad world of business. It labels the dreams and nightmares that keep executives awake at night — and what they really want to talk about when you are presenting a training proposal.

The accompanying figure uses the four points to locate some of the many trends and business problems we hear about today.

Types of Business Problems

Let's look at the four categories individually.

Customer Acquisition

The first problem of a business is to attract some customers. To paraphrase the movie line, you can build it, but if they don't come, you haven't got a business. Without dependable revenues you can't cover your costs, and revenues come from customers. Business leaders sleep better at night when they see the revenue trend growing from quarter to quarter, from year to year. Increasing revenues mean a positive trend in customer acquisition. In a free market where customers have a choice of several suppliers, business leaders also look at market share. A downward trend here signals a weakness in customer acquisition.

Two factors make up a company's strength in acquiring customers: the value of the product or service, and the ability to communicate that value to the customer. Thus, the customer-acquisition dimension has two subordinate groups of related business problems:

Product value: innovation, enhancement, line extension, acquisition, pricing or any other means of making sure the product line meets customer needs as well as or better than the competition.

Sales effectiveness: advertising, marketing, territory coverage, sales skills and any other means of assuring that customers *perceive* the value of the offer in spite of the claims of the competition.

In training terms, we are talking about people's ability, for example, to innovate, make good pricing decisions and sell effectively.

Customer Satisfaction

A business that loses too many customers is on a dangerous and exhausting treadmill. It must continually

---

FOUR TYPES OF BUSINESS PROBLEMS

PRODUCTIVITY	ACQUIRING CUSTOMERS
More with less	Differentiation
Lean and mean	Product diversity
Cost reduction	Innovation
Efficiency	Positioning/brand recognition
Reduced cycle time	Competitive advantage
Downsizing	Sales effectiveness
Teamwork	Market strategy
Measure: Profitability and cost-per-unit	*Measure: Revenues and market share*
CAPACITY	**SATISFYING CUSTOMERS**
Availability of raw material	Service quality
Labor pool (size and talents)	Responsiveness
Work-force diversity/capability	Switching costs
Core competencies	Value added
Cross-functional alignment	Customer focus
Coordination	Changing expectations
Supplier partnerships	Mass customization
Measure: Units-per-time and inventory	*Measure: Satisfaction scores and retention*

attract new customers just to stay even, but it can't really stay even because attracting new customers is more expensive than selling to old ones. The numbers that executives look at here are customer satisfaction scores and retention rates.

Assuming a product that performs as promised, there are two subordinate problems to worry about most:

Changing expectations. Customers may somehow change what they expect, making it more difficult to please them. Thus, any process or means that can anticipate, monitor, manage, educate or shape these expectations is important.

Lackluster performance. This one includes any mistake, failure, indifference or lack of attention or follow-up that causes the customer to be underwhelmed or that raises the appeal of switching to another supplier.

Common training goals in this area involve things like helping employees understand customer expectations, and teaching them to perform superlative service.

Maintaining Capacity

Another friend of mine, a senior vice president of a small company, was flying back from a sales call on AT&T. He turned to the production manager, who had made a strong impression during the call, and said, "What did we get ourselves into? Are you sure we can do this?"

Business worry number three: having the capacity and resources to deliver the goods.

The key measures here are units-per-time (How much stuff can you produce in an hour, a month, a year?) and inventory. The two main subordinate issues are:

Availability. Can we get the resources we need in order to meet our commitments? The question covers worries about shortages, the talent base, the labor pool, equipment failures and the like.

Coordination. This is the intangible management and cultural factor. How well do people communicate and align themselves on getting the job done and done right?

Here we begin to see the interrelationship of the different kinds of business problems. One of the biggest communication worries in business involves matching capacity to demand. The whole thing hinges on forecasting demand, which is why stomachs churn every year at budget time. That's when business leaders peer into the crystal ball and estimate how much capacity to fund (budget) in light of their best guesses about demand. The naive think about budgets in terms of funding their projects — a matter of slicing up the pie. The savvy think about budgets in terms of matching capacity to demand. If you can relate your favorite project (from literacy training to executive learning labs) to easing this pain, you'll find yourself on the inside track.

Jumping on a bandwagon is not necessarily the moral failing it is so often portrayed to be.

Productivity

Productivity relates to the cost of resources, or capacity. The idea is to get the most output for the least cost — to do more with less. Some people resent the terms used to measure productivity: cost per unit, worker hours per widget and profitability. To be part of the dialogue and decision making, we have to accept the legitimacy of the need to find an optimal balance among these factors.

The subordinate problems that business leaders worry about most are:

Cost of resources. The company wants to pay no more than the current market value for supplies, material, facilities, equipment and labor.

Waste. This can be any unnecessary cost due to inefficiency, downtime, scrap, overstocking, duplication, bottlenecks, cycle time, poor process design, disempowerment, bureaucratic red tape, etc.

In trainer's language these translate into worries about people's ability to plan effectively, research the best prices, work efficiently or implement good ideas.

It's also important to see how productivity connects to other points on the compass, particularly around the issue of matching capacity to demand. When do they cut the budget or ask for extra efficiencies? Whenever revenues aren't up to forecast — especially in the last two quarters. Productivity is the safety valve for poor planning.

Becoming a Business Problem

Now that we have our bearings, we can see how an issue becomes a business problem. Take quality, for example. In the 1960s and early '70s, product quality was not a particularly serious business problem. On the contrary, it was often seen as the enemy of productivity — just an extra cost that wasn't needed to acquire or retain customers. But when off-shore competitors hit the market with cheaper and better products, the compass needle started spinning and all points went on red alert. Today quality is a paramount business problem because:

• It takes quality products to attract customers.
• It takes quality products to keep customers happy.
• Quality process control assures reliable capacity.
• Continuous improvement results in productivity gains.

Those are the real reasons — the business reasons — why quality is a powerful bandwagon for training.

Post-test

So... what about globalization? Is it a business problem? Is it something to which you ought to hitch your training wagon?

Clearly, it's not a pressing business issue if all your customers and resources are domestic. But if your company extends across borders, then globalization brings an escalation of scope and complexity to the four primary business problems:

Acquiring customers. Globalization is a business problem to the degree that different national markets require different products (value) or tactics (sales effectiveness) to attract customers. Do your executives worry about employees' ability to compete in international markets? If so, you've got a business problem, one you might treat with special courses on innovation or sales effectiveness.

Customer satisfaction. The problem is to understand and fulfill the nuances of customer expectations in different cultures. Are your people all over the globe equipped to do that job? If not, you may be able to help with customer service training.

Capacity. Here the problem is how best to acquire, deploy and coordinate far-flung resources. From a human resources and training point of view, the key issue is coordination — the management of information and people. Are your executives concerned about getting employees around the world to work more effectively together and leverage one another's talents? Can you help with training on alignment, teamwork or planning?

Productivity. The corporation wants to take advantage of the least expensive resources in different parts of the world without harming overall capacity or adding wasteful duplication. These cost savings can only be realized if your people in various countries have the necessary skills and commitment — skills and commitment that you might be able to supply.

If top management is worried about these questions, and you see a way for training to help, then globalization is a business problem you can sink your teeth into. And so it is with any issue that floats across the horizon.

Suppose you're at a meeting in a lavish corner office, and the bigwigs are spouting business-school mumbo jumbo about "entrepreneurship and regaining a competitive advantage in a maturing market on the Pacific Rim." Try some clarifying questions from your understanding of the compass to penetrate the fog and hone in on the real business problems.

"So what you're saying," you ask, "is that we're having a harder time attracting customers in that market?"

"Yes," they agree.

"And the reason is that potential customers don't see the value of our product. Is that right?"

"That's right."

"Do you think the problem is with the product itself or with our people's ability to project its value against the competition?"

"A little of both," they say.

"Well, I've got some ideas about how we can address these problems with training..."

Now you're talking business!

Notes:

Training and OD: Separated at Birth?

For all their similarity of interests, training and OD are like feuding siblings who don't speak. It's time they started.

BY ALLISON ROSSETT

On an airplane somewhere between Denver and San Diego, an executive mused about why his training people and his organization development people couldn't seem to work together. He thought he was encouraging collaboration, but what he saw instead was foot-dragging.

"Is it something about our organization?" he wondered. "Is it something I'm doing? Is it the individuals involved? Or is this typical?" His questions forced me to admit that I think a gulf indeed exists between training and organization development (OD), at least more typically than not.

I first noticed the chasm more than a decade ago. During a consulting project at a manufacturing company, the training staff complained at length about a manager they considered unreasonable. Without exception, they attributed her faults to her background in OD.

Not long after, I suggested to a group of colleagues that we all attend an American Society for Training and Development (ASTD) luncheon presentation on the topic of organization development. Several of my training associates chose to pass, observing that OD wasn't particularly relevant to training.

Yet another example presented itself about five years ago. I was teaching a class on needs assessment for some training professionals in a computer company. One of the messages was that the data one gathers in assessing a performance problem will often point to solutions other than training — solutions like team-building, culture change, strategy alignment or feedback systems. One gentleman objected, arguing pretty much as follows: "I have a problem with this because we don't know about all those approaches. We aren't the people who handle any of that. We don't work with them. They aren't even located anywhere near us." There were nods all around. In a room with about 30 managers, nobody disagreed.

Such has been my experience of the relationship between the training world and the OD world. So the phone call from Sandy Quesada not long ago came as a surprise. Quesada was then a training manager at Amoco Corp. in Houston. She remembered that I'd been tracking the peculiarities between training and organization development, and wanted to know if I'd play a role in getting Amoco's training and OD units to work together more closely. (Didn't I think that their shared commitment to analysis might be a good place to start?) Within the month, someone at another company, this time in financial services, called to chat about a similar initiative.

Suddenly people are interested in collaboration between training and organization development. Why now? Maybe it's the quality movement with its belief in cross-functionality. Maybe there's growing recognition that what counts is results, and that business results depend upon alignment between what people are taught and what organizations actually practice and applaud. Maybe it's a newfound inclination to use systematic assessments to define solutions to performance problems. Maybe it's renewed customer focus. Maybe "performance technology" is finally shifting from idea to reality. Or maybe it's the collective impact of years of wasted opportunities. Whatever the causes, there is growing enthusiasm for aligning OD and training.

How might we go about that?

What They Do

Just what is organization development? Plenty of definitions can be found among practitioners and in the literature. (Lee Bolman and Terrence Deal's *Reframing Organizations* and Michael Harrison's *Diagnosing Organizations* are two favorite sources.) But the only way to achieve much agreement on a single definition is to sketch very broadly and, consequently, not very usefully: OD involves attention to diagnosis, strategy, roles, systems, processes and measurements that enable organizations and people to achieve their goals.

A more useful question is: What do OD professionals do? Here we can draw a more robust picture. Some create high-commitment work teams, an effort that often involves rethinking leadership and power relationships. Others participate in projects that transform organizational structures, beliefs, values, cultures and systems. OD people use a wide array of interventions, including leadership development, team-building, organizational design, culture change, strategic planning, facilitation of meetings and groups, conflict resolution, enhanced participation programs and performance management.

What, then, is training? *Webster's* defines it this way: "...to make a person or animal efficient in some activity by instruction and repeated practice..." Somehow that fails to capture the richness of the field I know and love.

So what do trainers do? Most analyze needs. Some build training courses. Others deliver courses. Some coordinate people and facilities. Many create instructor-led programs; some create self-study programs in print and technology-based formats. Trainers conduct evaluations, create job aids and electronic performance support systems, build multimedia products, serve as performance consultants, select and coordinate training vendors, coach employees in the workplace, establish on-the-job development programs and more.

Siblings...

Trouble is, every time I assign an activity to training or to organization development, I can think of an example that contradicts the classification — a training manager whose life is devoted to team-building or an OD person who is a skilled course developer or instructor. In many ways, training and OD professionals are siblings:

Both traffic in change. Training and OD practitioners agree that they have responsibility for growing their people and organizations, for playing significant roles in transformation. Amoco has now established an entity called the Organizational Capability Group (OCG), charged with coordinating efforts to bring about corporate change. Training and organization development are but two of many specialized units formally linked to enhance initiatives aimed at performance improvement. Says Katie Smith, practice area leader for instructional systems development (ISD) at Amoco: "When it first happened, I didn't have a clue about how it could work. Since OCG, many of our OD consultants are now in long-term productive relationships with a single client, and they are right there and positioned to leverage training and the other OCG service units."

Both are driven by clients' needs for improved performance. Whether the request is for a course on Lotus Notes or a curriculum to update the skills of auditors or assistance with strategic planning, training and OD professionals perceive themselves as responding to and serving their customers' articulated requirements.

Both acknowledge responsibility for customer education and business partnership. While being responsive to the needs that customers express, most trainers and OD people agree to some responsibility for developing the customer's understanding of performance improvement and, therefore, the accuracy of customers' perceptions of their own needs. In other words, professionals in both fields believe that the customer is not always right. More, they believe that ethical

---

TACTICS TO TRY, LAND MINES TO LEAP WHEN MOVING FROM TRAINING TO 'PERFORMANCE' FOCUS

BY DAVE ZIELINSKI

At a recent *Training Directors' Forum* conference in Tempe, AZ, performance consulting guru Dana Gaines Robinson, president of Partners in Change, described some tactics used in successful transitions from a traditional training to a "performance" focus, where training becomes just one of many tools — and often, the last tool — used to attack performance problems. These tips are taken from numerous companies Robinson has worked with to help make the change.

She also pointed to some potential land mines that should be anticipated and planned for in the transition.

5 Tactics for Successful Transitions

(1) Assign staff members to specific line clients. Structure your function so each person in the role of performance consultant has specific client assignments. *These assignments should be with specific people and not just a department.* Hold your people accountable for building and maintaining a strong, ongoing partnership with these business clients.

(2) Form a strategic plan for the transition. Involve as many training staff members as possible in forming a "big picture" for the transition. This plan should identify specific actions to be taken over a three-year period. At the conclusion of each year, review the plan and adjust accordingly.

(3) Proactively identify (with care) your first performance client and project. The most difficult performance consulting project is the first one. It is important it be selected so the experience is a positive one for the client — and for your department. Ideal criteria include a client who is a thought leader in the organization, is open to collaboration, and has a business need of some significance. *This individual can become a "marketer" of the performance approach to others in your company following a successful project.*

(4) Ensure your staff is clear about job expectations. For the majority of people in the training function, the day-to-day performance requirements *will* change. Ensure everyone is clear on what they are to *begin* doing and what they are to *stop* doing.

(5) Educate other HR partners in the organization on the performance improvement process and their respective roles in that process. If there are other departments that work in support of client needs, they need to understand the new performance focus of your group. Each group's respective roles and responsibilities regarding the process (especially as it relates to supporting a shared client) must be identified.

3 Land Mines To Be Wary Of

(1) Changing skill requirements. *It's highly likely some people on your current training staff will not be appropriate individuals for the transition.* This is because the requirements for success in a performance role are much different than the requirements for success in a traditional role. *Example: People who enjoy program facilitation and design may not want to be "partners" to line managers or assessors of performance requirements/data.*

(2) Working in "two worlds" during the transition. For a period of time — perhaps as long as three years — it's possible you and your department will need to straddle two worlds, working in both a traditional manner and in a performance manner. That's because it is rarely possible to completely stop what you are currently doing. *It is vital to be alert to the possibility and lure of being "pulled back" to the traditional approach only.* In other words, you will be changing tires on a moving vehicle.

(3) Committing time required to grow relationships with clients. The amount of time required to build strong client relationships cannot be underestimated. Time is required to meet with these individuals apart from the projects, as well as with team members of the department, in order to learn more about the various "new" jobs in the function.

practice often forbids giving customers exactly what they ask for. Instead, the professional is supposed to probe and study the nature of the performance problem, and sometimes disagree with the customer's proposed solution. ("Yes, I know you want a team-building course, but the problem here seems to be fuzzy goals, not poor teamwork.") As Jeff Lickson of The Consortium, a Houston consulting firm, puts it, both trainers and OD specialists are supposed to "Just say whoa" to hasty requests.

Both are committed to assessment and measurement. OD and training professionals espouse allegiance to searching analyses, continuous measurement, and basing their recommendations on solid data. Most trainers and OD people would hesitate to admit that they based an intervention on a hunch, or on a personal preference (for multimedia or visioning or whatever), or because the boss likes it. Practitioners in both groups take pride in diagnosis. There are, of course, cases that demonstrate that this is sometimes more a goal than a description of actual practice.

Both are committed to systematic approaches. Embedded in the literature and customs of both groups is a demand that practitioners go about their business systematically instead of "winging it." They are supposed to use defined processes and orderly approaches. They should have clearly articulated goals. Their activity should be data-driven.

In addition, another mantra is enjoying rekindled allegiance — systems thinking. The systems paradigm commits the practitioner to analyzing causes, using these root causes to define strategies, and establishing cross-functional and wholistic approaches to improve performance. In the training world, systems thinking has roots in classic books and teachings by people like Robert Mager and Joe Harless. Today, readers in both the training and OD camps are embracing works such as Peter Senge's *The Fifth Discipline: The Art and Practice of the Learning Organization* and Geary Rummler's *Improving Performance: How to Manage the White Space on the Organization Chart.*

... But Not Twins

Though there are many similarities between them, OD and training professionals tend to be keenly aware of their differences. The distinctions that follow are generalizations, valuable for the discussion they encourage, not for their application to any one setting or person:

Focus of attention. Historically, trainers have prided themselves on what they can do for individuals, while OD specialists have looked more toward the entire organization. More recently, members of both groups have been talking about the need to expand their views to encompass the work, the worker and the workplace. Though alliterative and appealing, this enlargement of perspective is far from a done deal and is complicated by the emerging importance of teams. Who serves teams? While the obvious answer is that we all do, teams present opportunities for both collaboration *and* conflict between trainers and ODers.

> **"Both trainers and OD specialists are supposed to 'Just say whoa' to hasty requests."**

Nature of the customer. There is a perception that the customers associated with organization development tend to reside at higher levels in the organization. In a mixed group of training and OD professionals, one OD specialist pointed to what she saw as a difference between them: "We work with the executives and I don't think you do." While the number of exceptions to this statement is probably growing, the trainers in the room didn't disagree.

This perception doesn't encourage trust, according to Cora Pendergast, a San Diego consultant with master's degrees in both educational technology and organization development. She notes that trainers are sometimes reticent with OD people, who tend to earn more money than trainers and whose role is to assess the organization and share information with an executive.

Perception of role and power. Another perception is that OD professionals are more typically found in strategic roles while trainers labor in tactical arenas. When pressed on this, both sides do some breast-beating, with trainers acknowledging the need to be more strategic, and OD people admiring the trainers' tangible tactical successes and the customer appreciation that comes from them.

An incident during a class on how to conduct a needs assessment illustrated how the differences in perspectives can play out. The group was working on a case in which an executive sought help with what was initially described as "messed up performance appraisals." We talked for 15 minutes or so about diagnostic strategies to ferret out the nature of the problems with the appraisals, and how to determine a good solution. We were, I thought, appropriately skeptical about training as the sole solution to this appraisal problem. But then an OD specialist in the class challenged our complacency: "I think we're jumping into fixing the appraisals too quickly. Before we look at randomly pulled appraisals and model appraisals, and before we interview supervisors and so on, shouldn't we be talking to management about whether the organization ought to reconsider its approaches to hierarchy, appraisal and performance review? You're assuming the leadership knows what it's doing with its performance management strategy." And we were. Few trainers are naturally inclined to challenge the basic assumptions underlying organizational practices, to push hard at the wisdom of a request, or to provide leadership in discussions of strategy and alignment. OD people are more likely to describe that as their role.

Where we live. At Amoco and elsewhere, most organization development consultants are entrenched in long-term relationships with clients, while training professionals tend to be peripatetic, engaging in more and shorter interventions for several corporate units. One effect of this is that trainers may spend more of their time on project management and documentation, since unfamiliar clients are more likely to demand a formal rationale for any intervention and to insist on seeing some concrete evidence of success. The positive side is that these demands encourage the kind of analysis and measurement that trainers say they want to do anyway.

Areas of comfort. Suppose a needs assessment reveals that the main cause of a department's performance problem is that its manager is inconsistent and capricious. How comfortable are you about going where that data wants to take you? If you're a trainer, the answer probably is, not very. This is a rather sweeping generalization, but more OD professionals than trainers are at ease in the realm of conflict, climate and feelings.

Computer-training manager Dawn Hall of Hunter Industries in San Marcos, CA, is forthright about it. "I didn't know what organization developers did," she says, "so I couldn't figure out how to coordinate with them. Now I'm getting them involved in conflict resolution and team facilitation. They're better at it than I am." Consultant Pendergast agrees, noting that OD specialists "take more interest in personal change and attitude, while trainers tend to focus more between the ears, more on skills acquisition."

Event vs. process orientation. While both training and OD professionals get tagged with reputations for analysis paralysis, OD people suffer much more from that image. Valid or not, the perception is that ODers love process and resist closure. Trainers, on the other hand, get credit for consummating their projects. But here's the rub: These trainers are then charged with being satisfied with educational events instead of pursuing the more elusive but higher-value systems fixes.

Some Marriages

The executive on the airplane isn't the only leader interested in improving the relationship between training and organization development. Now, finally, some companies are moving to blur conventional distinctions between the two. Like Amoco, they see it as a strategy for performance improvement.

Andersen Consulting Education. This St. Charles, IL-based group has received national awards for its commitment to training. But where once Andersen Consulting hired primarily instructional designers and technologists, the company now makes sure to select some people with formal training and experience in organizational design and strategic planning. It's a business decision, says Larry Silvey, a partner and managing director at Andersen; the firm isn't doing education for education's sake. The purposes are change, performance improvement and business outcomes. For that, Andersen needs a bigger and more cross-functional tool kit.

AT&T Universal Card Service. Linda Swanson, vice president of human resources at this 1992 Baldrige Award-winning company, says her unit is shifting to a more consultative role, where OD people, human resources people and trainers perceive themselves first and foremost as business partners to each other and their customers. Bob O'Neal, director of training at Jacksonville, FL-based UCS, puts it like this: "In the past, training would do performance analyses and come up with training and non-training solutions. Then we'd beg to put solution systems in place. The new organization formalizes all this."

> "We don't know about all those approaches. We aren't the people who handle any of that. We don't work with them."

The new collaborative goals are reinforced by the measurements the HR unit now uses to gauge its success. Instead of counting bodies in classes or the number of team-facilitation gigs it runs, the new organization will be judged by its ability to contribute to business results. O'Neal is laboring to link services to real problems in the organization and then to measure the improvements that occur.

The United States Coast Guard. The Coast Guard has been moving in this direction for several years, as indicated by the "Training Division's" name change to the Training and Performance Improvement Division. According to Lt. Cmdr. Terry Bickham, commanding officer of the Pacific Area Training Team, this is much more than a change in the letterhead. In July 1994, the Coast Guard commandant issued the equivalent of an executive order (COMDTINST 1500.23) articulating a new philosophy of training, education and development. The document recognizes the limitations of training without root-cause analysis and presses the organization toward systemic solutions. An attachment to the actual Coast Guard document demonstrates a much broader philosophy of performance, referring to a wide array of "job performance influences," like job aids, achievable criteria, policy, feedback, worthy tasks, confidence, strong leadership, timely training, coaching and more. The order ensures that trainers and OD specialists will cooperate in the effort, no matter their place in the organizational hierarchy.

Bickham cites the topic of leadership as a recent success. Historically, the Coast Guard offered formal leadership training in several locations and formats, each associated with the rank or enlistment status of trainees. Henceforth, all offerings, including those provided to midlevel enlisted people, will occur at the Coast Guard Academy in New London, CT. The idea of bringing together many levels of Coast Guard people at the academy represents a significant cultural change, says Bickham. "It says very strong things about the importance of leadership in our organization, top to bottom. It was the right thing to do, and it wouldn't have happened without the big-picture collaboration of trainers and organizational developers."

Aligning Training and OD

The relationship between training and organization development may be evolving, but it's certainly not happening everywhere. When pressed to describe the connection between training and OD in his company, a training executive at a large technology firm dropped his voice and admitted to managing it so that he and his people "didn't bump into the organizational development group." This executive is a strong advocate of shifting training's focus away from educational events and toward systemic solutions based on good needs assessments, and he was slightly embarrassed about the gulf between his people and the OD unit. He acknowledged the oddity of the rift, given his belief in cross-functional performance support, but he hadn't done anything about moving toward either acquaintance or alliance.

Situations like that serve neither the professionals nor their companies. Here are some suggested strategies for enhancing collaboration between OD and training:

• *Capitalize on high-level sponsorship.* This article began with an executive — not a trainer or an OD person but a client of both functions — who sat on an airplane and wondered why the two didn't collaborate. It was the Coast Guard commandant, not someone from training or OD, who could employ a directive to make collaboration the rule rather than an exception.

- *Develop high-level sponsorship.* If it doesn't exist, try to create it. If your organization's leaders are unaware of the possibilities, educate them. Cite examples of the cynicism generated when employees are trotted off to classes that have nothing to do with the key behaviors the organization really desires or rewards. Nearly every company has examples of unsupported training events. You'll likely have to look no further than mandated sessions in telephone skills, continuous process improvement, diversity or teamwork.
- *Demonstrate the fit with existing and emerging initiatives.* Is a quality-improvement drive under way at your company? That's a natural. So is the interest in "the learning organization." Peter Senge in *The Fifth Discipline* and David Garvin in a 1993 article on organizational learning in the *Harvard Business Review* both lament the cost of organizational boundaries and cheer the benefits derived from more permeable membranes. General Electric CEO Jack Welch identifies "boundarylessness" as a key tenet of GE's corporate strategy.
- *Create pilot collaborations.* Before enacting anything resembling formal reorganization, try some pilot projects. Measure their impact. Publicize the business results they achieve. Establish teams that include OD and training people, and assign them to help key clients solve performance problems. Create ad hoc and visiting relationships so that familiarity can encourage alliances.
- *Encourage people in each specialty to learn more about the other.* Focus on the commonalities as well as the differences. Use sample requests for training or OD assistance as the basis for discussion about similar and distinct perspectives and approaches. Together, read and discuss the work of Edgar Schein, Chris Argyris, Rosabeth Moss Kanter, M. David Merrill and Roger Schank.
- *Analyze what hinders collaboration.* There are often incentives that create distance and even competition between the two service units. Recognize the rivalry that can emerge in billable contexts, when both groups are trying to achieve their target percentages or recover their costs. Examine the history of the relationship. Work with the leadership of the two specializations to address these obstacles and transcend turf battles.

Drawing Pictures

The fact that it is hard to make any case at all *against* building alliances between training and organization development doesn't mean that those alliances are easy to bring about. Many trainers are genuinely sold on the idea of broader analyses and examining non-training solutions to performance problems, but that doesn't necessarily inspire them to reach out to OD specialists. The Coast Guard, Amoco, AT&T's UCS unit and Andersen, large organizations all, have chosen to bring specialized people together in structured and ad hoc ways. In other places, the trend is toward expanding the individual training professional's repertoire. One friend in government suggests that this individual-development strategy occurs because partnerships are perceived as too hard to effect.

OD and training are professions in transition, buffeted by shifts in priorities regarding empowerment, organizational structure, and specialization vs. generalization. The only certainty is management's desire for higher quality, lower costs, faster cycle times, and overall performance improvement. Eventually, these critical goals will precipitate more leveraging of training and OD through means narrow and grand, formal and informal.

At a training conference last year in Atlanta, Amoco's Quesada and I asked about 100 people to draw a graphic picture of the relationship between training and OD in their organizations. We got circles. We got squares. We got smiley faces and frowning faces. We got lots of white space. What we didn't get much of was overlap, proximity and arrows. What kind of picture would you draw?

Reengineering the Training Department

Learner-driven instruction on demand? More training for less money? Sounds like a pipe dream. But wait! What's that on the horizon?

BY BEVERLY GEBER

It was Claudia Davis' job to grapple with the fallout of the information age. As director of education for Hewlett-Packard Co. in Palo Alto, CA, she had to make sure that the company's legions of software engineers stayed current in a field in which the store of information changes so rapidly that their knowledge becomes obsolete in less than two years.

In the face of such a voracious need for continuing education, the old ways of providing training couldn't cope. By the time Davis' training department could fashion a new classroom course and deliver it to the engineers in the computer company, the information was already getting moldy. The situation was not only logistically vexing; it also endangered the competitiveness of H-P when its engineers did not know quickly about new advances in their field.

Yet that was not the only disadvantage of traditional classroom training. The costs of dragging engineers into classrooms continued to rise. Facilities, materials and instructor time all grew more expensive. But what troubled Davis even more was the time and productivity lost due to taking the company's engineers off the job for training. In the fiercely competitive computer industry, in which profit margins are often as thin as computer chips, the company couldn't tolerate frequent siphoning of its employees' time.

Davis was made vividly aware of all this two years ago when the education department had to teach H-P employees about object-oriented computer technology. Engineers needed to learn it right away, but others in the company needed to know about it as well. Davis calculated that so many people were affected that if she offered classes every day in 12 locations, it would still take more than a year to reach everybody in the company who needed to know.

So she turned to technology. Davis and her instructional designers devised a course on object-oriented technology that was geared to H-P. Then the company promised National Technological University (NTU), a videoconferencing company, that if it would transmit the course, H-P would guarantee that a certain number of subscribers would sign up for it.

That cut the cost of travel, since engineers could now attend the course through downlinks at their own workplaces. But it still meant that the engineers had to go into a room at a particular time to view the telecast. It would be ideal, Davis thought, to distribute the training to the engineers in such a way that they could learn what they needed at their own workstations when they had the time. So she took the next step.

Now, by using a three-way linking system that joins a computer, a videocassette player, and the satellite feed from NTU, engineers can record the classes as they're being telecast and watch them later at their desks. They can freeze the screen, which may show the contents of an overhead transparency that the professor is discussing, and use a computer-notes function to add their own comments to what appears on the screen. After the engineers finish watching the broadcast, they can print out their own personally annotated version of the content.

The new setup allows the engineers to move through the material at their own pace whenever they have time, a convenience that contributes to higher productivity. Although it costs money to telecast the classes and provide the engineers with desktop systems to capture it, the company is still saving money by eliminating the direct and indirect costs of classroom training. Currently, each setup used to deliver the training costs several thousands of dollars apiece, and not all engineers have systems. But Davis expects the cost to drop to about $400 within a couple of years, making the system easy to justify to top management.

"It's so overwhelming that nobody even questions it," Davis says. She calculates that in order to deliver five hours of classroom training, about 25 extra hours are needed for travel and incidental time. Multiply that 25 hours by the salary of the individuals involved and there's no need to bother calculating the direct costs of training, Davis says. "I just have to show [executives] the first set of numbers. It can't be worth it to let [trainees] spend 25 hours to get five hours of training."

And Davis believes that learning effectiveness is just as great — maybe better — with the new methods. In the past, a course with just five hours of content would probably be stretched to a couple of days in order to justify the travel. Trainers would undoubtedly throw in some information that trainees would need eventually but perhaps not immediately. Trouble was, by the time they needed to use the bonus information, they'd forgotten it.

The new arrangement may not be the consummate, never-to-be-improved-upon way to deliver training to engineers, but Davis maintains that it's radically better than the old way.

Davis and a growing number of her counterparts at other U.S. corporations are at work to reinvent the way in which training is conceived and delivered within their companies. At the same time, but to a lesser degree, they are also changing the way in which their training departments operate.

The popular term for this is reengineering. Briefly, it means radically changing a process, usually through the use of technology, to realize substantial gains in cost, time or service. In an earlier time, before the word was coined and popularized by Michael

Hammer and James Champy, authors of *Reengineering the Corporation,* it was called "doing more with less."

Training directors have always sought ways to wring more value out of their budgetary bucks. But those improvements tended to be modest and incremental, rather than the radical, revolutionary change that is sought today. Several trends have converged recently to bring about that sense of urgency within some corporate training departments.

• **Time.** As the H-P example attests, it is no longer acceptable for training to be delivered on a sluggish timetable. And it's not just generalized information for certain employee populations, such as object-oriented technology for engineers, that needs to be delivered before it goes stale. Consider, for instance, that many companies, in order to stay competitive, have accelerated their new-product cycles. In some cases, a new-generation widget that is slightly improved through the use of technology can be released less than a year after its predecessor. Ideally, training to support that new-product release should be ready before the product is made if the company wants to sell as many of the widgets as possible during the short shelf life they will enjoy before they, too, are made obsolete by the next generation.

• **Content.** The content of training courses used to be relatively static. That's still true of many subjects, such as time management. But other courses need to be changed frequently, perhaps because the state of the art of a particular technology changes. This means that companies must have the ability to deliver new content to employees without having to develop new classroom instruction or remaster a course delivered on interactive videodisc. Even so, the implication is that training is always represented by a course. That's not necessarily true these days. In fact, some companies are stretching the boundaries of the word "training." If the term can be described as information and instruction that helps people perform their jobs, then it is a small step to a world in which training departments help develop networked computer-based systems that deliver training modules as well as daily news and information to the desktops of the people who need it. For instance, Federal Express created an embedded learning system that will be available to the company's central service agents on their desktop computers. Besides training modules, the system will also carry daily updates that give the agents important information. If, for example, a snowstorm has just hit the East Coast, making it impossible to expedite packages in certain areas, agents would be able to tap a few buttons on their keyboards to find out which areas can be fully served and which can be only partially served.

"It can't be worth it to let [trainees] spend 25 hours to get five hours of training."

• **Place.** Things used to be simple. An instructional designer would create a course which, in due time, would be presented in a classroom. All the people who needed to take it would be ferried to the location in right-sized batches for two or more days of learning. Courses usually lasted at least two days in order to justify the costs of bringing trainees from around the country — or around the world — to a central location. Content could always be found to fill up at least two days' worth of training. And if the trainees did not immediately need the information being thrust at them, they probably would sooner or later. Hopefully, they'd remember it when they needed it. Many companies are deciding now that such gatherings are far too expensive and time-wasting — as well as being an often untimely method of learning — to justify frequent use. Their preference is distributed training, in which information is put at employees' disposal, sometimes through an electronic performance support (EPS) system, at the moment the employee needs it. "Nowadays, if someone wants to do training by satellite or computer, it's considered an exception, and they have to go through all sorts of approvals, whereas it's easy to get approval for a classroom-based course. In the future, the opposite will be true," says Marc Rosenberg, district manager for education and training in AT&T's corporate human-resources department in Somerset, NJ. He is involved in a corporatewide rethinking of the role and delivery of training within the company.

• **Technology.** It is, quite simply, the enabler. There is nothing new about the perception of centralized classroom training as expensive and inefficient. Five years ago, training directors could envision distributed learning and information on demand, but they couldn't produce it. The technology was a barrier because it was prohibitively expensive and not especially user-friendly. But as the march of technology pushes prices lower, and as more people learn to use computers as something other than fancy typewriters, both those barriers have started to crumble. The result is significant change in the way in which training is delivered. Davis says that up to 65 percent of training at H-P is now delivered outside the classroom. Larry Silvey, managing director of Arthur Andersen Consulting Education in St. Charles, IL, says he has seen major changes just in the past two years in what technology can offer training. His division developed a highly sophisticated, CD-ROM-based simulation that helps teach the company's consultants how to consult. It presents an imaginary client company, along with specifics of the client's situation, and asks the student to give the company some valuable advice. The new course, which takes a typical trainee about 40 hours to complete, replaces a 60-hour program of individual study and classroom instruction. Although it was expensive to create the course, Silvey says that Arthur Andersen saves about $10 million a year in training and payroll costs by delivering the course on CD-ROM.

All of these driving forces have converged to force change within some training departments. "We just don't have the luxury of using the old methodologies anymore," says Maryanne Johnson, director of the leadership center within the Center for Professional Development at U.S. West Inc., in the Denver suburb of Lakewood, CO.

Few training departments are making the kinds of radical changes implied by the term reengineering. More common are situations in which training contributes to reengineering efforts elsewhere in the company by providing instruction that helps employees take on new roles, says George Bennett, CEO of Symmetrix Inc., a Lexington, MA, consulting firm that specializes in reengineering.

It may not be possible for a training department to get maximum benefit from a reengineering effort if the rest of the company isn't doing it, says Bennett. But reengineering the training department can still produce handsome results.

Training departments that are on the reengineering path generally are lodged within large companies that have thousands of far-flung employees. The companies also tend to be high-tech or communications firms, whose employees are already comfortable using sophisticated technology. They might be organizations with visionary leaders who are pushing the training departments toward reengineering. They might be companies in financial pain, whose leaders are asking tougher questions about the utility of money spent on training.

"Training is a hefty investment," Rosenberg says. "Training and HR have these big bull's eyes on them that say 'overhead.' The training department that says, 'We've trained 20 percent more students than last year,' is in trouble." In other words, a training department concerned only with counting the number of students in seats probably isn't measuring whether the students learned any-

HOW THE TRAINER'S JOB CHANGES

All this talk of reengineering the training department brings up a point of intense interest to the average training-department employee: Will my job change and, if so, how much?

The answer to the first question is: Yes. Depending on what kind of job you hold and whom you ask, the answer to the second ranges from "a little bit" all the way to "prepare for whiplash."

Many of the companies already in the midst of reengineering have seen the duties — and hence, the required skills — of trainers change.

Sometimes the changes have been relatively minor. Almost all the training departments that are making greater use of technology to deliver training are insisting that everyone become much more knowledgeable about technology. Surprisingly, even high-tech companies such as Apple Computer Inc. have found that their trainers needed heavy doses of computer-literacy training in order to prepare them for a new way of delivering instruction. Some companies, such as Arthur Andersen and Co., have had to add more graphic-arts specialists and technological wizards to the training department to be able to produce a new class of computer-driven courseware.

Many training directors believe that the people who populate training departments in the future will hold different occupational titles than they hold now. Classroom instructors, for instance, ought to be beefing up their résumés as soon as possible.

"One of the things we have to face is that we still have a lot of people in the training community who are oriented toward classroom activities," says Jim Hite, a training manager with Northern Telecom's Learning Institute. Many of these trainers aren't at all comfortable working with technology and can't fathom that there are many topics that no longer need to be taught in a classroom, he adds.

Just 25 percent of the training offered by Apple Computer to its U.S. sales force is conducted in a classroom, which means the company needs many fewer classroom instructors than it once did. As part of its effort to reengineer, the training department analyzed the skills it now needs in its staffers, rewrote almost every job description, "posted" the jobs within the training department, and hired anew for all the positions. Some people settled into a rough approximation of their old jobs, but others had to scramble to retrain themselves for new positions. For instance, the training department has many more "project managers" than before, a position that requires a wide knowledge of most aspects of training — including technology — and an ability to get a group of specialists, each working on several projects, to meet deadlines.

But even the instructional designer's job changed at Apple, says Lucy Carter, director of Apple's worldwide performance system. Much more than in the past, instructional designers need to be able to design courses that are delivered by technological means. They also no longer have the luxury of taking 18 months to design a course. Now, Carter says, a course can be designed in about two weeks. How? For one thing, the training department uses a sophisticated instructional-design expert system that allows trainers with no formal instructional-design experience to create a prototype. Then an experienced instructional designer fine-tunes it.

At Federal Express, there has been a big drop in the demand for classroom instructors. Just a few years ago, a classroom instructor may have spent 80 percent of her time in the classroom; today that figure has dropped to 40 percent. Peter Addicott, senior manager of training and development for the company's southern region, says that those trainers are now spending more time doing internal consulting with line managers. The company hasn't had to shrink its training staff, but Addicott notes that the number of training-department employees has stayed constant for six years while the number of workers companywide has doubled in the same period of time.

Will the training department need fewer people in the future? Yes, says Maryanne Johnson, director of the leadership center within the Center for Professional Development at U.S. West. Claudia Davis, director of education for Hewlett-Packard, doesn't believe that fewer trainers will be needed, just smarter ones. For instance, she says, "We don't have instructional designers. We need people who are performance technologists."

Davis sees a rising need for trainers who are better at "scanning the environment" for new information and breakthroughs. "The role of education is scanning for ways to meet the business needs in a shorter time frame," she says.

And, by extension, the role of the reinvented trainer is to find those new ways. It may require other kinds of skills. As Carter puts it: "You can sit in a garage all night, but it won't make you a car. You can be a trainer all your life, but you might not have the skill sets to take you forward in this environment." — B.G.

thing — or whether the skills they did gain are helping the company at all.

Rosenberg suggests it's essential that the training department begin to think of itself as an educational resource whose goal is to serve customers well with the minimum amount of hassle to them. Starr Eckholdt, president of the Alliance of Organizational Systems Designers, a Winston-Salem, NC, consulting firm that specializes in reengineering efforts, admits that a reengineered training department is easier to describe than to create. First, he says, you figure out what your customer needs. Then you eliminate or reduce cycle times in order to deliver information to employees and give them resources to build their skills. The shorthand version: shorter time frames and higher impact.

A reengineered training department, in Rosenberg's vision, is one that knows it delivers value because it measures that value. It delivers its products and services in the way that is most convenient for the user, even if it means delivering training and information to employees' homes. A reengineered training department almost surely uses technology to improve its processes and deliver its services. It probably contains fewer people than it did before, and the ones who remain probably use sophisticated, automated tools for instructional design.

According to Eckholdt, a department that wanted to reengineer itself would begin with the question, What are we trying to achieve? It's an old question, he admits, but those in charge of the training function have to take a fresh look at it, freeing their minds of the way things have always been done.

If the training department is trying to produce highly effective employees for the organization, it must map the processes it uses to mold ordinary people into productive, valued employees. "When you look at it this way, you reframe your thinking around the product you're trying to produce. You ask, 'How can we do it better than we've ever done it before?' " Eckholdt says.

Ideally, he says, in this creative stage, training executives should be reaching for breakthrough ideas, not incremental improvements. For instance, the inclination in many quarters would be to streamline the existing curriculum and make it easier for employees to sign up for courses. But, says Eckholdt, what if the training department could come up with a way to meet training needs in a somewhat customized way, within weeks of identifying the need, and take the solution straight to the customers? What might such an arrangement look like? It might not include a curriculum of courses at all.

Despite the heavy technology bent of its strategy, reengineering does not mean that classrooms will be eliminated.

To date, very few training departments have completely overhauled themselves. Most often, reengineering begins with one or two significant changes in the way in which training is delivered. It builds from that point, provided that training directors can be convinced that learning is as good or better than before, and provided that the costs and cycle time can be reduced.

Silvey says Arthur Andersen has pinpointed three goals of its reengineering effort. First, it wants to use technology as much as possible to reduce cycle times, increase productivity, cut costs, and improve learning results. It wants to use the best practices it can find in other companies and universities. And it wants to create an electronic performance support system for its employees in field offices.

Despite the heavy technology bent of its strategy, Silvey says that reengineering does not mean that classrooms will be eliminated. In fact, Arthur Andersen's CD-ROM consulting simulation now is used sometimes in the classroom to create a more authentic learning situation. Trainees work in teams to advise the make-believe company contained in the CD-ROM program, just as they would in the real world. Coaches in the classroom help guide them, just as an Arthur Andersen senior partner might in reality.

At Northern Telecom, the communications company in Nashville, TN, the training function set up an EPS system that supplements the five-day training course given to new managers. Jim Hite, a manager for the Northern Telecom Learning Institute, says that the EPS system contains practical information the manager can capture at the moment she needs it. For instance, the system contains detailed information and examples of how Northern Telecom managers are expected to draw up budgets. The EPS system didn't do away with the need for a class to orient new managers, but it reduced dramatically the number of times new managers had to bother someone else for answers to their questions.

A different kind of need at U.S. West led to a laptop-based learning system for almost 400 of the company's top managers. The reasoning is, Johnson says, that if the company is going to compete effectively in a new technological age, its top decision-makers need to be knowledgeable about wireless and multimedia technology.

Previously, the company brought executives together for a series of informational meetings. But it made more sense to let the executives learn about the new technologies on computers at their own pace, obviating the expense and time of flying everyone to a central location for a course. An executive retrieves the information through a laptop computer that hooks up to a CD-ROM player, fax machine (for reporting test results), videocassette recorder, and the Internet data base.

When the executive begins the program, she takes a pre-test that identifies the gaps in her knowledge about technology; that assessment produces a "map" of the learning program that shows the executive how to access information to plug the gaps. The program contains 10 modules, each built around a particular technology. When she is finished, she takes a post-test to measure what she learned.

The company found that it had to make available "coaches," subject-matter experts who could answer any questions the executives might have while going through the material. The coaching system provided the hand-holding some computer-reticent managers needed, as well as providing the course designers with tips on how to improve the program. Eventually, it will be made available to all employees of U.S. West. In the meantime, Johnson says, the company is expecting significant cost savings from delivering the instruction on laptops instead of pulling its most expensive employees off the job for a day or two of classroom training.

Another high-tech company, Apple Computer Inc., is also busily reinventing the way in which it delivers training. In the process, Apple has drawn together the training, advertising, public relations and documentation functions in order to coordinate all the information that goes to trainees. Lucy Carter, director of worldwide performance systems for the Cupertino, CA-based company, says that when she examined the previous new-product training and information system from the point of view of the company's 20,000 salespeople, she was overwhelmed by the volume of material.

The company released 72 new products last year, and for each one, salespeople typically received four or five CD-ROM disks, four or five videotapes, and a huge pile of paper. None of the four departments that sent the information was aware of how much the others were sending. "It was a great amount of information representing a huge amount of time and money, and it wasn't improving anybody's performance," Carter says.

She gathered a task force that analyzed how salespeople used their time and learned about new products. She helped organize a benchmarking project to find out whether other companies were using alternative delivery methods. She sent people to conferences about EPS systems. And she convened a worldwide Apple training council to mull how the training function could better meet the needs of trainees.

One of the outcomes of that council was the process that now exists to inform salespeople about new products. Called Apple's Reference Performance and Learning Expert (ARPLE), it is an EPS system that is distributed to individual salespeople through computer file servers in 60 locations around the world. Not only can users call up information on new products, they can also use an expert system to create a presentation for a particular product. Eventually, says Carter, the sales rep will be able to enter information about a particular client, and have the expert system suggest a strategy for selling to the client.

But the beauty of the new system is that users are no longer inundated with information flowing from three or four pipelines. The PR, advertising, documentation and training departments pool their information to eliminate redundancies before sending the information out to salespeople. It wastes less time and money on the corporate end, and saves the salespeople from wading through useless information.

Carter suggests that what makes ARPLE different from the average EPS system is that it is a multifunctional effort to improve performance that looks at the company's systems from the point of view of the user. "I've seen some EPS systems that look great, but when you look at the target audience, you see they're also receiving 96 other things they have to see and do," she says. "Our effort was not just to make training function differently but to make the organization function differently and to have the organization support the individuals."

Judging by the path of progress in the companies mentioned so far, reengineering typically begins with efforts to improve the process of *delivering* training within the company. If those changes lead to improvements in the training department's internal processes, great. But there have been fewer efforts to reinvent the way in which the training department itself functions.

Arthur Andersen has cut its review times for new training courses by one-third by doing "rapid prototyping" of new courses.

This is entirely understandable. After all, the trainer's charge is to deliver instruction as effectively as can be. If quantum leaps are possible, they ought to apply to the department's core responsibility. Efforts to improve processes within the training department, without radically rethinking the role of training within an organization, may be little more than rearranging the deck chairs on the Titanic. But there have been a few attempts to reengineer the way in which training departments operate, most of them arising from efforts to reengineer the delivery system.

The training department at U.S. West, for instance, is trying to redesign its computerized systems to create one interlocked, fluid system to replace the hodgepodge it now contains. Because several of the systems don't talk to each other, there exists a series of time-wasting, paper-based "handoffs" that slow down the whole training process.

For instance, one computer system contains employees' training records and another contains reservations for classes; the classes themselves are listed only in a catalog, which is updated and mailed to employees at regular intervals. Employees needed to check the catalog for a course they wanted to take, and reserve a spot. But the trainers had to deal with two different computer systems in order to check to see whether the employee needed the course and schedule him into a class.

With a new system, which Johnson says will be online soon, the employee sits at his desk and taps into one seamless system that contains information about the courses available and what his skill gaps are. Soon, Johnson hopes, the employee will be able to access certain training modules right from the system, without having to attend class. In the meantime, Johnson plans to speed up the scheduling of classes and reduce the need for the catalog.

Arthur Andersen's Silvey says that his department has cut its review times for new training courses by one-third by doing "rapid prototyping" of new courses. In the past, instructional designers may have put together the "perfect" training course only to see it mauled when it went through a sequential review by 10 people. Now, the instructional-design team creating a technology-based course can produce a version that is strictly vaporware, and call together the 10 reviewers in one room to see it and comment. The result is a much shorter time to design a course.

Hewlett-Packard has found ways to produce a CBT course in two weeks. Among its tricks is its use of a template that allows it to author more quickly, and its ability to "repurpose" segments of previous training products, Davis says. What she means is that H-P might take a snippet of a course and use it in another way in a new course. Maybe a piece of video used in a performance-appraisal course could be used to buttress a different learning point in a CBT course on diversity. This ability to reuse material in new ways is essential in cutting the time it takes to produce training. "There's not a lot that is new," Davis says. "What's important is our ability to repurpose and reconfigure, which saves time."

Technology has allowed a great many advances in the workings of the training department, as well as the way in which instruction is conveyed to employees. Ten years ago, it was possible to wish for something like an EPS system that would provide brief training modules and coaching available on the spot to employees at their desks; unfortunately, the technology didn't permit it.

Today, it's possible to wish for a learning system that is completely learner-driven and mobile. Perhaps it's a system that gives the learner an unlimited multimedia extravaganza that also automatically links him by e-mail to others learning the same material within the company. The system might be accessible anywhere — including a car. Perhaps it allows the learner to fill knowledge gaps by using public data bases. To accomplish that, of course, there would need to be an as-yet-uninvented piece of software that would allow the user to pluck the precise piece of information he needs from a data base, such as the Internet, without getting bogged down in its labyrinths.

AT&T's Rosenberg acknowledges that it's possible to imagine all kinds of wondrous advances that will bring us closer to the ideal of a true learner-driven training system. Hardly anyone in the training community could disagree with such a vision, he contends. But there are a few potential obstacles to the fruition of such a dream.

First, and most obvious, is technology. In some cases the technology simply doesn't exist yet to make the dream come true. In other cases the technology is available but it carries a shocking price tag.

Peter Addicott, senior manager of training and development for Federal Express' southern region, believes that mobile learning — anywhere, any time — is the key to his company's training future. In fact, he can glimpse it now in the tools used by Federal Express' delivery people. Each courier has a mobile device linked to a central system that can tell her where a package is at any given moment.

> "I think part of what's holding us back as a society is our comfort with the classroom environment."

There is no reason, says Addicott, that those systems can't also deliver an EPS-like learning system. No reason, that is, except for money and the computer hardware and software it will buy. It probably won't happen right away, Addicott says, but he hopes to have such a system in the near future.

Those limitations — money and technology — are the reasons that this potential revolution in learning will be led, once again, by large companies. They are the ones with the deepest pockets and the strongest motives to switch to an electronic, learner-driven system.

But there is another barrier that may foil the revolution: the learner. "I think part of what's holding us back as a society is our comfort with the classroom environment," says Apple's Carter.

Northern Telecom's Hite says he often gets requests from line managers wanting to have a performance problem solved. Almost always, he says, the manager wants Hite to put together a classroom-based course. And Northern Telecom is not a low-tech company.

Trainees sometimes resist computer-based training, too, because they're not used to learning in that way. Johnson says that when U.S. West introduced the laptop-based system to teach its top executives about the latest advances in technology, it overwhelmed them at first by delivering the entire collection to them in one chunk. "We gave them the laptop, and the CD-ROM, and the videos, and the paper-based systems, and it was just too much," Johnson says. The company later discovered that some trainees needed to be able to call a coach to talk about the information. U.S. West has learned that it must continue to cater to employees' comfort needs — in other words, their desire for human interaction.

Will this mean that companies will always and forever need to provide a classroom option so that trainees can forge bonds with others? Not necessarily. After all, we have reached a point where romances are carried to the brink of a formal engagement through the use of data-base bulletin boards and e-mail. It's just possible that 15 years from now, when Generation Xers have ensconced themselves solidly in corporate America, a tiny fraction of instruction will be delivered in classrooms, and everyone in the training community will look back in wonder at the marvelous inefficiency of the system that exists today.

10 Ways to Undermine Your HRD Effort*

You may not agree that each of these errors is fatal, but at least be aware that some heavy-hitters see potential danger in them.

BY RON ZEMKE

Call these "learnings" — lessons garnered from seven years of interviewing the best and the brightest in the field. Call this a primer of surefire ways to blunt the organizational effectiveness of your training and human resource development HRD effort. Consider it a Christmas present from the heavy-hitters and go-getters — those individuals who have raised their training and/or HRD efforts to positions of prominence and impact in their organizations and who have, over the years, been willing to take time to tell *TRAINING Magazine* how they did it.

Warning! You won't necessarily — and needn't — agree that every one of these "ways to whiff it" is a devastating policy or a fatal faux pas. You may even see one or two as success principles rather than blunders. Fine. But be aware that someone sees a down side or potential danger in the idea you cherish.

In truth, none of the pros we have talked with would decry all 10 as disastrous ideas. But each is a practice that has been cited, convincingly and frequently, as having imbedded within it some seed of organizational self-destruction. Each has, at the very least, stood the test of remaining intriguing to us over time. Stitched together, we feel, the 10 make up a thought-provoking sampler of ways to turn an effective training and HRD effort to mud.

ERROR 1:
Fail to define the role of HRD in your organization.

Ben Tregoe of Kepner-Tregoe, Inc. in Princeton, NJ, and Geary Rummler, who heads The Rummler Group of Summit, NJ, both have argued that to be optimally effective, the head of the HRD function must understand and agree with top-management's concept of what the organization is trying to become. And the HRD effort must be structured in such a way as to help accomplish *that* mission. Should your department function as a corporate university? As a performance-problem-engineering team? The answer lies not in some mystical measure of right and wrong, but in discovering the most appropriate tactical fit with organizational strategy.

Being strategic and effective in your HRD efforts, knowing who you are and are not, what business you are and are not in, requires that you take the time to think through and publish a clear-cut mission statement and a menu of responsibilities. Without such a charter you will never be able to evaluate and modify your HRD function, and you will dilute your chances of becoming a key part of the organization.

ERROR 2:
Allow HRD to report to middle management.

Some of the finest people in the world — some of our best friends — are middle managers. But when it comes to clout, the kind needed to ensure a long-term involvement in HRD, you need positive support at the highest level. The chief executive officer (CEO) is ultimately responsible for attracting, developing and retaining talent in the organization. To whom the HRD unit reports is the choice, ultimately, of the CEO. If, by design or neglect, the unit reports to middle management, with little or no access to upper management, it shows something important about the CEO's concern for and interest in developing people. At best, the top dog has an impoverished idea of the contribution people-development efforts can make to the development of the organization.

Under these conditions, the HRD manager will never attain the posture necessary to be really effective in the organization. The least the HRD manager should settle for is reporting to a senior officer close to the executive office. The ideal setup, of course, has the HRD officer reporting to the president, managing director or CEO.

At Olin Corp. in Stamford, CT, president John M. Henske considers centralized control of HRD an operating necessity. To ensure proper attention to the area, Henske established a corporate HRD team, headed by the vice president of administration, that reports directly to him. Team members include the employee relations directors from each operating group and from the corporate staff, the medical director, compensation chief, management staff and personnel services director and the director of development and training.

As a result, training director Boris "Bo" Sichuk is accountable for the quality and effectiveness of programs run by every operating group of the corporation. He is directly responsible to the HRD committee and, through it, to Henske. That's pretty good positioning: good enough that Sichuk was able to budget an unheard of 80,000 hours of start-up training for a new plant opening.

Obviously, Sichuk has access to more resources and influence than HRD people whose direct reporting level is significantly lower. In addition, training and HRD results are highly visible.

ERROR 3:
Claim measurable bottom-line results for HRD efforts.

The contention that training and

---

*The concept of cataloging particularly effective ways to "screw up" owes its origin to Dr. Olaf Isachsen, president of the Institute for Management Development, Oakland, CA. It was spawned during a 1978 interview when Isachsen was vice president-management development for Wells Fargo Bank in San Francisco. Since then he has had a great influence on their shape and number.

HRD efforts can prove their bottom-line results may be the greatest myth ever concocted by the profession. Some place along the way, we in HRD have convinced ourselves that our efforts can show a direct, measurable contribution to profits. Some suggest we aren't doing our jobs if we don't try to claim so many cents of profit per share for our activities. It's a fantasy that can rise up and bite us.

Ian E. McLaughlin, president of Training and Education Consultants, Inc., brings the point home with this story: "When I was training director for Del Monte Corp., I once ran before-and-after tests to prove the value of a specific training program. We did an outstanding needs analysis, put on a terrific program and the results were top-notch. The following three months saw this district move to the top third in sales of the item we wanted to see improvement in. I turned in a report showing dollar increases and everything else I could think of.

"Then the deluge! The product manager claimed credit for his support of the effort. The local sales managers said they had concentrated their efforts on the item after our workshop, and claimed credit. The regional sales manager pointed out that if headquarters wanted a sales workshop on one item, it obviously must be important, so he had exerted pressure on the item.

"All in all, I learned several lessons from the episode. First, as training director I should never try to take sole credit for increased sales results... and sometimes maybe not even a little bit of credit. Second, profitability is never a one-department or one-action result. Training should be built into marketing plans just as are advertising and promotional activities; training is part of the total action plan, not a poor relative and not a panacea. Third, a better measurement for me is having a trainee return home and a few weeks later write, 'Hey, I followed your ideas and I just closed the biggest sale of my life! Thanks!'"

Question: How many other staff people make such an absurd claim? The controller? The treasurer? The janitor? The typing pool? Research and development? Of course they don't. HRD, like every staff function, exists to support people on the line; to help line management and line operatives attain superior performance. Self-aggrandizement only squelches the motivation of line personnel and contributes to unproductive conflict.

Answer one final question: If the organization has an unprofitable, over-budget year, how many cents per share of that outcome are you willing to be accountable for? We can't have it both ways.

If this one upsets you and you still feel the need to show bottom-line results, perhaps you'll appreciate the view of Jay Beecroft, who until his recent retirement was top trainer at the giant 3M Company. "No training group can expect to gain influence without committing to operational results," he says. But, he adds quickly, "A training manager has a responsibility to realism. Management must know what is and is not possible through training, even if it detracts from the image."

ERROR 4:
Allow the HRD staff to "play act" as line managers.

When still a corporate HRD officer, Olaf Isachsen characterized his job as that of an extra head and hands for line managers to use in solving problems. "My job, like the job of every staff manager, was to be a resource to line management. They make the profit, we don't. Their profitability pays for our luxury of being able to take some time, step back and help them 'grapple with unknown concepts.'"

The problem is, we sometimes confuse thinking *with* and thinking *for* line management. If the HRD staff is making decisions for line managers or making unilateral moves that usurp the time line people budgeted for productive pursuits, the staff is "playing" line manager.

This indicates that performance criteria for both line and staff are inadequate, which puts the HRD director in a no-win situation. Line managers are almost universally gifted at withholding commitment from decisions to which they have had no input and for which they were not responsible. Facilitating a line manager's decision-making is appropriate; accepting responsibility for making decisions the line manager would prefer to abdicate is inappropriate.

A humiliating personal example may make the point. As an eager-beaver training director for a major New York financial institution, I had the bad sense to tell a senior personnel VP that he needed a certain genre of supervisory training because his turnover rate of 17.5% was too high. His response: "It is my job to decide when turnover is too high or just right. It is your job to find and focus the data. Don't ever attempt to usurp my responsibility again."

From there, he proceeded to get nasty. But he was 100% right. I had attempted to do his job, to play line manager, and that was *not* what I was getting paid for.

Frequently, trainers are asked to decide if training is needed. The real job is to work with management to determine whether training — or any other intervention — might be an appropriate response to a given problem. But in the end, the decision belongs to line management.

Tregoe suggests that the HRD job at its best is a data-gathering job: a search

---

10 WAYS TO BLUNT THE HRD EFFORT

■ Fail to define the role of HRD in your organization.

■ Allow HRD to report to a middle manager.

■ Claim measurable bottom-line results.

■ "Play" line manager.

■ Use "other-directed" assessment techniques.

■ Perform in the classroom.

■ Track and report activities.

■ Hire a large in-house program development staff.

■ Buy fads.

■ Exempt HRD from HRD.

© Performance Research

for information in and outside the organization about conditions that will have an impact on its long-and short-term existence. And how can you resist this line from Beecroft: "Our most critical task is to help line managers spot the problems, to sort real problems from perceived problems. Once the problem is identified, most people can find a reasonable solution."

ERROR 5:
Use "other-directed" assessment techniques.

According to Allen Tough of the Ontario Institute for Studies in Education, the typical adult engages in five learning projects a year. These projects or, as Tough defines them, "highly deliberate efforts to gain and retain certain definite knowledges and skills or to change in some other way," typically consume 100 hours of work or study. Eighty percent of the time they are planned and executed by the individual on his own; 73% of the time they are job-related. The most common motivation is a desire to get better at, or develop new skills for, a specific task. In short, people learn because they want to, and they most frequently want to when they find they need to improve their ability to do something related to their jobs.

Assessment by a superior, an assessment center or a battery of standardized tests is "external" or "other-directed" assessment. The individual "judged" in this manner to be in need of learning is likely to reject the assessment as inaccurate.

Self-assessment tends to be more credible. The individual must be able to respond to an authentic situation and interpret his or her performance without an assessor's aid. While "other-directed" assessment can be perfectly valid from a technical standpoint, self-assessment tends to result in the instigation of a learning project more frequently than does external assessment.

A condemnation of the assessment-center concept? It might sound like it, but it isn't. Nor does assessment-center guru William C. Byham of Development Dimensions International in Pittsburgh interpret it as such. Says Byham, "Developmentally oriented or career-planning assessment centers do combine self-evaluation with the assessment-center process itself. This is especially true in diagnostic centers where the individual is there only for his or her own benefit and there is a greater level of trust and openness."

ERROR 6:
Spend a large percentage of your time in the classroom.

The head of HRD is a manager first and a specialist second — or third. Like every other manager in the organization, the training director is responsible for the total performance of a unit or department. If the HRD chief insists on being the star classroom performer, he or she eventually will jeopardize his or her image with peers as a "fellow manager." Worse yet, senior management may come to regard the HRD department as "Sam/Samantha and his/her band of classroom crusaders" rather than as a group of people capable of making a meaningful contribution to the company's goals.

Isachsen wrestled with the problem of whether or not to take the stage and chose to demur: "My mission when I was at Wells Fargo was to create conditions that would cause line managers to improve, but without putting HRD in the limelight. I had to forego the pleasures of the classroom-trainer role."

A different view is taken by Ray Crapo of the education and training branch of the New York State Office of Court Administration. "The training director," he says, "should be a teacher/participant/facilitator of instruction, not just a management expert. And it is up to training directors to 'sell' this idea to top management so that management will respect them as much as it would a consultant who brings in the same program and expertise." Consequently, Crapo does train in the classroom from time to time.

Two knowledgeable people, two different opinions. But consider a final question: What one thing do managers and executives fear most? Give up? Time and again, surveys have shown that executives are most fearful of speaking in public. Trainers *live* to be on their feet talking. Unless you can find a way to turn the difference to your advantage, why risk being judged "not like us" by executives with chronic flop-sweat syndrome?

ERROR 7:
Track and report activities.

If your year-end report to senior management reads, "...892 people attended 2,489 hours of instruction in 1982 through 103 course offerings..." you probably are blowing it. You would be better off tracking and reporting on change. Changes in performance, productivity, even attitudes, would be more meaningful than a tabulation of classroom hours.

Reporting that "the HRD unit assisted the word-processing department in efforts to decrease employee absences and the percentage of return work" would be an improvement. Asking program participants, their subordinates and superiors to evaluate changes in the participants' behavior over time — and summarizing those changes when reporting to senior management — would be better still. The tracking and reporting of *activities* suggests a belief on your part that being busy counts. In fact, only results count.

Paul H. Chaddock, vice president of Boston-based Lechmere Stores, a division of Dayton Hudson Corp., uses the concept of critical ratios to measure his management development efforts in the belief that "we should make our measurements as parallel to the accounting measures used in the organization as possible. The senior management of most companies is taught to understand reports that talk of inventory expenses, capital, costs and so on. Our measures should at least parallel those. And we should report information in ratio form. Management is used to looking at percentages and ratios. We should adhere to that approach. It is comfortable and has credibility as well."

Chaddock has found five measures useful in his work at Lechmere and elsewhere in the Dayton Hudson organization.

- **Placement ratio:** comparison of promotable or placeable internal talent with talent brought in from outside.
- **Backup continuity:** comparison of available, qualified managerial backups to the number of slots for which backup is judged appropriate.
- **High performer-retention ratio:** comparison of people evaluated as better-than-average who leave the company to those who stay.
- **High potential-usage ratio:** comparison of the percentage of managers rated as capable of two levels of advancement in five years, to the percentage of those who have, in fact, moved up.

• **Management effectiveness ratio:** a set of fairly flexible comparisons — top-management payroll vs. total payroll, exempt vs. nonexempt employees, payroll vs. cost of sales or net sales and other measures for tracking management effectiveness.

ERROR 8:
Hire and maintain a large, in-house program-development staff.

As we mentioned earlier, most adult learning takes place at the adult's pace, in the adult's own mode of preference and at the adult's own direction. Aside from our contention that mandatory classroom training struggles against these facts, the in-house development of programs has five other potential problems.

• In-house productions generally are limited by the resourcefulness of in-house employees. Their skills and abilities alone determine the quality of their programs.

• Sooner or later, activities become important "track and measure" items because of the constant need to justify a large in-house staff. This moves the focus away from helping others perform better.

• Internal programs become predictable, safe and boring as the ceiling of internal talent is reached.

• If you build a program internally and it bombs, a crisis ensues. If you buy a program, try it out and discard it, your liability is limited.

• Keeping the in-house staff busy eventually tends to become the pre-eminent HRD management concern, and training programs come to be seen as the only solution to performance problems. If you are zero-base budgeted, as you should be, most management time will be spent talking others into attending your programs and authorizing the development of new ones.

Isachsen recommends thinking of the data-processing and information-management functions as analogous to the training function. "The computer-systems people don't do a systems analysis and then go out in the garage and build the organization a computer." Of course not. They buy a computer, adapt it to the system they designed and move on. "Why shouldn't training people be allowed to follow the same model?" the crafty Norwegian asks.

A corollary: If you don't have an internal development staff, you will have to buy or lease programs when you have a problem that can be addressed through training. The temptation is to work with the last vendor who brought in a winner for you. Take care. No vendor can possibly have the best answer to all problems. But beyond expertise, becoming a captive of a given vendor damages one's organizational credibility. Once you begin hearing comments like, "Well, Harry, what XYZ program are you pushing this year?" there is no need to ask for whom the bell tolls.

In Beecroft shorthand, this rule reads: "No training department can be all things to all people. We have to bring in outside talent and help continually just to stay even with progress. The future is in problem analysis, not program building. To sell to the need, you have to know the need."

ERROR 9:
Follow the fads and fancies of the field.

The sign on your door should read: "Vendors with dubious products beware." Current "in" things should be investigated rather than dismissed out of hand, but the HRD director who goes in search of "some of that behavior-modeling or right brain-left brain or assertiveness-training stuff" simply because everyone else is doing it, has fallen into a trap.

There are no shortcuts to performance improvement. The job is to create conditions within the existing reward-and-punishment systems that will foster lasting improvement. Sometimes that requires knowledge and skill programs; sometimes it requires change in the system and/or culture. Usually it requires investigation and consultation.

A corollary is that the HRD group, to be most effective, must avoid the appearance of having pet social causes as well as pet training programs or training solutions. As Olin's Sichuk puts it, "You can have all kinds of great social values, and you should. But if you're interested in selling those values and not in problem solving, then perhaps you're better off as a consultant outside the organization."

ERROR 10:
Exempt HRD from HRD.

If the HRD department does not take its own medicine, others will be skeptical. Aside from the embarrassment of the "cobbler's children syndrome," professionals in HRD must be aware of the intellectual and emotional impact of HRD efforts on the client organization. And, of course, HRD units need performance improvement as much as do other units. Sometimes they even need to bring outsiders in to facilitate their internal development.

If you have a professional staff, when was the last time one of your people was hired away by a line manager impressed by that person's talent and promise? Do you have formal, written development plans for your department? If you believe that career development and career planning are conservation measures — that they keep us from squandering valuable resources — how would you explain an HRD staff without internal development plans?

To drop one final Beecroftism, "People who don't grow continually become inefficient, then ineffective and finally obsolete." That's just as true of trainers as it is of managers, CEOs and engineers.

A last word

The HRD function can have a significant impact on organizational effectiveness, efficiency and long-term survival. Without the right people with the right skills in the right places at the right times, that survival is in serious jeopardy. To ignore the wisdom implicit in these 10 little land mines is to put the development effort, and ultimately the organization's survival, in jeopardy.

Is 'Just Training' Enough?

All courses and activities must be aimed at developing the organization.

BY STEPHEN P. BECKER

As training manager, you have a responsibility to your organization that goes beyond developing and implementing training programs and systems. Like all other managers, regardless of function, you have a general task of helping the organization develop. You must think of yourself as an *organizational* manager first and a manager of training, second.

Your opportunity to manage organizational improvement is greater than that of many other managers because training has a unique characteristic. It frequently gets many employees into job-related discussions and activities in an atmosphere of relative openness and trust away from the workplace. If the instructor is any good, and if the learning groups are structured properly, honesty usually prevails. The result is that participants in training programs often volunteer information about organizational problems which they see or which affect them directly. They also may provide clues to, or symptoms of, organizational problems.

This revealing process can normally be expected from participative training methodologies. Of course, all this good stuff will disappear into thin air if you perceive your role strictly in terms of helping learners achieve specific objectives. But if you also perceive yourself as manager of organizational improvement, then you will be seeking those clues and symptoms of patterns which will indicate needed changes.

Let's look at some organizational problems which you could discover as a consequence of conducting training programs. Remember, these needs may have nothing to do with the training program itself, which may be very successful and badly needed. The side benefit derives from your ability to identify areas requiring organizational improvement. You also may be able to develop some ideas, direction or strategies for initiating changes.

The first problem that you might identify is conflict. You may be conducting a training program on negotiation skills and after several sessions realize that there is great conflict between two senior purchasing agents. They both may be buying components for the same project. Because of their conflict, their subordinates are also in conflict, suppliers are confused, the purchasing department is not meeting its requirements, and other departments such as physical distribution or production are all losing ground. In addition, customers are not satisfied because they are not getting the service in terms of delivery that they were promised. It is possible that the entire operation has been slipping and could be improved by reducing or at least controlling the conflict.

As training manager you could be satisfied to know only that both purchasing agents have the required level of negotiating skills, or you could become concerned with the larger organizational issue of reducing the dysfunctionalism of their conflict.

Another example of potentially costly conflict may be found in high-technology organizations. Assume a new product is being developed. There needs to be cooperation between research and development, design engineering and manufacturing. Because of the great pressure for task performance, as well as the risks to personal careers that are usually on the line in such situations, conflict is common. As training manager you may be able to gain insight into this conflict as you conduct training programs related to the development of the new product.

It may be possible for you to contribute toward the reduction of any conflict you discover. How you would reduce it would depend on the organization, the people involved, and yourself. You may just tell somebody else who could help, provide individual coaching to key managers, initiate an organizational-development effort, plan new kinds of training programs, or hire a team-building consultant. Your concern at this point is not with strategy. What is important is that as the participants in training programs cause you to become aware of and sensitive to organizational problems, you take some responsibility for helping your organization to overcome problems and meet goals.

Behavior Maintenance

In a particular training program, you may be helping people to learn new management skills for which there is not enough organizational support. This second organizational problem can be classified as "behavior maintenance."

For instance, you may be conducting a training program for first-line supervisors on the subject of labor relations. You may be covering labor contracts, law and discipline procedure, as well as preventive-discipline techniques. Through the reaction and responses of participants in the training program, you may discover that most department managers really do not delegate labor relations responsibility to first-line supervisors.

No matter how good the training program is, if the participants are not going to be able to use what they learned back in the plant, the training investment will be wasted. You, as training manager, must take the appropriate steps to help the supervisors get responsibility for labor relations. If you don't, the supervisors will be frustrated (or relieved) and you will look foolish because everybody will know that training just isn't realistic. In this case, the learners could have achieved every learning objective but done nothing differently when they went back. The organization would have better-trained supervisors, but it would not get improved performance from them.

A third organizational problem you may become sensitive to is related to images. As a result of observing and listening to training program participants, you may realize that employees have a consistency of images. These images result from the way people believe they are treated.

Employees may believe that top management is snobbish and doesn't care very much about anybody below the level of plant manager. Production people may feel inferior to sales people. Sales people may think that they can't win because every time they start to make some money, sales management will change the structure of commissions, quotas or territories. Manufacturing supervisors may believe that the unions "hold all the cards" so that there is no way the company can get rid of a bad worker. Many production managers think that safety inspectors are just a nuisance who make no real contribution. Many people in smaller organizational units believe that they are considered unimportant, even though they may have important jobs.

All of these kinds of images can take an intangible toll on the organization. Such perceptions and attitudes affect relationships and performance. It's hard to measure, but there is a definite organizational cost because of an image or set of images that in fact may not be correct.

As training manager you are probably more aware of such images than anybody else in your organization. You also may be in a position to make proposals that can work toward correcting false impressions. At the very least, you can clarify these images for selected managers or groups of managers so that they can decide whether they want to try to change them. Many top managements are amazingly naive about attitudes held by their employees.

In addition to identifying opportunities for conflict reduction, behavior maintenance and image improvement, you can gain insight into many other problem areas, including: how well employees understand organizational goals; the general level of commitment to achieve goals; whether people feel a sense of membership and belonging; what problems are seen as important; and whether there is sense of security and pride in the organization. You also should be on the lookout for individual problems, such as a person who is obviously in the wrong job.

The basic point is that with a decent, functioning training department, proper objectives and successful programs, you will have a huge amount of organizationally important information revealed to you. Using it constructively could enhance the health of your organization — and your position in it.

Notes:

Decentralizing Training

A balance of bureaucracy and independence usually works best.

BY BRIAN McDERMOTT

Centralized or decentralized? Both of these philosophical approaches to training have strong advocates, but it seems that training executives on both sides of the argument, even when defining their programs as one or the other, are actually seeking a delicate balance between the two extremes.

Control Data Corp. is in the midst of decentralizing *all* of its corporate staff functions, according to Michael Hopp, director of human resource development and research. Historically, the company always has been centralized. But, because of the slump and stiffer competition in the computer industry, Control Data is reorganizing, trying to more clearly define and support its overall business strategy and to quicken its reaction time to its markets, Hopp says.

"The question is, are we best positioned to be able to succeed in the future? Is our corporate staff properly organized to achieve corporate objectives?" For training and development, he says, that means determining where responsibility should be placed for developing each employee group.

"We've always been a little decentralized in training. Our organizations that rely heavily on technical knowledge and skills have always been responsible for their own training and development. We've had little central responsibility for those groups, with the exception of the management and sales representatives, but even with those employees the various business units have had the flexibility to address their specific needs."

The directed move toward decentralization, Hopp says, is designed to ensure that responsibility for all staff functions is held in the most logical parts of the organization. "But to say that training could or should be totally centralized or decentralized is a little bit of a red herring. It's too simple a concept. As we analyze this, we'll find there are segments of the company that logically need to look more centralized for the economy of scale, or because of similarities in theme or culture. Others will need more independence.

"As we decentralize, however, we're working with the attitude that we have some values that all the organizations within the corporate structure should have in common. It may be that one of our corporate training objectives will be to help our various business units translate those common messages so the ideas can be woven into management throughout the company. We may not be mandating particular courses, but we'll be making certain that the key messages and values are communicated.

Control Data has used an outside consultant in the initial analysis of its structure, Hopp says. "Some people think of this cultural change as an earth-shattering event, but I think decentralization will be a fairly long process. If we look back three years from now, we'll probably be able to say, 'We've changed quite a bit.' But it will take the retrospect to see the slow, subtle changes."

A Case for Centralization

There's an ongoing debate at Carlson Marketing Group about what the corporate training department's role should be, says April Schmidlap, manager of training and development. The company uses centralized and decentralized training, but up until a year-and-a-half ago there was no corporate training staff.

"One of our biggest problems is the real lack of understanding of what training is all about," she says. Schmidlap's department — two people — handles all the professional skills training for an employee force of 1,200. Technical skills are taught in the various departments by subject-matter experts. "It's not unusual," Schmidlap says, "that training evolves in an organization, starting with coaching, then on-the-job training, and then moving, as we have, into formalized training. Now that we have a formalized department, how should it be operating?

"We're looking at some of the obvious advantages a centralized function would offer: a clearer overall direction and more uniformity in design and evaluation procedures. But there is significant resistance from people who support the already established decentralized training system.

"The solution to training needs in the past has been perceived as a matter of finding the people who do particular jobs best and letting them do the training. I'm not opposed to using subject-matter experts, but there is some recognition now that these people don't necessarily know all there is to know about training. Somehow, I've got to tactfully help these people understand there is a better way to train, that there is a lot to understand about the purpose and theory of training, about measurement and up-front analysis... and that our biggest concern is for the uniformity and quality of operations.

"We can't be all things to all people, but I believe there has to be a solid [reporting] line through our department for all training so we can properly assess and evaluate what we do.

"We've been getting a lot of verbal support from management for these ideas, but we are struggling. We are working desperately to get them involved in supporting and reinforcing training. I feel so strongly about centralizing our efforts because our program is so new. To get off on the right foot, we have to be clear on what we are doing; then we can develop flexibility."

Merging Cultures

American Savings Bank (ASB) dropped its preliminary plans to establish regional training centers in 1981 when, spurred by deregulation of the banking industry, it participated in a three-way merger, says Amelia Rego, director of training.

"The culture and environment of the banking industry, specifically savings banks, were so provincialized then that each bank thought of itself as separate from the rest of the banking system. 'We do things differently here' was a common attitude. If we regionalized our training, that attitude would probably have permeated, and we couldn't have that. We're a financial services company now, not merely a savings bank. We are working for a new culture and a new vision, so it helps to have people coming in from different areas to talk with each other."

However, part of developing a centralized program for the bank was inadvertent, Rego says. Initially, she was hired to deliver *Professional Selling Skills*, a Learning International program, which, along with a semi-formalized teller training program, was the sum of American Saving Bank's training efforts. "It was left pretty loose as to how I would work, but one of my goals was to eventually also set up formalized training." The centralized location Rego now uses for all training — except a "road show of new products and services" — was selected because it was an empty space in a building the bank owned.

In a larger organization (ASB has 1,100 employees located in and around New York), Rego says she would feel a stronger need for a more decentralized training formula. While employed at the GE Executive Development Center, she says, she worked with "lend/lease instructors," managers who were trained to deliver training modules at their regional locations, their own training centers, or satellite sites.

"If I were starting a new training department, I would look first at the organizational setup. If it were located predominantly in one area with easy accessibility to headquarters, I would lean towards centralizing. If it were national or regional, I would look at centralizing for the things that unify an organization, but would also look at setting up regional training sites. And I would look at the money available; if there was little money, I would centralize and plan to travel."

Fitting Strategic Plans

Ray Merritt performs the centralized-decentralized balancing act on two levels as training manager for Martin Marietta Aggregates, a 2,100-person division of Martin Marietta that produces crushed stone for construction projects. On the company level, Merritt trains employees in 13 states at 90 different locations. He also uses training programs provided by Martin Marietta's corporate training staff, which to some extent serves all of the corporation's 60,000 employees.

"One of our overriding objectives is to make sure that training is tied into the company's and the corporation's strategic plans. We feel we can do that best by developing a consistent approach to employee and manage-

Balance is the keyword when deciding between a centralized and decentralized training structure.

ment development. To do that we have to centralize our course development, and the order and priority of how those courses are delivered.

"But we leave the selection of who attends up to the districts. They know best what needs their people have. We're also decentralized because we don't have a training center, I go to our locations and offer the training. We find that more cost and time effective than to have guys from the Midwest come to Raleigh [NC].

"We also get input from the field through surveys and personal contact. If demand is strong enough for a particular kind of training, we put together a pilot and see how it works. For instance, we've had a lot of success with Blessing/White's *Managing Personal Growth* in that kind of situation. But we won't go full-scale until we try something with our district people to see if it is relevant."

Merritt says, "I don't think a centralized training operation would be as effective for us as our mobile organization. Everything we do becomes a logistics problem. Training has to be tied into our jobs. Our business pushes people for time; they are concerned about money because each district operates as a profit center. Our training has to be related to the bottom line. We can't be seen as a burden."

On the corporate level, Merritt takes advantage of that training staff's ability to also function centrally or on-site. He sends middle and upper managers to a corporate *Advanced Management* program in Bethesda, MD, but brings the staff in to conduct an *Effective Supervisory Practices* program for lower-level managers.

"The big advantage to sending middle and upper managers to Bethesda is that they're with people from other parts of the corporation and get a view of what is going on throughout the organization. And regardless of their businesses, they find that the management and people problems are pretty much the same.

"With the first-line supervisors, we find it's more effective to have people together who are in the same business and going through training for the first time. Also, we might put 80 people through this program and far fewer through the *Advanced Management*. So, from the cost standpoint it is cheaper to do it in-house."

Merritt says, "If we had more people to do training, I imagine I would spread them out; put a specialist in Des Moines or Omaha and make that person responsible for a region. I would maintain our decentralization on a smaller scale. We can keep in better touch that way. We can decide what programs to do companywide. Or, on a district level, people can tell us what they'd like to have and we can control the quality and consistency we need.

"That's what fits our management structure best. And we've learned how important it is to make sure the direction training goes is supported by top management, that training be tied into the overall company direction and development."

Dignity in Decentralization

Ken Bardach warns that imbalance between centralized and decentralized training, as a subset of overall management and development, can be devastating. Bardach, formerly a trainer with John Deere and Harris Corp., is director of executive programs at the Boston University School of Management.

"A business system that is too centralized," Bardach says, "creates bureaucracy and pushes the decision making away from the grass roots. At the other extreme, you become a holding company and you lose any potential for synergism.

"There is a delicate balance that is needed. Balance isn't as sexy as extremism, but it is a very important watchword. You need good thrust and momentum, but everything ties into other things. Training is a subset of development; it means growing people, linking needs to performance appraisal and career pathing and more. To expect all units in a company to do that well on their own... well, it just doesn't happen. You need a corporate or centralized model to coordinate it. Innovative training and career pathing and performance appraisal are great, but if they're not consistent with the company's climate or goals, they don't make sense.

"But if *everything* comes from the core, it feels like things are being imposed and as if there is no choice but to implement as instructed. To not get ownership is detrimental. At the very least, you have to give people the latitude to customize and build upon the core you create.

"This kind of decentralization, I believe, is the sum and essence of dignity for the individual. There is nothing worse than a company that is too bureaucratic, one where a president makes a declaration and thinks, 'It's done.' People want to be self-actualized implementers, not just implementers.

"That is the balance you have to strive for. And I have seen a lot of organizations struggle by not constantly working for that respect and interaction."

Control Data's Hopp says, "Clearly, neither centralization or decentralization is a panacea to solving training problems." Much like the continual swing of support between liberal and conservative politics, Hopp says, the pendulum swings, too, between the changing needs of particular training departments at particular times.

Malcolm Warren, director of training and organization development for CVS, told attendees at a Training Directors' Forum Conference: There is no organization structure which is correct [for every organization], and no organization structure in existence is correct for long. There are many solutions to getting people to work together effectively."

Notes:

Centralizing Training

A look at how one company answered, should we?

BY RICHARD D. BOWSER

The training department of the new Equitable General Insurance Company had always been involved solely with providing licensing, product, and sales training for the Equitable life agents, who would soon begin selling auto and homeowners insurance in eight southwestern states. The question was then raised: Should the training department also provide training services for those company employees who would be underwriting and servicing the new Equi-Gen policies?

Ultimately, top management decided to have the training department assume responsibility for all company training programs.

Before reaching this critical decision, management took a long, hard look at the advantages and disadvantages of centralized training. To assess the potential value of a centralized training department, they asked — and answered—some basic questions.

What are the advantages of a centralized training department?

- *It relieves the line supervisors of time required for training*, thus improving production by allowing supervisors to concentrate on their production responsibilities.
- *It reduces training time.* Since the new employee would generally be trained away from his work area, there would be less distraction, allowing him or her to concentrate on learning the material. This approach also allows supervisors and coworkers to concentrate on their regular duties, free from the distractions of a new trainee. By the time the new employee comes to the job, he or she will have acquired the basic skills and be able to start producing right away, causing minimal disruption of the work flow.
- *It fosters professionalism in training.* Just as skills of a manager differ from those of a salesman, so do the skills of a trainer differ from those of a supervisor. A supervisor's job is to manage people and to keep the work flowing smoothly. A trainer's job, on the other hand, is to prepare the new employee to begin effective production.
- *It provides for better control of training.* One problem with training conducted by line supervisors it that there is seldom enough time to do an adequate job. Line supervisors, pressured by the work flow, often end up giving the new employee only a brief orientation and introduction to the work setting. Often an older worker is responsible for helping a newcomer "learn the ropes." Usually, the new employee takes production time away from the older worker by asking a lot of basic questions. And the new employee doesn't really learn what he or she needs to know because the training lacks an organized method or format. A centralized training department is able to: a) research the need for skills training; b) determine the best method of providing this training; c) administer the training in a logical step-by-step program, making sure the trainee learns everything he or she needs to know; and d) follow up to assure that the trainee has acquired the necessary skills and to do necessary remedial training. In addition, a centralized training unit is able to continually improve and modify training programs to meet changing needs.
- *It reduces duplication among departments.* Since many new-employee training needs are identical or closely related in content, a centralized training department can train in combined classes, using equipment and materials tailored to meet each individual department's training specifications. Thus, a centralized training department saves money; there is less duplication of equipment, materials, etc. And a centralized training department eliminates the need for a part-time trainer in each department, thus allowing employees to concentrate on their production responsibilities.

What are the disadvantages of a centralized training department?

- *Line managers and supervisors "lose control" of the training.* The issue of control is generally not a problem when the responsibilities between the line department and the centralized training department are clearly defined at the beginning. As a staff operation, a training department must, of necessity, work closely with each line department to assure that training is correctly administered. In the end, the responsibility for training still rests with the line department, but the actual hands-on training can best be done by the training department.
- *Line supervisors have technical expertise which trainers often lack.* This disadvantage is overcome when the training department utilizes line department personnel as "resource" people to develop and administer training materials. Thus the trainers can acquire technical expertise from various resource people — who are not taken off their jobs and whose daily production is not interrupted.
- *Expense is reduced without a formal training department.* In truth, without a centralized training department, each line department has to purchase its own equipment and training materials, thus increasing training costs rather than reducing them.
- *Line department training can put a new employee into production immediately.* This is true only if the new employee already has the basic skills necessary to do the job. And even when the employee does have these skills, he or she must learn the new company's procedures before effective production can begin.

Will a centralized training department take work away from the line managers and supervisors?

The answer is both "yes" and "no." Yes, it will take some work away from the line managers and supervisors because they will no longer be responsible for administering initial training to new employees. No, it will not take work away because they will still have the ultimate responsibility for seeing that their people are adequately trained. A centralized training department will relieve the supervisors of the need for personally administering initial training, thus allowing them to concentrate on their primary job duties.

What should be the objectives of a centralized training department?

The primary objective should be threefold:

1. To get new employees into effective production within the shortest possible time;

2. To increase production levels of all employees; and

3. To prepare current employees to assume positions of greater responsibility.

The best method for meeting these objectives is a five-step "systems" approach to training-program creation.

• *Initial needs analysis* — to determine exactly where training is needed within the organization.

• *Development of program objectives* — to determine what the trainee should be able to do upon completing the training that he or she could not do before.

• *Design and development of the actual program.* The trainer works closely with technical experts in each of the line departments to make the training program technically accurate.

• *Testing and medication.* The program must be tested to make sure that it both teaches the material and meets the objectives set for it. After initial testing, modifications and improvements can be made.

• *Implementation and administration.*

In what areas of training should a centralized training department be involved?

Before answering this question, it must be determined which areas need training. In most cases, a centralized training department is involved in all training programs, including initial company orientation, job skills training, communications training, supervisory and management skills training, and administration of industry courses (IIA, CPCU, etc.). In addition, the centralized training department can serve to tie together diverse departments within a company, continually reminding them that the company has one primary operating objective.

Based on its answers to these questions, management at Equitable General Insurance Company decided that training should be considered an investment in human assets rather than an expense. They have seen that investment pays dividends in greater organizational growth, greater efficiency on the job, reduced operational expenses, and, eventually, increased profits.

Notes:

What's Wrong With Corporate Training?

We preach that training is a competitive necessity — and then fill our catalogs with courses that do everything except help the business compete.

BY GLORIA COSGROVE
AND ROY SPEED

Training has an important role to play in the restructuring of American industry that is now taking place, but you would never know it from looking at most corporate training departments. Senior executives haven't taken the trouble to nail down the role of training in their companies, and they consistently underestimate its value as a tool in developing their businesses. They have come to view it mainly as a bone to be tossed to employees — a perk when things are going well, a morale-booster when they're not.

Training departments, for their part, have done plenty to encourage this view and very little to steer training in the right direction. They have failed to demonstrate the usefulness of training in achieving management objectives, and thus have thrown into doubt the legitimacy of training's contribution to the organization's primary goals.

Before we go further, let's clarify a point that too often goes unspoken in discussions of "training" as a whole. Anyone who bothers to examine the world of corporate training quickly notices that there are two different realms of training activity, with quite different purposes.

The first kind of training addresses the skills needed to perform a specific job: how to drive a forklift, how to use a computer system or software package, how to distinguish and sell insurance policies or financial instruments. While people may argue about delivery methods (formal vs. on-the-job training, for instance), no one doubts the basic legitimacy of this type of instruction. Everyone understands that, somehow or other, job-skills training must be done.

The second kind of training is a little more difficult to define, but it's where the big money usually is spent. This training is intended to support broad management objectives and the performance of the organization as a whole. It is this kind of training that we are especially concerned with here.

In larger companies, far too many of the people who manage and staff corporate training departments see their jobs in a limiting and ultimately self-defeating way. They practice what we call the catalog approach; they are obsessed with providing handsome catalogs of training programs. And senior executives, to the detriment of their companies, have allowed this approach to flourish.

A Catalog of Obsessions

The catalog approach may have seemed like common sense when it first evolved. But in most companies it has degenerated to the point where training is seen as essentially superfluous — nice but hardly necessary. The catalog approach is characterized by a number of common training department obsessions. Here's a short list:

• *Providing courses.* Training managers believe that their job is to offer training courses — the more, the better. Once you accept that your purpose in life is to provide courses, your time and energy get channeled into selecting them, scheduling them, advertising them, filling them, getting classrooms and equipment for them, checking attendance at them and so on. You become a porter for administrative baggage. At the bottom of this obsession is the illusion that activity equals results, and thus that more courses mean greater accomplishments.

• *Pleasing the crowd.* If it's your job to provide courses, then it would be embarrassing if nobody came. To avoid this specter, training managers must fill their courses. Consequently, they end up catering to popular tastes. The obsession with pleasing the crowd partly accounts for the growing role of fashion and fads in corporate curricula, as illustrated by the rapid translation of best-selling management books into best-selling training programs. After all, executives are suckers for a good fad, just like the rest of us, and if you're providing courses that have the right buzzwords in their titles, management tends to assume that you're bringing in the latest and greatest.

• *Making employees feel good.* We all know that corporate restructurings and downsizings have been hard on employees whose jobs are eliminated; but they also are hard on those left behind. Training managers have reacted by providing more programs they think might improve morale: courses in stress management, boosting self-esteem and so on. These crowd-pleasing programs also help ward off the embarrassment of unattended courses — hence the popularity of the "personal growth" model that so many companies' curricula now seem to be built around. Senior managers acquiesce in the plot, thinking it an easy way to do something (please, anything!) about morale.

• *Fixing problems.* Training managers who have followed the path outlined thus far will inevitably begin to sense that their efforts are not exactly essential to the organization's driving goals and purposes. Observing all the heads rolling down corporate hallways, training managers naturally begin to fear the ax themselves. The challenge then becomes to appear useful. And when you want to appear useful, your savior is problems — any problems. Because if you're a training manager, you can almost always position training (i.e., you) as the solution to the problem. Question: How often are "needs assessments" initiated not to uncover real business needs and determine the most promising solutions for them, but rather to enable training managers to make a case for their own continued existence?

The catalog approach, then, is a trap from which it is not easy to extricate yourself. Like the emperor with the new clothes, you're vulnerable to the simplest doubts and the most childlike questions, such as: How is training adding value to this organization? Such questions strike fear in the hearts of training managers. The mania for evaluation and hard data that has arisen in the past few years is at least partially a response to their panic.

If you find yourself mired in the catalog approach, you probably shouldn't be thinking in terms of fixing the training function. You're going to have to think more in terms of recreating the training function from scratch. And that simple question — How will this activity add value to the organization? — must become your touchstone. It instantly reveals the absurdity of certain measures of how well you're doing your job (number of classes, number of participants, cost per person) and the validity of others.

The Problem With "Fixes"

If you want to refocus (i.e., fix) your approach to training, your first instinct might be to conduct a needs assessment. But a needs analysis in no way guarantees that you'll get your training efforts on the right track. In fact, even the most sincere needs assessments sometimes serve only as examples of what can go wrong when you simply try to fix what already exists, rather than rebuilding from the ground up.

To illustrate, suppose that a company is undergoing drastic downsizing. The training department, wanting to be useful in this difficult time, conducts a traditional needs analysis, asking the question: What skills do our employees need? The conclusion is that they need programs in managing and understanding change. Accordingly, the company begins cycling hundreds of employees through seminars that teach them (or purport to teach them) how to cope psychologically with change and uncertainty.

But at some point the company's managers realize that such programs are irrelevant if not downright distracting. The problem originates with the question the needs analysis was designed to answer. Instead of, What skills do our employees need? the question should have been, What skills does the organization need?

A new needs analysis, designed to answer the second question, concludes that what this particular company desperately needs is to move forward. The organization has a change-management problem, all right, but the change it needs to encourage right now is to get people to think in terms of short-term results. It needs a companywide focus on defining short-term goals and achieving them. The generic coping-with-change seminars are contributing nothing to that purpose.

> "Once you accept that your purpose in life is to provide courses, you become a porter for administrative baggage."

So what shall we do? If we can't just "fix" the catalog approach, should we dump training altogether? Any organization that does so at this point had better pray that its competitors do the same, for at no time has the training industry been better poised to serve American companies. The proliferation of new training technologies and more efficient delivery mechanisms adds up to one thing: a resource that companies ignore at their peril. The rest of the world is waking up to this fact — which explains why the United States is viewed in other countries as a kind of training mecca.

If eliminating our training department would be a bad idea, what are we to do with it?

Know Your Organization

Let's review the crux of the problem. Over time, the average training department's real goals have had more and more to do with its own continued existence and less to do with realizing senior management's strategic objectives. Many training managers don't even know precisely what the corporate strategy is, let alone how the training department might serve that strategy.

So here's the first question we must answer: What precisely is the business strategy? One place to begin is with the company's strategic plan. It will at least give you an idea of what the company's articulated priorities are. Don't assume, however, that reading your company's strategic plan is sufficient preparation. It is nothing more than a preliminary step.

The next task is much more difficult: Compare the company's articulated goals and priorities with its real goals, as demonstrated by its actions.

Suppose that executives start trumpeting a devotion to "innovation champions." A training manager might be tempted to conclude that training should support that value — by offering seminars on creative thinking, for instance. But how are champions of change and innovation actually treated in the company? When they raise their heads above the crowd, are they praised and promoted, or do entrenched middle managers lop off their heads as soon as they're visible? It is a training manager's responsibility to analyze the real reward system. You must be intimately familiar with all such disparities between professed values and real actions. Only then will you understand how pointless it would be to spend a lot of money on creative thinking seminars.

What we are suggesting is that it is virtually impossible to recreate the training function in a company without understanding the company's underlying structures. More and more companies are professing "values" along with specific strategic objectives, a trend fraught with danger for training managers.

To illustrate, suppose word comes down from the top that the company will adopt the "team" concept; senior management wants greater emphasis on teams. Which of the following initiatives would be appropriate?

A. Launch a new series of team-building workshops for line employees.

B. Sponsor a series of management summits in which all work is to be reorganized and all functions redesigned in alignment with the team concept.

C. Investigate: Find out what management means by "the team concept" and — more important still — which real-world objectives management is trying to accomplish by forming teams.

We suggest that you resist the usual training responses and select the last approach. Chances are, alternatives A and B would both end up reinforcing the view of training as a function completely separate from mainstream result-getting. Alternative C, on the other hand, would enable you to address your actions, whatever they might turn out to be, to the real intended result — rather than the activity that happens to be the flavor of the month. This shift, away from a focus on activities and toward a focus on results, is one key to ensuring training's ongoing relevance and contribution to the organization.

The company's strategic plan provides at best a skeletal picture of where senior executives would like the company to be. And even if that picture does appear to jibe with the real goals, training managers must flesh out the skeleton by determining the qualities, skills and approaches managers and employees would need to run the company in a manner consistent with the objectives. Two essential steps in this process:

• Examine the work force. Where do the employees currently stand vis-à-vis the desired qualities, skills and approaches?

• From the start, before you train anybody to do anything, put some measurement systems in place. Choose measures that track progress toward specific management objectives.

A final word of warning: Resist the tendency to commence with sweeping change or to start with the toughest challenge ("If we can do it there, we can do it anywhere..."). Instead, look for receptive areas or audiences, and focus on a limited number of specific results. Build credibility from there.

Rebuilding on a New Foundation

Any manager of a catalog-oriented training function who undertakes the kind of organizational analysis we've described will soon draw a conclusion: If training is really to serve the company's strategic objectives, the training department has to be recreated.

As with all restructurings, retooling the training department can be a painful process. The department frequently must be rebuilt from the ground up, starting with new assumptions about training's fundamental raison d'être, and redesigning not only the menu of programs, but the way those programs are selected. It means establishing direct communication channels with senior managers and keeping an eye on their changing objectives. Also, since those objectives may change abruptly, it means being able to stop on a dime, make hairpin turns and, from time to time, dismantle the whole department again and reinvent it in yet another form, one that better serves the new strategic priorities — whatever they might be.

If American companies are to make better use of the training function, training managers must take the lead. They must apply to their own departments some of the advice about fundamental change that they've been preaching to the organization at large. They must set out not to "fix" their departments, but to recreate their functions from scratch.

Notes:

The Training Control Room: Creating Your Vision

Looking for a 'vision' for your training department? Try thinking of it as a factory control room.

BY MARTIN M. BROADWELL

One measure of a successful human resource department is its quick response to the organization's training needs. That's easy to say. It's even easy to measure. It's just hard to do. And it remains hard to do despite all the tips and techniques we hear about how to do it: how to run a quick-and-dirty needs analysis, how to develop an informal network of workers and line managers who can tell us where the fires are burning so we can put them out, and so on.

Maybe we've been going at it backwards. We generally think of training as a troubleshooting function. That's the mental framework in which we operate, and most of the techniques we use are geared to the troubleshooting mind-set. Suppose we changed our perception of training's role from one of troubleshooting to one of trouble preventing.

Suppose we were to redesign the training department as a sort of "control room" for the organization. Like a well-functioning control room in any manufacturing plant, the training function would be ready to react instantly to the first sign of impending trouble. How might such an arrangement work?

The Role

Whether it be a mill, a factory, a refinery or a power plant, there is always a place where all the important activities, from anywhere in the facility, can be monitored — and adjusted. The people who operate the control room have a unique job: They sit around and hope for nothing to do. For the most part, when they have to take action it's because something is not going correctly out in the plant. The pressure is too high or too low; the temperature is too warm or too cool; there is a break in a line. The control room has needles and gauges and computer readouts and bells and alarms — all kinds of on-line, immediate indications of how things are going right now.

The fact that the people in the control room often have little to do or aren't rushing around trying to look busy is a function of the job, not a sign of their uselessness. If they've done their job well in the past, and the operation they're monitoring was well-designed in the beginning, the facility should be running relatively smoothly.

Essentially, their job is to identify flaws in equipment, materials or operator functioning. Much like fire fighters, they mostly wait around to be called — but then they have to be ready to act quickly and effectively. Unlike fire fighters, however, they don't wait for a fire to act. They have the means in place to anticipate or predict possible hot spots. The measure of their worth is not in how well they extinguish fires but in how well they prevent fires from breaking out. So it should be with a good training organization.

The Big Picture

Let's look at the characteristics of a well-designed control room and see how far we can carry the analogy. First, the control room gets a total picture of what's happening in the operation being monitored. There is feedback from all parts of the mill or refinery, or at least from all those parts that have a large impact on the core operation.

When the control room was originally designed, its "architects" got assistance from everyone concerned: design experts, managers, professional specialists and skilled workers, all concurring in what information needed to be fed to the monitoring location. Since everyone recognized the importance of the control room function, there was little bickering. People agreed that information must flow from all critical points, and perhaps from some periphery areas as well. This information web was installed at the beginning, then added to or improved as new technologies or operations developed that required new monitoring capacities.

Those in charge of delivering training to the organization should have this same total picture. Training experts have preached "needs analysis" over the years, but the process almost never works in the manner we're talking about here. The problem may be that we've relied too much on one tool — a cumbersome one at that — to gather all the information we need. Needs analyses usually take a long time to prepare, a long time to administer and a long time to interpret, not to mention the time it takes to react to the findings and get the needed training in place.

There are other possibilities, some already in place, that could give us a better total picture. For instance, most organizations have some kind of performance appraisal system. It is the means by which those who are both knowledgeable about and responsible for behavior tell the organization how well things are going. Organizations find this a ready source of determining training needs — provided that the performance appraisal really is a good indicator of significant behavior, measuring specific performance against meaningful standards.

If the people responsible for gathering this performance data can make it available to those concerned with monitoring behavior for training needs, then it is a simple matter to convert the information into useful training courses. But it must be across-the-board data, not just a spattering of information from some departments or work levels but not others. Most especially, it must represent the judgment and insights of the experts: the managers and workers themselves.

Historically, the "personnel" department kept up with the appraisal results, and the "training" department looked after the training. In many cases they never communicated with each other, even though the two departments reported to the same vice president. This is like keeping information away from the control room because it is too delicate for the operators to know about.

There is another existing source of training needs that rarely gets noticed. Most organizations are replete with reports and forms and operating data that describe how things are going in functions such as R&D, production and sales. These need to be funneled to the training control room. If production is down, a training alarm should ring. If sales are down, the needle should go to yellow or red. If the board approves a new plant or a major expansion, bells should ring and whistles should blow. And it's not just trainers who should react to this inflow of data. Everyone who sees the information ought to look automatically to the training function to take action.

Every training class offers additional data about training needs. Suppose that alert instructors actually listen when trainees explain why things aren't working as they should. Suppose the instructors understand that they are hearing "control" signals. They would respond to the warning lights by recording the information, passing it on or investigating further.

Similarly, good course-evaluation sheets should be more than happiness ratings; they should serve as a collection mechanism for control-room data. These trainee-comment sheets offer a great sampling of what's going on out there in the world being served by the training department. Actual training needs surveys can be taken from this legitimate cross section of the organization's population.

Speed

Another feature of the effective factory control room is the "immediacy" or present-time factor. The information flowing to the control room must describe the state of affairs as it is right now, not sometime later when a reaction would be too late to help or when serious damage already has been done. A stuck valve or an overheating boiler isn't something that can be fixed at somebody's convenience. This points up two needs: The information must get there as the problem arises, or before, and the control room must be capable of taking action quickly and appropriately.

> "The information flowing to the control room must describe the state of affairs as it is right now, not some time later."

So it should be with the training operation. The information-gathering devices we mentioned (and others, of course) must come as close as possible to giving us present-time data. Predictive data would be even better. But unless we can respond quickly, having the data is not very helpful. This means the training organization must have enough expertise and experience to analyze performance problems quickly and intelligently, and to design and deliver good instruction.

The training "control room" cannot be staffed only with new people or borrowed people or people who are familiar with the business but not trained in treating malfunctions. It must include a core of skilled professionals who are prepared to react to trouble and able to anticipate possible problems enough in advance to do preventive training.

There will always be a need for new people and even borrowed people, but it would be foolhardy to leave the training control room in the hands of inexperienced operators — just as it would be silly to do so with a factory control room. The staff must have the expertise to read the data and receive support from management for making the correct response.

Closing the Loop

A final look at the analogy tells us we'll need to follow up on the actions taken by those in the control room. Did the valve close and was the pressure stabilized? Did maintenance arrive in time to stop the leak? Were the appropriate people notified in cases in which further management decisions were needed beyond the control room's authority or ability to respond?

The training job isn't completed when we have taken action. It is only finished when the deficiency is taken care of. This means going back to the original sources of data to see if we now get proper readings. Perhaps the indicators will tell us that we overlooked something in our initial response. For instance, maybe this wasn't entirely a training need after all; maybe some policies or procedures need attending to.

Good training control room operators would sit in a critical seat in the organization. They'd have the opportunity, the obligation and the thrill of keeping things running smoothly. Pretty exciting "vision," eh?

4 Ways You Can Make Training a Strategic Business Imperative

This award-winning training unit stays plugged into top management in the company.

BY DAVE ZIELINSKI

Keeping current on the strategic direction of your company — no small challenge these days as plans shift about as often as the wind direction — remains one of the best ways to ensure training efforts don't become marginalized. That's not much of a problem at Geisinger Health Systems in Danville, PA, where training manager Georgia Geise and her team have worked for years to tie training and consulting services to key business needs by developing close relationships with the company's leaders.

Geise and her staff lobbied the CEO and other top executives to have lunch with the group in mid-October 1994 to talk about a mandatory change management process underway at Geisinger. "For two hours we sat and picked their brains about hot issues in managed care and the direction of the organization," Geise says. "In turn, they got to hear our latest proposals for team-based training for the company."

It's those hard-won, high-level connections that helped the team garner a *Training Directors' Forum Award* in the category of tying training services to business imperatives.

Ideas for Increasing Training's Influence

Here are some of the ways Geise's seven-person training team has made education pay off for the organization:

• **Get the CEO's ear.** Accumulate a series of training successes, and making sure the rest of the company knows about it via marketing efforts. Geise says in her 18 years in the training field, "I have never had as much support for the function as I have now, and never had this many trainers on staff." One reason is the staff has stepped out of the training box to continually generate new ideas — and not always traditional training solutions — for performance problems.

• **Help manage change.** Geisinger Medical is going through a significant cultural transformation, moving from a traditional hierarchal structure to one that is more team based. To support the shift, Geise's team created a system-wide change management process. The training has these components: a two-hour workshop, *Mastering the Challenge of Change*, presented first to senior leaders, then to 7,000 employees; a train-the-trainer session that prepared over 26 line workers to deliver training; and a level 3 measurement tool to assess training transfer.

• **Focus on building teams.** Teams are key to the company's success, so Geise's team offers team-building interventions to departments and clinics throughout the system. The intervention is a three-stage process: (1) individual interviews with all team members; (2) follow-up reports with recommendations; (3) experiential training, group facilitation, and departmentally specific skill training. The department also offers what it calls "change agent" service, where clients can choose from a menu of options to help them facilitate change via a six-step protocol, Geise says.

In addition, the company's performance appraisal system is becoming team-based, and training is developing new job competencies for team leaders and team members, says Geise. Among team member competencies, for instance, are skills like flexibility, conflict management, planning, and conducting meetings. Leader competencies are similar, but include skills like coaching, relationship building, and decision making.

• **Facilitate information sharing.** In conjunction with senior managers, the team developed an *Executive Leadership Program* for 140 senior level physicians and administrative leaders. The program's goal is to get leaders to share "best practices" with their peers, build relationships, and to develop more consistent and innovative leadership practices. Titles of some of those courses include: influencing through effective communication, service excellence in health care, techniques of financial decision making, and strategic planning.

There is also a mandatory general leadership curriculum for anyone in the company who is in a leadership position, or aspires to be. It is a multiphase program that includes a 36-month learning cycle.

Meeting the Need for Shorter, Targeted Classes

The team also developed two new training concepts in response to requests for shorter, more targeted training interventions. *Style Clinics* are

> Working hard to capture the ear of top managers and making sure the right people know about training successes ensures this training function is a hot ticket.

abbreviated sessions that focus solely on case studies and feedback in relation to how managers come across to their employees and team members; *Skill Clinics* are shorter sessions that deal with specific skill topics like writing skills, assertiveness, and so on. The need for shorter sessions is particularly important in light of the eight to 10 courses many employees will take as part of the mandatory team-based training.

"That's a long time away from jobs," Geise says. "We are working hard to take the 'nice to have' stuff out of all of our courses, and to focus only on those skills or knowledge employees absolutely need on the job right away. We're not going longer than three hours for any given segment."

An assertiveness training course that once ran eight hours was first cut to four hours, for example, and then shortened again to two hours, "without losing much impact," Geise says. The course includes a detailed overview of what assertive behavior looks like, then asks employees to role-play in triads.

Notes:

Working With Top Management

Linking to corporate plans is an advisable training strategy.

BY BRIAN McDERMOTT

General Motors is engineering corporate cultural changes because earnings have sagged. The U.S. major-appliance industry is tightening operations to fend off foreign competition. Even IBM and AT&T, once bastions of security and profitability, are cutting costs and eliminating jobs. Businesses of all sizes are more frequently equating efficiency with survival, and the message ringing clearer than ever for trainers is, "Contribute or be gone."

Perhaps the best way to assure that a training function contributes toward reaching organizational goals is to directly link all education and skills development programs to corporate strategic business plans. Often, however, that is easier said than done. Many companies operate without formal strategic plans; others pass them down to the training department reluctantly, in fragments, or with little explanation or understanding of how training fits in.

In the best situations human resources people are integral parts of the strategic planning process; in the toughest situations they fight for the same information given freely, and with great expectation, to the operations areas. Somewhere in the middle, it seems, is the most common situation: Human resources folks are peripherally involved in formulating strategic plans, but primarily responsible for reacting to management dictates.

Patrick Pinto, an industrial psychologist and a facilitator for the annual *Training Directors' Forum Conference*, believes that a training director — and a training function — solidly linked to corporate strategic business plans can play a leadership role in setting organization strategies. There are at least three arenas in which that linkage can be improved, Pinto says: structural, cultural and political.

Structural Links

"Traditionally, strategy determines the business a company is in and how it is going to survive. The business plans based on that strategy allocate the resources and determine where a business is going and how it is going to get there.

"When you think in terms of strategic planning meetings, the HRD people, at best, are on the fringes. When the strategy is set and the plans formulated, the senior managers then turn to the HRD person and ask the stupid question, 'Can you support this plan?' No one is going to say, 'No!' There might be some respectful dissent, but that person will support the plan. There really is no choice.

"These plans have direct implications for human resources management, and training in particular. What I've talked about is an example of the plan leading human resources development (HRD). The best situation, however, is when human resources people are at the table formulating these plans, emphasizing what moves can be made based on the capabilities and competencies of the work force. Unfortunately, that is not happening much if you are talking about HRD."

In his experience, Pinto says, structural changes in organizations — taking training out of the personnel department and making it directly accountable to senior management — have improved training's link to business plans. The direct connection to upper-level executives, he says, increases the likelihood that HRD people can influence strategy.

Cultural Links

"Strategy and culture go hand-in-hand, and I believe that we trainers are unusually positioned to deal with culture. We understand it. We can measure it. We can provide interventions to modify it.

"Many organizational leaders don't really understand culture. They understand business decisions, but those decisions are made in context of the culture. The factors may include the company's policies on promotion from within, its emphasis on internal development, its reliance on its own research and development. The company may not favor growth through acquisition.

"Trainers, I think, should identify for top management those aspects of the culture that support or detract from the company's strategy. Trainers can articulate these things for those who don't have the language or the instruments."

Political Links

The third linkage factor, Pinto says, is political, which extends from learning the company's business to honing individual influence skills.

"Implicit in the definition of strategy is that all of a company's activities are integrated. That means trainers have to understand how the business works if they are going to integrate.

"Personnel people, including trainers, tend to whine more than others about the lack of respect they get regarding their business knowledge. But I don't think there is any function that is uniquely or more strategically positioned than any others. It may be that we whine because we rely too much on our technical skill base. There is a naiveté that a lot of HRD people possess. We believe there is a right and a wrong way to do things. We have a sincere belief in the basic goodness of humanity, in truth and beauty and light... that good will win out.

"We hide behind that, however, instead of getting out and learning the business and the political aspects of the company. I'm not talking about lying through your teeth or backstabbing, but we can't simply promote ourselves because we know more about training than anyone else in our organizations. We'd better. But that's not what's going to impress senior management.

"We've got to wake up to the political realities. We've got to be team players and understand what impacts the organization. At times we have to ignore the organizationally destitute and invest in the winning parts of the business." Pinto also suggests:

• Get the basics right. Make sure the training department provides the services that are needed and expected before being too concerned about participating in the formulation of strategic plans.

• Offer your expertise to facilitate or to find a facilitator for corporate strategic planning sessions. Remember, however, if you facilitate you may limit your ability to contribute content to the discussions.

• Offer facilitator expertise to the various strategic business units in your company, especially if you can't link at the top levels. It can earn you credibility.

• Save a failing endeavor. It takes experience to know when your risks in such a venture are minimal, but it also takes patrons and sponsors. Find out who the clear winners are in your company and hitch up, unashamedly.

• Remember, you'll never be able to leave the training function if you don't have a strategic focus on business. Who would want you?

Earning Credibility at 3M

The political aspects of positioning training are somewhat reduced for Tom Mehring at 3M Corp. As manager of the graphic arts training and development department, he reports to the marketing directors in that division. He says, however, "You have to earn the right to be involved in strategic planning."

3M is a fragmented organization, Mehring says, where directives from the corporate level are filtered down to the divisions and incorporated into five-year plans. "In training, we take that information and build programs to support the strategies identified. As in all operating functions, we have to prioritize. There are many more programs that are needed than we have resources for, So, we go back to management and review the requested programs in light of those resources and make decisions."

Mehring says his involvement in strategic planning sessions helps him in such discussions to understand the delicate balance managers must achieve between short-term profit needs and the long-term investments needed to fulfill strategic plans. I helped facilitate the process, but I was also contributing information about 25 percent of the time. I learned a tremendous amount. Training really is a support function. We have some limited impact on the direction of the business. The critical thing, though, is to have an in-depth understanding of where the business is going."

Despite what the business media have described as a shake-up to reinvigorate sluggish profits at 3M, Mehring says, the demand on training hasn't changed much. The long-term goals and requirements for profitability are constant. "Our training situation is improving, however. Our credibility and the impact we have been able to make is growing. And the more credible we become, the more we are allowed to get involved with critical business issues." For example, Mehring says, his department recently completed an expensive — and successful — cross-training program in support of a switch in market direction. "Now we're looked at to help in other areas."

"You have to earn the right to be involved in strategic planning."

Mehring says, "I feel very strongly that we can sit and cry about the lack of respect for training or we can start building the right to have it. We can do a good job with what we're allowed to do, then broaden our focus and arena. Some of that is happening for me now with my involvement in strategic planning. But I am constantly trying to get more and more involved. Then I will understand the whys of our business; then I'll have the ownership in the plans that I need."

Mehring's efforts have included:

• Coming up with and sticking to training solutions that he feels are needed to develop people effectively.

• Volunteering to facilitate meetings not related to strategic planning in order to increase the receptivity to training.

• Working to eliminate the stereotype of the training function providing only classroom activities, and promoting the idea that trainers are the experts to turn to in people-related matters.

• Taking what strategic planning information is available to training and using it to plan proactively: canceling, altering or developing programs as needed, and on his own initiative, rather than waiting for directives from management. (To aid in this process Mehring creates a matrix, identifying major strategic issues in the left column and listing all current courses along the top of the grid. Courses that don't help fulfill the strategies get pushed to the bottom of the priority list.)

Philosophical Connections

Dan Powell Smith was hired as director of management development and communications at Pennsylvania House because the company was looking for help in better implementing its strategies.

The home-furnishings company wants to be the leader in its segment of the market, Smith says, and bases its plans on three obsessions: service, existing for the customer, and respect for the individual. "The biggest problem with statements like that is that if they are not reflective of what is really going on, the people down in the organization say, 'That's fine, but we don't really operate that way.' When I fell into this job it appeared, from the long-range plans and the mission and objectives statements that had been written, that we needed development at every level of the company.

"Basically I have found my job in management development is tied to that value of respect for the individual, whether it's our employees, vendors or whomever." The process of integrating training, Smith says, has been evolutionary. Previously the training function was largely administrative, but now, based on performance, has been able to have more impact.

Smith says:

• His organization development efforts have concentrated on working with key managers to develop organization plans, which now drive succession planning efforts, as well as planning and development for people in their current jobs. The result has been more intelligent placement of individuals during a time of rapid growth for the company.

• He has been involved in producing a system and training that dramatically improved the company's performance-appraisal program.

• He has worked to better prepare line managers for their roles as trainers.

"I think you have to be patient. These kinds of changes take dogged determination. It took me more than four months to prove that the training we were going to use (Zenger-Miller) was what the organization needed. You've got to be a little stubborn; not bone-headed, but confident and competent.

"My feeling is that you also have to be personally and philosophically in line with what an organization wants to do. I think I automatically had some credibility because I believe so strongly in the need to respect the individual, and the company is moving in that direction. I looked at some companies that were diametrically opposed to what I believe. I'm lucky not to be there."

Emphasizing Action at Hasbro

Profits at Hasbro Inc. soared 85 percent annually from 1980 to 1985, according to *Business Week* magazine, making it a leading toy manufacturer in the world. Jim Good, the company's one-person training department, works to integrate HRD into Hasbro's business cycle by:

• Emphasizing results.
• Making sure training relates to goals.
• Instituting succession planning.
• Working to solve immediate needs.

"A simple example: Because of complaints about people skills, I've done supervisory training on all three shifts. I've been here at 1 a.m. on Saturdays. It's not tough trying to sell managers on linking training to their plans. Managers want to get things done. We don't talk about it, we do it.

"The important thing is to manage people with respect. Be fair. Listen. That all happens from the top of the company. I'm just a part of the process. I've got to work with the people in compensation and benefits, employee relations and staffing. We've got to work together as a team and just try to have some fun."

Meeting Immediate Needs at GM

As manager of employee training for the General Motors Acceptance Corp. (GMAC), Larry McElwain's major assignments come down to him from his vice president.

"In a smaller organization it might be good for me to be involved more directly in strategic planning meetings. But here, someone has to be [between the strategic planning group and me] to determine needs so I can provide the best service. Otherwise I would only ever go to meetings and never get anything done."

GMAC's planning process includes input from the personnel department, McElwain says, which manages human resource development as a subject area, rather than a specific staff.

"At this point we're very content with what we are doing in strategic planning and training. We still have to put out some fires, but we are looking much further ahead than we have in the past."

There is a great expanse between policies set on the corporate level and his immediate training responsibilities, McElwain says. "There is always room for improvement; at times connections break down, but the communication links are quite good. Information usually gets to you quite expeditiously."

Although his connection to strategic planning is indirect, McElwain says, "I believe you've got to know what has the attention of the people above you in order to meet the needs of the people below. What are they looking the hardest at? If that is political, it's political. I just call it doing my job."

Notes:

Do We Still Need Formal T&D?

Concerned training executives sound off.

BY DAVE ZIELINSKI

In a spirited discussion on the Internet, a group of concerned trainers recently explored the question, "Do organizations still need formal training and development?" At issue was whether training as it exists in many companies today — housed in a designated staff department, relying more heavily on formal classroom instruction than on-the-job "as needed" learning, and staffed largely by non-subject-matter experts — is best suited to help companies tackle competitive challenges going into the next century.

Here's a sampling of their thoughts:

The Future: Training "Brokers" in Line Units?

"If by 'formal' training and development we mean the generic vanilla corporate programs on time management, customer service, and so on, then we no longer need it. If by formal T&D programs we mean strictly classroom delivery, then we no longer need formal T&D.

"However, if by formal T&D we mean the ability to analyze the business needs of the organization and competency needs of its employees, and the ability to design, deliver, or administer education that weds the needs of the business with required competencies of employees, then we desperately need formal training and development.

"As long as there is an executive who says, 'Train 'em,' we need someone to counter with: 'Why? Is classroom training really the right answer to meet the business need/performance problem? Could this not be done instead with job aids, CBT, action learning, mentoring?'

"I suspect, however, that the days of large training departments are over. A small — even a one-person — training department that does needs analysis and evaluation, and facilitates or does design before seeking other delivery methods, might be the appropriate model for the future. This small department would make the buy/build decision and act as recruiter, occasional instructor, and 'broker' for given line units and external/internal delivery and design resources, who might be plumbers, programmers, or, perish the thought, managers in the real world."

— *Susan Keen, Sunquest Information Systems, Tucson, AZ*

Needed: A Comeback for Quality OJT

"Whatever happened to on-the-job training (OJT)?

"As the rate of technological change accelerated, system complexity grew faster than the informal OJT systems could accommodate, resulting in vast variances in the quality of training. Industry responded by first identifying subject-matter experts (SMEs) who would train groups of workers (still sort of OJT, only with less one-on-one), then by formalizing training departments as the quality continued to be below acceptable levels.

"Unfortunately, in the name of organizational standardization, areas where OJT would have continued to be acceptable were also transitioned to formal training.

"How about the present and the future? One trend I've seen in today's environment is that the declining training budgets of downsizing companies have collided with ISO 9000 requirements in such a way that OJT has made something of a comeback, particularly in the less-technical manufacturing processes. In the future, I suspect the technology of electronic performance support systems (EPSS) will be at least a partial, probably majority, answer to the lack of consistent quality in OJT in the technical areas. EPSS will do this by providing an electronic 'coach' that always gives consistent, hopefully correct, guidance and instruction just as the worker needs it to accomplish 'real work.' That's what OJT really does, right?

"The bottom line for T&D professionals? Our task is legitimate — it just may not be the same job description we've grown to know and love over the past 10 to 20 years. Increasingly, we are challenged to expand our skill sets to be able to address 'performance improvement' as the main objective, rather than 'training.' In my mind, this is a long-overdue sea change, as it finally focuses our profession on a business-oriented, measurable result, rather than on a process. Process focus tends to only proliferate programs, but not always provide solutions."

— *Will Pearce, manager of training and performance systems, TBM Consulting Group, Durham, NC*

Trainers' Trump Card: Diagnosing True Nature of Performance Problems

"A big plus for trainers/performance consultants: the complexity of determining the optimum solution to performance problems. While it would be great if all line managers were adept at performance analysis, in my experience most are not. T&D adds value by helping managers assess situations to determine whether training is warranted or whether something else, which may be less costly, is a better solution. And T&D can disseminate this capability if we concentrate more on helping managers learn to analyze performance discrepancies first, and only then to choose solutions.

"Even when training is indicated, it can be difficult for line managers to discern a quality program. I'm sure most of us have clients who have selected a training program or resource that failed to provide a quality learning experience. Formal T&D adds value by serving as an interface between our clients and the vast universe of training products and services out there. Skilled instructional designers can create or evaluate training programs and recommend those that truly fit.

"Again, it would be terrific if our profession could develop processes and tools that would allow line managers to do these analyses and selections themselves. For now, I remain convinced that acquiring this expertise is an ongoing, full-time job, one not well-suited for the manager who is concerned only with getting the job done. Until we can find a way to equip managers with these skills, T&D will be a key organizational resource."

— *Stacey Williams, InterActive Dynamics*

The Value of Systematic, Organized Learning

"To answer this question, we should ask: 'What is the most efficient and effective way to learn a given subject in a particular situation?' In some cases, self-directed learning may be the answer. However, I challenge you to compare our libraries to our learning system. What separates us from the animals is our ability to learn from the experience of others *and* to build on that experience. That is what libraries represent; they are a managed resource representing a particular library's knowledge set.

"What does this have to do with T&D? Suppose knowledge and experience was not captured in libraries but just books or other media scattered in various unrelated places. Like the monkey at the typewriter, the potential learner may stumble on the resources needed and may be lucky enough to develop some multiple perspectives that broaden, rather than narrow, the learning. However, it is much more efficient to manage learning through gathering and packaging information relevant to tasks at hand and delivering it to the student, as he or she needs it. Someone — the librarian, mentor, trainer, etc. — acts as the resource to package this information so the student is free to continue performing the assigned job rather than running around searching for it. In a business environment, this includes linking company strategies and goals to the learning.

"I am not talking here about what a training organization should look like or its size, I am talking about the need to 'manage' education. Even when it is outsourced to different vendors, there must be a glue to give it perspective in terms of the business, and to keep the product and costs honest."

— *John H. Reed, training supervisor for the Exxon Corp.*

Notes:

2 Case Studies Show How Training Can Play Major Role in a Restructuring

Easing the pain of a downsizing effort.

BY DAVE ZIELINSKI

When it comes to supporting the victims and survivors of downsizing, training plays a variety of roles, many of them on the periphery of the process. But we've found two departments that have carved out more prominent and influential roles. They've done it not through classroom work, but largely through use of performance consulting interventions and by creating "embedded" training in the work environment. Their focus has been as much on supporting job redesign, workload redistribution, and time management skills as it has been on helping victims and survivors deal with the emotions of change.

And their experience underscores a key point: The more process reengineering and job redesign their companies did *before* cutting people loose, the better off everyone was when the downsizing dust settled.

Training: Reorganization's "Nerve Center"

At Mallinckrodt Medical Inc. in St. Louis, the consolidation and closing of plants has led to the loss of some 500 jobs in the last two years, says Rich Meyers, director of organizational development. Meyers' staff managed three of those layoffs — not a role familiar to most training functions. "There's no question our performance consulting experience, and the project management skills we've demonstrated in the past, were reasons we were given this role," says Meyers. "Had we been more of a traditional training function, we probably would have gotten the word after the fact about what was going on. And that would have been long after we would've had an opportunity to influence or guide the process."

Meyers' support was two-pronged, designed to help both laid-off workers and survivors:

• *Supporting downsizing victims:* The company's philosophy is to inform those affected long before they're actually laid off, "so they can make an orderly transition in their own lives, and also continue to contribute as informed and respected members of their teams," Meyers says. Mallinckrodt will be closing a plant in upstate New York within a year or two, and the 300 affected employees have known about it for a year.

Meyers' staff assumes the following roles in the process: help determine selection criteria for those who are to be let go, manage that selection process, manage all outplacement services and track success rate of those being placed, arrange security and escorts, educate supervisors on how to deliver the message about the layoffs (and train the HR people who accompany supervisors into those meetings). Meyers says he taps some external resources to help in these roles.

• *Supporting downsizing survivors:* Meyers' staff offers some general workshops for independent survivors, but the majority of their time goes into specific consulting support for affected work groups.

On the general course side, a half-day workshop called *Moving Forward with Change* is required for all remaining supervisors, and is open enrollment for others. "It's about dealing with the shock and emotional ups and downs, and to help folks understand what they're going through is perfectly normal," Meyers says.

That's followed with one-day workshops called *Managing Your Career in a Changing Environment*, where participants get help in assessing their skill strengths and weaknesses, determine whether current jobs are a good fit, and so on. Finally, there are individual career development planning workshops for survivors. "These all have as their focus recovering from trauma," Meyers says.

But the biggest immediate concern for surviving employees is often how to pick up the slack for departed coworkers without killing themselves, and here is where the consulting experience of Meyers' staff pays off. "You have to show people how they're going to function after their colleagues leave — that's a big source of anxiety."

His staff worked with three business units heavily affected by job cuts, and where there were the biggest disruptions in work flows or job design: new product and technology development, information management and technology (IM&T), and the sales group.

The most important part of the process happens at the front end of the downsizing — and is a big reason why the IM&T group is faring better than the other two groups in downsizing's aftermath, Meyers says. "IM&T built the clearest vision of how it was going to change to keep performance high following the reorganization. We probably needed to do a little bit more process reengineering in the other two groups before we downsized," he says.

With the IM&T group, for instance, the post-downsizing planning involved moving away from decentralized data management to a more centralized structure. That meant selecting some new computer platforms and application packages, and "assessing what systems employees were going to use and who needed to use them before we even decided who would be laid off," Meyers says. That allowed Meyers' staff to help build new competency models around new tasks and workflows.

Meyers consulted with IM&T on defining "new goals, roles, and responsibilities" for staff members, on setting work-duty priorities, on where to find the right training resources for specific needs, and offered other reengineering support. His group also did some team-building training.

The sales group is having a bit of a harder time, Meyers says, because salespeoples' roles changed more dramatically. The group shifted from a hierarchical structure where salespeople called primarily on clinicians to a very flat structure (from 15-to-1 to 30-to-1 reporting relationships) where they call more frequently on hospital executives. The new product and technology group is in the same boat. Shifting to a matrix management structure from a vertical structure was "very foreign to some people in that group," Meyers says. "They are scientists, and they tended to feel the changes were just a distraction from their real work, which is at their lab benches."

Ways to Embed Training in the Workplace to Support Redesigned Jobs

Downsizing and resulting job redesign continues to be fast and furious at BellSouth Telecommunications in Atlanta. Suzanne Snypp, director of network training and performance support, says most jobs in the technical organization are being redesigned as a result of the major reengineering effort. Her mission is to support technical task workers like service technicians, dispatchers, engineers and network monitors who troubleshoot network problems. "Every job that touches something in the network is being rethought right now," she says.

The primary way she supports the change is not through classroom interventions, but through increased use of "embedded" training like job aids, on-line documentation, expert systems, and other troubleshooting tools employees can call on without leaving their work areas. "We are in a sense working ourselves out of training jobs," Snypp says. "We want classroom training to be minimal, and to place the education within the system."

One sign of that transition is that Snypp no longer is responsible for course development. "I've given that up, and now do only client consulting around front-end analysis and how best to use existing curriculum," she says. So, for example, if a client has a new job design and a resulting performance challenge, Snypp will send out a human performance technologist to do a front-end analysis and some consulting. "If we find training is a solution to the challenge, we send the request over to course development. But if we find, as is more often the case, it is a culture, work environment, or a job design issue, we use other approaches."

Some repositioning of the training function is a result of the downsizing hitting home: training lost about 30% of its people in the last two years, Snypp says, much of it support staff. One response was for training to form a new group it calls Performance Improvement and to relocate course development to a small, centralized nucleus. Many former "trainers" are now performance technologists assigned to consult with units affected by downsizing. The centralized course development structure has worked, Snypp says, because "too often in the past we found different parts of the organization were creating courseware around the same subject matter, so this decreases our duplication." In addition, she is outsourcing a greater amount of her department's work.

As technical jobs are redesigned at BellSouth, Snypp works hand-in-hand with job designers at the start of that process. Once tasks for new jobs are roughed out, her group creates a competency model. An outside consultant conducts a series of interviews and focus groups with remaining employees to help determine specific behaviors needed for these jobs. Snypp then reviews those findings with subject matter experts and others to ensure they're on target, and groups competencies from most-to-least critical. Her group then creates consulting contracts or recommends curriculum to support the new competencies.

---

5 WAYS TRAINING CAN AID DOWNSIZING EFFORTS

What can training executives do to deal with the need for new job skills and coping mechanisms in the workforce after a downsizing? Here are five strategies to help ease the corporate pain:

1. Have a contingency plan in place, even in good times, to present management when the prospect of a significant layoff looms. The preparation will speak volumes about training's commitment to care for survivors, and provide yet another chance for training to prove its value.

2. Too often, the emphasis is only on helping survivors deal with *emotions* involved in the change — dealing with anger, stress management, survivors' guilt — yet many survivors find themselves without the job-related skills to handle their new or expanded responsibilities. Make sure there are training or consulting resources in place to help survivors learn new duties, and give them process improvement support that helps reduce non-essential work.

3. Be prepared to offer voluntary courses after hours or on weekends to help survivors cope. After a layoff, employees may be seen as "too busy" to attend training during normal work hours. And don't plan on billing anyone for your time. Budgets are probably stretched as tight as schedules.

4. Don't neglect first-line supervisors and middle managers. Too often the focus is only on how layoffs negatively affect the front line.

5. Find and tap the expertise of line workers who have experience in areas such as time management, process analysis and flow charting, grief counseling, and other soft skills that may help survivors. It'll not only take a bit of the burden off an already taxed training function, it will give those survivors a stake in making the post-layoff atmosphere healthier. — D.Z.

CHAPTER 2

PARTNERING WITH LINE MANAGEMENT

Marketing Training to Management

Management support is elusive key that must be sought.

BY BRIAN McDERMOTT

When management comes calling for training it's simple for a competent training director to get a program approved. But line managers don't always know when training can solve their problems, and convincing a troubled manager to spend on training can be a struggle. Even when a manager says yes to an idea, that support can wane when it's time to commit the resources and the people. That's when sales and marketing most obviously come into play.

Sales and marketing, though, are inextricable and constant parts of a training director's job; not to be done one day a month or be easily spelled out as job objectives. Ed Gerlich, training administrator for Blood Systems Inc., estimates he spends up to 50 percent of his time on a daily basis selling, and even with that much effort he figures it will take a full year to gain approval for the training he believes his company most needs now.

"Our people are very technically oriented. They're technologists and nurses and very strong in the technical aspects of our community blood services. So it's easy to sell management on training in just about any technical area, especially because we are in the throes of the big AIDS scare. But, when we talk about areas in which I think our people have weaknesses — supervisory and management skills — I get resistance.

"I've put together a proposal and I'm trying to convince management that, if we are proactive, this kind of training will help us in the long run, that supervisory training dovetails with the problems we're having on the human side — turnover, [equal opportunity compliance], discontent, and low morale.

Gerlich has sold his management on some supervisory training. It took seven months to approve a $25,000 investment in televisions, videocassette recorders and a contract with Deltak Training Corp. (Naperville, IL) for use of films at each of Blood Systems' 23 locations. It took less time to approve a $50,000 renewal contract, but that, Gerlich believes, is not enough to meet their needs. He has invested six months in his current proposal and expects it will take six more months to put the program in place.

Gerlich is capitalizing on his company's reliance on certification processes to improve their training procedures for managers. In medical areas, he says, employees cannot even draw blood if they are not certified. He has proposed that supervisors must be certified as management and supervisory skills trainers before they can be promoted. That, he says, will provide him entree to a team of education coordinators in the field and create a cost-effective system for delivering a variety of training programs.

"Based on my 27 years experience, the best advice I can offer on selling training to management is to transfer training from a staff function to a line function. Do your homework. Ask responsible line officers what they need. Give it to them. Let them help teach it. Thus, training sells itself."

No Pat Answers

The pat answer about how to sell training to management, according to Joseph Andrew, director of training for Tom Thumb Convenience Stores, "is that you have to equate training with bottom-line results, dollars and cents, which may mean using turnover studies or extensive evaluations and measuring cost effectiveness. But I think the issue is much larger than that. Increasingly, CEOs are realizing that people are their greatest asset and will also, through the year 2000 and beyond, be their scarcest resource. The challenge is to convince CEOs that margins and bottom-line results fall into place when people know how to manage the people that work for them. If we increase our training budgets for that purpose, we can increase our bottom lines."

Andrew, who has been with Tom Thumb for only 10 months, believes turnover in the company has already been cut greatly as a result of boosting the standard training for store managers from one to six weeks. Previously Tom Thumb's training was almost exclusively technical. The plan is to make the course 30 percent technical skills, 70 percent people skills.

"It was easy to get the six-week program approved. My CEO was convinced that training was a key for us. He wasn't sure what it was he wanted, but he knew we needed it. So I involved myself with him on a regular basis. I told him what the program was all about and what the effects would be. The next step is to increase our budget. So far I've done things inexpensively. We need more sophistication."

Andrew estimates he spends one of every eight working hours "strictly selling," but believes a significantly greater amount of his time goes indirectly toward gaining management commitment for his ideas and programs.

Selling the Biggest Needs

At AAA Michigan, a company that is rapidly diversifying, "the demand for training is enormous," according to Lynda Greenblatt, director of human resources development. "People at the top of the house say we need management training. People in the lower ranks say, 'What about us? The company is changing, how are we going to be prepared to meet its demands? What about our career development?'

"The product managers say they need specific technical training for their people in order to respond to the organization's demands. In the last five years, through all our changes, we've responded primarily to that demand. Our management and supervisory training, to our shame, has fallen apart; it has gotten old and tired. Now we're looking at this whole thing to figure out how, as a training department, we can meet the big needs of the company. We're looking at training as a partner in the business, looking strategically at how we can put our talents, efforts and dollars where the greatest impact will be felt."

The sales and marketing challenge, Greenblatt says, is to overcome one of the ill effects of over-centralization: supervisors forgetting that training is part of their jobs.

With the help and support of AAA's planning and management team, Greenblatt's group has decided it will no longer do technical training.

"We will be instructional-design oriented. We will do what we do best: consult on performance issues, design programs for people who need them, provide the company with quality control, train trainers so that line supervisors can get back to developing their people. We'll focus on developing a strong management program and get serious about succession planning and career development.

"In terms of selling — which can seem shallow — I don't want to sit in an ivory tower figuring out what the company needs and then have to sell it. My people are going to do a marketing plan. We are going to treat it from a zero-based budgeting perspective, looking at what should stay and what should go. Eventually, we will charge back for all our training. That can be risky, but we're banking on our belief that we will do it so well that managers will want it."

To promote this new training direction, Greenblatt says, she is creating a management development review board and taking advantage of the access she has to AAA's president and executive vice president.

"You absolutely have to have political connections. One of the things I took away from Leonard Hirsch's presentation [at a Training Directors' Forum Conference] is that if you don't get dirty and are not willing to lose,

SPRINT TURNS TO 'ACCOUNT MANAGERS' TO HELP MARKET ITS TRAINING SERVICES

The chief training arm of telecommunications company Sprint in Kansas City — its University of Excellence (UE) — had a dilemma: It was offering top-notch training and organizational development services, but business unit heads were often not aware of how training could help them, or they actively resisted UE's appeals, says Karen Mailliard, vice president of HRD.

The solution was a new communications and marketing campaign highlighted by the creation of UE "account managers" assigned to 15 Sprint business units.

Choosing Account Managers

The ideas are outgrowths of a move to centralize training at Sprint, with the University of Excellence as the centerpiece. Mailliard helped launch the University in 1991. "My challenge was to go to 23 business units and convince them if they transferred their head count, dollars, and facilities to me, I would do a better job of training and developing their people. Well, people just don't give that up unless they're pretty sure they're going to get a better product. It was a tough sell."

Even with this new structure and a flurry of new training activity, Mailliard says busy executives were often unaware of what UE could do. "We had been sending out reams of information about our services, reporting back to the line with data, and doing presentations, but because telecommunications has become so competitive, our executives just didn't have time to read it," she says.

Mailliard's solution was to create UE account managers. Members of the U of E's staff are now assigned to specific business units to educate them about UE services and analyze performance problems in partnership with them. "They report to each unit executive, and their job is to act as a 'marketeer' and liaison to that executive and his or her team," she says. "Then, they bring that performance analysis data back into the university so we can help them determine the best solution."

How does she choose account managers? "We put them through role plays — hypothetical meetings with business unit heads — and also use assessment tools. It's a posted job."

Account managers create their own "account plan," just as if they were on the sales force. The plan states they'll have a certain number of contacts with managers, attend a certain number of their staff meetings, and so on. "They are measured in performance reviews based on their customer team's evaluation of their worth to the team as a training liaison," she says.

Because of the concept's success, Mailliard now has more executives asking for account managers than she can fund.

Benefits of Rating Line Managers According to Training Advocacy

Mailliard and staff also decided to begin placing key executives in five categories based on their perceived level of advocacy for training: 1) active advocate, 2) passive advocate, 3) neutral (aren't using training, or express no discernible opinion about it), 4) passive adversary, and 5) active adversary.

With help from a local consulting firm (Corporate Communication Group), UE staffers — with account managers doing the bulk of the work — started identifying those who were neutral or non-supportive, and tried to move them along the continuum toward "active advocates." The consultant helped account managers identify specific communication or behaviors that made managers fall into a particular category.

Advocacy is two-pronged, Mailliard says: "We define advocacy as not only supporting the U of E's efforts, but also how interested the manager is to continually developing employees."

One example: the head of Sprint's network organization was leading a reorganization and came to Mailliard for help with managing the process. "As the result of working with an account manager who educated him on what we could do, he became an 'active advocate,' and now refers regularly in his written communication and speeches to the help we were able to give him."

people are not going to perceive you as being part of the game. If you are a peripheral part of your company, you are always going to be scrambling around on the outside. Training directors tend not to be business people. Often they come from academic environments, and part of that is good. On the other hand, if you are not perceived as a partner it is very difficult. We must become knowledgeable about our businesses. We have to make a concerted effort to do that, and we have to do it on our own time."

Greenblatt suggests: Get to know the finance people, the marketing and sales people, the folks who are running your business. Know what they do and what their problems are. Know the directors and managers at your own level. If you don't have access to senior executives, figure out how to get it. Become part of the strategic planning process.

"This is all part of my own plan. It's not easy to do. It's easy to say the words, but it's a different story as to how to get to the point where people see me as having the solutions to their problems."

In one particular situation, Greenblatt says, it has meant occasionally taking a reluctant manager to lunch, working to forge a relationship he would never initiate. It has meant setting up meetings he would never call. It has meant bringing in a third person with whom the manager could communicate better. And it has meant getting to know that manager's needs by questioning not only him but people who work for him. It has also meant, Greenblatt says, moving the message about an important need upward through the organization so that pressure could trickle back down.

"It's a matter of being resourceful and of not being blinded by my own point of view. It is also my role to be ready when there is an open window. You have to be prepared to respond when you start doing some of this stuff."

Compliance vs. Commitment

Edwin Nolan, manager of human resource development programs for Eckerd Drug Co., says, "We have to beat people away. Everything is seen as a training problem, so we hardly do any marketing, except in the process of trying to gain commitment and having people understand how to use our service."

Nolan says, "A major pitfall in marketing training to managers is to confuse compliance with commitment. You need more than an 'OK' from senior management. What you see from senior management as approval may really mean, 'Go ahead, I won't get in your way.'

"The easiest way to avoid this, although it is difficult to implement, is to involve senior management in your needs analysis. Ask them what they want, how it fits their business plans, who the subject matter experts should be. Review your findings with them. Have them attend pilot sessions. Incorporate their ideas into your rewrites. Keep people in the loop because you can get into trouble when you try to be your own sponsor."

Notes:

Power Brokering in Training

Here's an eight-point strategy for training managers who want to increase their budgets, broaden their power bases and save money for their organizations.

BY LARRY WINTERS
AND JO DIMINO

Training departments have a power problem. The problem is that most of them have no power — or so little that distinctions between "some" and "none" become hard to draw. And the reason this is a problem, regardless of your attitude that organizational politics is a shabby subject, is that power, in and of itself, means nothing more nor less than the ability to get things done.

In most business environments, power is associated with budget size and control of expenditures — with how much money you've got and your authority to decide what to do with it.

If the organization invests in a specific department or activity, it is committing itself to making that activity successful.

Although most competent training and development (T&D) managers could more than justify their contribution to any operation, their departments tend to be viewed as staff support, with little or no impact on the organization's bottom-line profits. Resulting budgets (and policy commitments) are meager in comparison to those given the majority of line functions.

Historically, T&D managers have tried to defend their expenditures by demonstrating "back-end" behavioral changes and productivity improvements. But these contributions are extremely difficult to document, especially when operating managers are likely to cite non-training factors (such as salary increases, incentive plans and work-place adjustments) as contributing to those improvements.

Suppose that, instead, you practice a bit of classic, solid management strategy: Focus your attention on a budget line item — in this case, training — and document how you could reduce expenses without reducing the quality or quantity of service.

How can you, as manager of training and development, increase the size of your budget and use the resulting power boost to increase your company's profitability? You can do it by gaining control of all T&D expenditures throughout the entire organization. Within 12 months, the eight-point program we'll outline here will produce a strategic shift in your organization's balance of power — a shift toward the training department — and will solidify certain changes within the organization to sustain that shift.

What we're talking about is a power play, carried out on the organization's own terms. And yes, we're speaking of empire building. A disreputable term, that, but only because it is associated with managers whose determination to build empires outweighs (or negates) their desire to serve the interests of the organization as a whole. In short, empire building is a negative force only when it produces negative consequences or fails to produce positive ones.

If you can build an empire that serves the company — and everyone in the company — better than they are served by existing empires, you are not Darth Vader.

With no apologies for the term, therefore, we'll explain that this power play is made possible by the simple fact that employee training in this country currently represents a multi-billion dollar business.

If your organization is at all sizable, chances are that thousands of dollars are spent every year by various department managers for seminars, films, books, consultants, computer software and other training-related items. Each manager, restricted by departmental boundary lines, is unable to purchase in volume and therefore unable to negotiate the best price available from vendors. In other words, if vendors are selling directly to individual operating managers, the dollars spent by those managers probably are undiscounted.

What's happening under this all-too-common arrangement? Not only has the T&D specialist lost control over the quality of many company training programs, he or she also lacks the power to negotiate potentially substantial savings for the organization as a whole.

The strategy outlined here is challenging and may not appeal to the faint of heart. But it can be tremendously rewarding for those not afraid to broker in the elusive commodity of power.

Step 1. Network

Interview a representative sample of profit-center managers. Your task at this point is not to convert skeptics, but simply to gather information on how they spend training dollars. The trade-off for their cooperation is your promise to save money for their operating units while increasing training opportunities for their people.

If you can get them to support your concept of stretching their budgets through volume purchasing of training, so much the better. But trying to argue your way through all possible objections is exhausting. Concentrate, instead, on managers willing to help make the concept work, or on likely converts. Effort spent with these people is well worth the time.

But for heaven's sake, exercise some tact. You're talking about taking money out of this manager's "pocket" and putting it into yours. You needn't present your idea as something you are determined to do regardless of what this particular person thinks. You simply have an idea that may work out extremely well for everybody. If the information you gather from the skeptic and from other managers indicates that you *can't* make good on your promises, you will, of course, drop the plan. And this is true. Unlikely, if they're all buying training individually, but true.

Once you have chosen your network of contacts, what's the best way to gather the vital information? You might want to conduct a person-to-person survey or use a questionnaire. Written questionnaires about financial matters tend to make people nervous, however, so explain at the outset that your main desire is to understand the *intent* of the expenditures, as well as the sums per se.

But make it clear that you do need the sums. And you'll need to know the *actual dollars* spent on training for a selected 12-month period, as opposed to the amounts that have been budgeted. Be sure to have the managers indicate exactly what they purchased: cassette programs, seminars, outside consultants for in-house programs, college courses, periodicals, newsletters, correspondence courses and so on. Travel and living expenses should not be included in the totals.

Step 2. Analysis

Start by segmenting your responses. List the types of training purchased, the dollars spent, and the vendor or provider of the service. Begin to look for patterns in purchasing — similar categories of topics or needs, recurring vendors, etc. If certain responses need qualifying, especially if the survey was in the form of a written questionnaire, follow up with a personal visit to the manager.

Keep in mind that your data represents only a sample of the total training dollars your organization spent.

You do not have a categorical picture of your company's expenditures for the previous year. But if you have sampled responsibly, you ought to be able to make some pretty good projections.

Step 3. Decide

Question yourself. If the power to disburse all of this money were indeed in your hands, what would you do? Based on your operating managers' expressed needs, how would you allocate the dollars most effectively for them and for your company's balance sheet? Be especially careful here, because the decisions you begin to make now will be prime contributors to the ultimate power you broker for yourself.

Step 4. Contact

Get in touch with reputable outside training vendors, including the ones selected by your sample managers. Suppliers will be more than willing to discuss training programs and packages with you, make suggestions about the most economical way to use your designated budget and, most importantly, outline any discounts available to you as a volume purchaser.

Don't be satisfied with reading about these programs or listening to sales people describe them. Attend seminars yourself, wherever possible, and get your hands on samples of other products to test in your company.

An increased ablity to *get things done* will do wonders for training's reputation.

Step 5. Organize

Now that you've done your homework, put your facts in order. Document the actual training dollars spent during the last 12 months and compare this amount to the number of employees trained. Highlight your discoveries about how volume discounts would affect the total price tag in relation to the number of people trained.

Make sure you have a good, strong story to tell and that the approach you've developed is efficient, effective, timely and, above all, economical. As a precaution, show your proposal to a financially astute colleague; he or she may be able to spot any questionable assumptions or statistical holes in your presentation.

Step 6. Meet

Arrange a meeting with your company controller or, if appropriate, with the chief executive officer. Explain that you have identified an area in the corporate budget which you feel can be reduced by 15%, 40% or whatever figure applies.

Start by sharing the results of your survey. Then outline your findings concerning the potential savings with volume purchasing. Your primary goal at this point is to present facts and figures objectively. Let the figures open the door for the revelation of your intent to save the company money by becoming the sole purchasing agent for training.

Step 7. Follow-up

Don't let a good idea wither on the vine. Any suggestions brought up by the controller (or CEO) should be incorporated into your proposal immediately. If necessary, reevaluate any items or approaches which met strong objections during the meeting, and search for alternate methods. You won't want to compromise your goal, but as in any realistic situation, a few adjustments may be needed to push the proposal over the corporate hurdle.

When you draft the final copy of your plan for the controller, send a copy to your immediate superior. Power building is by nature a play of strengths against weaknesses, and at this juncture you're negotiating from a position of strength. It may take some courage (and some tiptoeing) to keep your research to yourself until you're ready to relate it to dollars-and-cents benefits, but you'll have to try; it's too easy for a charge of "empire building" to be hung around your neck *before* you've accomplished anything. In this case, time is your leverage, so use it to your best advantage.

Step 8. Publicize

As soon as you've gotten any positive feedback on your completed plan from top management, start sharing your results with line managers. Recruit their cooperation and support. Emphasize the fact that they're not losing funds, they're gaining better-trained staffs — both quantitatively and qualitatively — and they're making a greater contribution to the profit picture their operating units present.

These eight steps definitely will require hard work, initiative, imagination and, perhaps, a thick skin. But many training managers who have tried this strategy have accomplished considerably more than the enhancement of their power bases within the organization. They also have achieved some or all of the following objectives:

• The ability to contribute — on a continuing basis — to the profits of their companies.

• Increased respect for their training and development expertise from line managers.

• A better understanding of the

training needs of *all* company employees.
- The ability to report to upper management on the *exact* training activities going on within the organization.
- Access to the type of data necessary for planning future training programs in line with company growth projections.

In other words, the training empire you build with this strategy is going to be one that serves the needs of the organization and its people. Your increased ability to *get things done* will pay off for everybody. And if, in the process, bigger budgets and greater commitments from upper management accrue to you, these are simply the results of well-performed power brokering at work.

Notes:

Added-Value Negotiating

'Win-win outcome' is easy to say, but often hard to pull off. Here's a step-by-step process for building balanced deals.

BY KARL ALBRECHT
AND STEVE ALBRECHT

All of us are negotiators at various times in our lives, whether we know it or not and whether we like it or not. While we generally think of a negotiator as someone formally appointed to represent a country or a corporation or a union in some matter of great importance, the truth is that most of the negotiations in the world happen on a much smaller scale.

People have to make deals in many areas of their lives: getting a new job, getting a promotion, getting married, getting divorced, buying or selling property, renting an office or an apartment, leasing a car, settling a dispute at work or going into a business venture with someone else. We negotiate much more often than we realize.

But most of us aren't very good negotiators. It isn't a skill we learn in any deliberate way. It seems to be something we're supposed to "pick up" somewhere along the journey from childhood to adulthood.

We generally don't pick it up very well, judging by the difficulty human beings have getting along with one another. Even supposedly seasoned negotiators run into all kinds of trouble. Just a few examples tell the tale.

California Gov. Pete Wilson collided with the state legislature not long ago over key budget provisions. Wilson kept vetoing their submissions and they kept refusing to submit the budget he wanted. Result: The state government ran out of funds and couldn't even pay its employees' salaries. For several months, the government ran on IOUs redeemable in the future at 5 percent interest.

In Australia, the airline pilots' union decided to strike for wage increases of 20 to 30 percent. Their tough negotiators faced off against the tough negotiators of the airline companies and the government. The strike dragged on for months. Result: The government dissolved the union, but not before the economy came to a virtual standstill, tourism to Australia was in shreds, and hundreds of small companies that depended on tourism were driven to the wall.

In recent years, some businesspeople have come to believe that the traditional idea of negotiation as a form of combat is seriously flawed. The strategy of presenting the opponent with an unfair offer and expecting him to counterattack with an equally unfair demand, on the presumption that the two parties can somehow fight their way to an acceptable middle ground, is becoming obsolete.

A new era, with new and more complex problems and issues, calls for new thinking. We are beginning to understand that negotiating is a complex social and psychological process, usually going well beyond the basic economic proposition that most people tend to start with. It calls for a more skillful way of interacting and a more thoughtful approach to balancing the interests of all parties. Hence all the talk we hear about "win-win" negotiating.

Over the past decade or so, we have been developing a method called added-value negotiating (AVN). AVN draws upon the ideas of many thinkers who have explored and developed the concept of negotiation as a process of adding value to a deal rather than one of extracting or conceding value from the other party. We think it represents a real advance.

How does added-value negotiating differ from the more familiar concept of win-win? The most obvious difference is that AVN employs the idea of "multiple deals." Instead of offering one deal and hoping to beat it into shape, AVN calls for the creation of several deal "packages." It's usually easier to find an acceptable deal when you can choose one from many. Since each alternative is based on a mutual understanding of interests and the options that can meet them, both sides get a sense that the negotiating process is balanced and fair. We've found that the method seems to change the entire psychology of negotiations.

Most people do want to negotiate cooperatively. Most do want to end up with a good deal and good feelings as well. Most probably would agree with this list of desirable objectives for a negotiating process:

- The two of you can meet and talk on a reasonably cordial, cooperative and stress-free basis.
- You can reach agreement fairly efficiently, without a great deal of wasted time and effort.
- The deal you work out is balanced; that is, it offers satisfactory value for you and satisfactory value for the other party.
- You have a positive relationship by the time the process is complete.
- You would be willing to do business together again given the opportunity.

Again, most people would like negotiations to work this way. They just need to be able to see a way to do it. Telling them to approach the situation with a win-win attitude isn't helpful enough. That's where AVN comes in.

Added value negotiating is like a road map we can use to help us *arrive* at win-win outcomes.

AVN boils down to this five-step process:
1. Clarify interests.
2. Identify options.
3. Design alternative deal packages.
4. Select a deal.
5. Perfect the deal.

Let's take the steps one by one.

1 Clarify Interests

Before you can even begin to formulate some possible deals, you must know what you want and what the other party wants out of the negotiation. The AVN method starts with a search for interests on both sides. What are the needs, desires and aspirations that each party seeks to satisfy?

These interests can be separated into two distinct categories: subjective and objective.

Subjective interests are judgmental. They relate to needs that are intangible, personal and perception-based. For example, the desire to generate good will in business or the desire to foster a long-term relationship with the other party.

Objective interests are measurable, tangible, observable, concrete. Think of cash or the deed to a building or access to a computer.

One of the easiest ways to clarify the interests involved, both subjective and objective, is to use a four-square chart called the Window of Interest, as shown in Figure 1.

This simple chart allows you and the other party to enumerate your interests in a plain, readable form. It also points out mutual interests.

One or both parties can create the Window of Interest. It helps to start the negotiation process rolling quickly because it gets both parties talking and documenting their interests on paper. Thus, the negotiation opens with an emphasis on productivity rather than posturing, overblown emotional issues or long harangues.

2 Identify Options

Every negotiation involves a number of elements of value — the tangible and intangible assets that can be traded off in the process of arriving at a satisfactory deal. Once you've clarified both parties' interests, take stock of the elements of value available in the negotiation, both tangible and intangible. Ask yourself these questions:

1. What can I give them that they need?
2. What can they give me that I need?
3. How can we both add value to the deal?

Elements of value generally can be divided into five categories. Here are the categories and some questions to ask about each one.

• Money: How much is involved? How will it be paid? Under what conditions? When?

• Property: Is it intangible or tangible? How much property is there? Are we negotiating for all of it or portions of it? Where is it?

• Actions: What will you agree to do (or refrain from doing) for the other party? What will the other party agree to do (or refrain from doing) for you?

• Rights: What rights can they give you? What rights can you give them?

• Risks: What risks are apparent in the deal? What risks may be hidden? What risks could you take? What risks could the other party take?

Another paper-and-pencil model comes in handy here. The Option Tree shown in Figure 2 helps you keep physical track of the various elements of value.

3 Design Alternative Deal Packages

What makes AVN so different from most other negotiating methods is its use of multiple deals. Instead of creating one offer and trying to force it onto the other party, as in win-lose negotiating, you design two, three or several possible deals. Using a "Chinese menu" approach (pick something from Column A, something from Column B), you can scan the Window of Interest and the Option Tree and create a series of deals, each with its own special appeal.

A few things to consider as you design various deals:

• Build the deals so that each one includes options in each of the five value categories.

• Design deal packages, which are various combinations of the value elements that balance the interests of both parties.

• Each deal should offer a different way to balance interests, through a different arrangement of the value elements.

For example, suppose two departments in an organization need a sophisticated desktop publishing system. The system is too expensive for either department to buy on its own. So they're considering pooling their resources in some way that would meet the needs of both. This requires negotiation.

Working together, they have pinpointed their key interests and identified elements of value in the five cate-

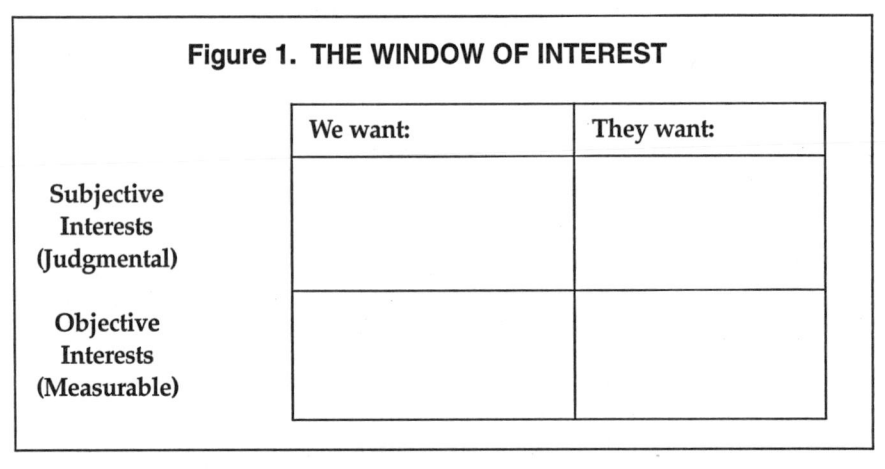

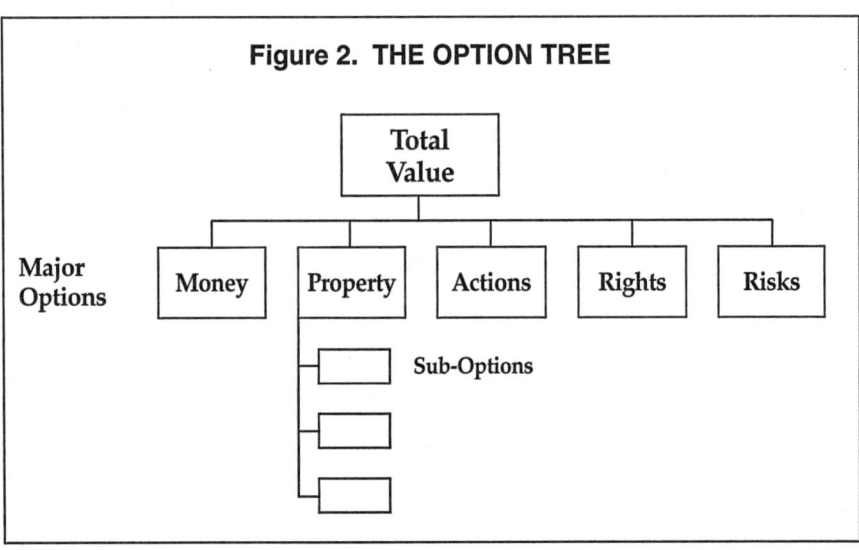

Figure 1. THE WINDOW OF INTEREST

	We want:	They want:
Subjective Interests (Judgmental)		
Objective Interests (Measurable)		

Figure 2. THE OPTION TREE

Total Value

Major Options: Money | Property | Actions | Rights | Risks

Sub-Options

gories. "Money" options have to do with how much they're prepared to spend for the system, how they will share the expense, and possibilities such as having one department buy the system and cross-charge its use to the other. "Property" options might involve who owns the system for capital-budget purposes, who has physical custody of it and who will have access to it under what circumstances. "Actions" might deal with who handles the procurement, who sets up and checks out the system, and who provides training for the users. "Rights" could include the allocation of available time and policies for rush projects. "Risks" might have to do with handling warranty repairs, extended warranties and safeguarding critical data.

Working with these options, the departments could create a number of different deal packages. For instance, one package might look like this:

• They buy the system jointly, with Department A paying 60 percent and Department B 40 percent.
• Department A has rights to 60 percent of the available user time, and Department B to 40 percent.
• The system will be located in an area readily accessible to both.
• They will ask the facilities department to look after physical security and capital inventory.
• They will sell unused capacity on the system to other departments, and split the proceeds 60-40.

That's just one possible deal package. Other packages could be radically different. Still others might vary from this one on only a few points. With many deals to choose from, the two departments are highly likely to agree on an arrangement that meets the needs of both.

4 Select a Deal

Once you've created at least two or three deals, it's time to become more critical and analyze them carefully. If you designed each deal on your own, taking the other person's needs into consideration, you'll have to give her time to evaluate what you have put together. You also may need to take some time to evaluate the packages from your own perspective, making sure these really are deals you want to offer.

AVN is neither difficult nor stressful, especially compared to the tug-of-war of a win-lose negotiation.

As you analyze each deal, look at it in terms of the following criteria.

• *Value:* How much value does the deal incorporate for each party? How much value does it create in total?
• *Balance:* Does the deal offer equal or comparable value for all parties?
• *Overall approach:* Do the elements of the deal fit together into an effective solution for all interests?
• *Appeal:* Is there at least one deal that is feasible — a package that all parties can say "yes" to?

If the answer to the last question is "no," you need to go back a step. Take a harder look at the Window of Interest, the Option Tree, and the type and scope of the deals you designed. Come up with something different.

When you sit down with the other party, discuss only what you think are feasible deals (if none turn out to be attractive to the other party, design some more, either separately or together). Compare all feasible deals, and settle on one you both like.

Once you both agree that there is at least one acceptable deal on the table, it's time to move to the last step.

5 Perfect the Deal

People have a tendency to want to rush things as they reach this stage of the process. There is more involved at this point than just dotting the "i's" and crossing the "t's." This is your chance to make sure you've covered all the important details, that the relationship is still healthy and that you have a written agreement that all parties can live with.

It's important to refine the selected deal, make sure it's balanced in terms of total value and assure that all the parties are comfortable with it. Once you've chosen the deal that works best, you can tighten up various particulars, perhaps add extra items of value and hammer out the details together.

Many people find, to their great relief, that getting through all five steps of the AVN method is neither difficult nor stressful, especially compared to the tug-of-war of a win-lose negotiation.

AVN is based on openness, flexibility and a mutual search for the successful exchange of value. It allows you to build strong relationships with people over time. But the main advantage of added value negotiating comes down to one thing: better deals than could be gotten by any other method.

Notes:

What to Avoid When Shifting from Training to Performance Consulting

A conciliatory rather than strident approach helps win the confidence of skeptical line managers.

BY DAVE ZIELINSKI

The rationale that Dan McCarthy, director of performance improvement at Rochester Gas & Electric in Rochester, NY, gives for his training group backing away from classroom training in favor of performance consulting is a common one these days. "We'd been getting more pressure from management — they have expressed some dissatisfaction over training's impact on the business," he says. "But even without that pressure, we knew this is a change we'd have to make."

The group launched the new approach by first changing the department's name from human resource development to "performance innovation," and changed staff titles from HRD specialists to "performance consultants." The group also fundamentally altered its mission statement. "We held up all of our efforts and courses against the new mission, and said if there is not some visible contribution to performance improvement, let's stop doing it," McCarthy says.

It was more than just idle talk — the function ceased doing career counseling, for instance, because it no longer had evidence of a clear contribution to company performance. On the other hand, McCarthy says the group stopped doing some things it shouldn't have. One example: facilitating meetings. "It was something we did a lot of, were very good at it, and we got a lot of business from. But we didn't see it as fitting the performance consulting profile, so we decided not to do it anymore.

Don't Assume Everyone Believes You're a Performance Expert

"We've learned there's a heck of a lot more to it than just changing your name and focus," McCarthy says. The group also created a new logo and flyer to aggressively promote to line managers the "new" business training was in. So what happened? "Nobody called. We did all the stuff the textbooks and consultants said to do, but managers weren't knocking down our doors bringing us their performance problems."

So they returned to the drawing board. The first move was to bring in some respected external training consultants and pick their brains about best practices. One local consultant from Learning International introduced the group to the concept of "earning the right," or the idea that trainers/performance technologists can't just assume they have the respect and credibility that makes line managers immediately want to use their services. "Sometimes that process of earning credibility means doing some difficult things," McCarthy says. "For instance, when a manager asks for a training program and you think training isn't the answer, you can't just give her a 10-minute discourse on why training is a bad idea. We might tell that manager we can indeed meet some of her training needs, but at the same time we'll start our own investigation and do a needs assessment. Then we'll report back to the manager, saying 'in addition to these training needs, there are some other things we discovered we need to talk about.' " McCarthy's group might then cut a deal — they'll do the training in exchange for a chance to do some follow-up performance consulting with the group.

And instead of completely writing off those previously mentioned meeting facilitation duties as outside the realm of performance consulting, they now see them for the golden opportunities they present. "Instead of the neutral role of facilitation in the past, we have a new set of ears listening for performance problems. So after the meetings, we might come back with a specific proposal to a manager for some consulting assistance, based on what we heard in the meeting," he says. "We've gotten some consulting business that way." For instance, in a recent meeting McCarthy facilitated, the subject of process improvement came up. He followed up later with a manager, explaining his group's success in process improvement consulting with one work group. "Giving them even one small example of success is a lot better than saying: 'We can do this — trust me.' "

3-Step Example of Performance Consulting in Action

One example of the group's evolution in performance consulting: The company was having trouble managing collectibles, and a new collections manager who had gone through a negotiations training course was recommending it to all of his people. "Had he called me with that request four years ago, I would have told him, 'No, we don't have negotiations training in our catalog now, but if we get large enough demand, we'll consider adding it next year.' Two years ago, I would have said, 'We don't have the program,' but I'd find a course for him out there in the market. This time, though, we said, 'Yeah, that sounds like a good idea,' but at the same time went to work on our performance consulting plan."

Here's what he did:

• McCarthy asked the manager if his group could do some needs analysis in the form of one-on-one interviews with collections folks. He showed the manager the process he wanted to follow, using consultant Dana Gaines Robinson's "performance relationship map" as a guide.

• His people came back with a report listing six problems inhibiting collections performance. The biggest: inconsistency in the process used to negotiate collections agreements with customers.

PERFORMANCE TECHNOLOGY BEST SOLD TO LINE MANAGERS IN 'PLAIN BROWN WRAPPER'

One challenge in introducing "performance technology" is getting line workers to understand that training is only one of many solutions to performance problems. Equally challenging is getting past many line managers' beliefs that the consulting process is a threat to their own skills and turf.

Here's a few tips from R. John Howe, chief of training in the employment standards administration, U.S. Department of Labor, Washington, DC, to help get past those barriers. Howe has had some success using performance consulting, but admits he still has a long way to go.

- For demonstration projects, start with a real problem operating management needs to solve — "preferably something where it has become clear that sound training either hasn't and won't work." Pick something small and with a short time frame, so the client can see both the work processes entailed and any results quickly.

- Don't mount the project as something you're doing "for" the client but rather as something you're doing "with" them.

- Start where the client is and don't explain performance technology from the consultant's viewpoint. Introduce the concept only in its most basic form. "A friend of mine calls it marketing performance technology in a plain brown wrapper," Howe says.

- Don't expect a client with whom you've worked on a successful performance technology project to remember on her own that the training function has this kind of capability. "Because the client had to be organically involved in order for the project to be successful, their own experience may be — even if you were very useful to them — that they solved it themselves.

An effective performance technologist may be nearly invisible to the organization — and will necessarily pay the price of that invisibility." — **D.Z.**

- McCarthy presented the information back to the manager, and now is assisting him in implementing a more consistent, defined process for negotiating payment agreements, "which is a lot different from his original request of a generic negotiations class for everyone," he says.

McCarthy also recommends another idea — something he picked up at a *Training Directors' Forum Conference* — to help market the process to line managers. He now holds workshops for those managers on how the performance consulting process works, and how it differs from training. "Through that exposure, we have picked up some additional consulting work," he says.

Resources to Help Build Your Staff's Consulting Skills

- Dan McCarthy, performance improvement manager at Rochester Gas and Electric, recommends two books he says "are good roadmaps for making the leap, filled with conceptual frameworks and how-to's from the real world about building new skills and strategies."

The first is *Performance Consulting: Moving Beyond Training*, by Dana Gaines Robinson and James Robinson, $32.95, (800-707-7769).

The second is *Future Training: A Roadmap for Restructuring the Training Function*, by James Pepitone, $18.50, 800-707-7769.

- Will Pearce, manager of training and performance systems at the TBM Consulting Group in Durham, NC, suggests the book, *The New Language of Work*, by Danny Langdon, past international president of ISPI. Says Pearce: "It offers a systematic approach to describing the components of work, then uses that as the basis of describing the factors that affect human performance in the workplace." Call ISPI, 202-408-7969, $25 for members, $27.95 for non-members.

- David Ferguson, senior project manager in client training and performance support at GE Information Services, recommends these classics as good primers for understanding performance technology and building consulting skills:

1. *Analyzing Performance Problems*, by Robert F. Mager and Peter Pipe. Says Ferguson: "It's as relevant today as the first edition back in 1970." Center for Effective Performance, 770-458-4080.

2. *Human Competence: Engineering Worthy Performance*, the 1978 classic by the late Thomas F. Gilbert.

3. *The Handbook of Human Performance Technology*, by Harold D. Stolovitch and Erica J. Keeps, editors. An 800-page compilation from several practitioners and organized into sections. Call ISPI, 202-408-7969, $75.

- The list wouldn't be complete without mentioning Peter Block's 1981 classic, *Flawless Consulting*. Many consider it the bible of performance consulting.

Improving the Status of Training

Partnership with corporate leaders is training's key to elevated status.

BY BRIAN McDERMOTT

The Dream: Management begs for the training department's input and advice on any issue of strategic importance to the organization. There are no new ventures, no new products, no shifts in corporate strategy or management practices without first consulting the training and human resources development professionals to get help in spelling out the can-do's-can't-do's, the long-term implications, the short-term priorities.

The Reality: It just ain't so... but many training executives are striving hard toward that wished-for relationship, and some are making progress.

In some organizations the reality does approach the dream. But even in the most enviable of situations the relationship can fade or change dramatically when business trends demand. What trainer wouldn't swoon at the thought of replacing their existing budget with the $900-million budget Jack Bowsher inherited at IBM when he took over as director of education? However, Bowsher told attendees at *TRAINING Magazine's* conference, one of his first and most important challenges was to upgrade the use of training technology to cut costs, or to find some other creative way to contend with the $200 million budget cut proposed by management.

The consensus among participants in the *Training Directors' Forum* White Paper Project is that improving the status of training in an organization is tied more to being a skillful manager than a knowledgeable training professional. Training expertise is essential. But what training executives do as managers in deference to helping meet broad business objectives — communicate, plan, politick, respond — is where most effort goes in trying to increase training's strategic importance within the organizations represented by the White Paper participants.

The recommendations generated by the participants fit loosely — with overlap — into four broad categories: communication skills, planning and execution of executive responsibilities, understanding and responding to corporate objectives, and professional skills. Each of the specific ideas about how to improve the status of training in an organization, however, points back to one underlying piece of advice: Do whatever necessary to be in sync with your organization's business and objectives, and work in partnership to improve that business and meet those objectives. The specific recommendations follow.

Communication Skills

Recommendations in this category range from suggestions about specific ways to phrase inquiries to management, to which managers to choose to focus sales efforts toward.

- Position yourself as a facilitator of organizational meetings with senior executives. Offer to plan and facilitate a planning or team-building retreat for executives, then "work like crazy to make it excellent." As a result, managers may turn to you for help in the future.

- Give feedback to senior executives about training's successes in terms with which they are familiar. Track budget information, attendance and evaluation reports, the number of training hours, the cost of hours and training, attendance rates, the number of contacts needed to fill courses, and post-training evidence of the actual skills being used on the job. Provide that kind of information — even if not requested — quarterly, if not monthly.

- Chart return on investment in terms of time and money saved as a result of training, and get supervisors to sign off on such reports.

- If possible, demonstrate bottom-line results of training efforts. Calculate the results in terms of additional sales, for instance, or savings made because of improved negotiating skills.

- Interview senior executives about why management development doesn't work, then use that information to improve your offerings.

- Offer condensed courses to managers so they'll know what to expect for their subordinates sent for the full programs.

- Be partners with other members in the personnel areas. Bind the human resources functions, and involve other HR people in training when appropriate.

- Focus your efforts on new executives so you can help set their biases about training. Or, work with executives on the way up in the organization who will remember your contribution to their development.

- Find a key leverage point in any proposed project and get something working quickly.

- Advertise your successes. When negotiating with a manager about a training program, cite examples of how the program has helped that manager's peers or superiors. Be honest, too, about your failures.

- Give the company feedback on how it's doing from the human resources perspective, especially in comparison to competitors or exemplary organizations.

- Treat company management as valued customers.

- Consult with management about their needs. That is, don't ask what training they need, ask what problems they have and figure out what you can do to help; their perceived needs are the ones managers will find time to address.

- Work to create a doctor-patient relationship with managers. (When you visit the doctor you don't walk in and say, "I need 500 ccs of penicillin.")

Planning and Execution of Executive Responsibilities

- Work to make the training department a required stopover for managers climbing the corporate ladder.

- Review strategic plans for each department or division, and work to become a partner in that planning process.
- Link training efforts to the bottom line as an investment, instead of an expense.
- Move quickly when responding to clearly identified organizational needs.
- Tie the training and human resources development plans to the corporate strategic plan.
- Work to have budgets within your organization include time designated for managers to attend training, work as trainers, and for staff people to attend training.
- Develop processes that support and maintain goals identified for forming partnerships with management. Training curricula, policies, procedures, and budgets have to reinforce the plans you make.
- Work to gain influence with key managers in all functions.
- Reorganize the training group, when appropriate, to meet the changing needs of your company.
- Strive for visibility at all levels of the organization.
- Hire qualified staff members.
- Measure results, not activities.
- Be customer focused. Meet the needs of employees, not your own needs.
- Get commitment from managers to be responsible for the development of their own people, and position yourself to work as an advisor or resource in meeting those developmental needs.
- Whatever you do, do it well.

Understanding and Responding to Corporate Objectives

- Address senior management needs with the programs you offer, and include senior managers in the needs assessment, planning, and delivery of courses.
- Tie course objectives to the strategic objectives of the organization.
- Devise programs that encourage or require bosses to buy in, that are utility driven, offer ongoing reinforcement, and can be carefully evaluated.

7 WORTHWHILE AND OVERLOOKED REASONS YOUR EXECS SHOULD INVEST TIME IN TRAINING

Tom Brown is CEO of Management General, a Louisville, KY-based consultant to a number of Fortune 500 firms. He wrote this article to convince more top managers to become involved in their company's in-house training efforts.

Since the early 1980s, the use of internal corporate training programs to develop managers has been growing. The problem is that too many internal programs lack the presence of some very important players: the company's top echelon. Too many VP-and-above types feel internal training isn't worth their time. If they're going to be developed, they want to fly home with a sweatshirt from a Top-10 university, business cards of impressive classmates from other companies, and signed copies of their professors' books.

But top execs who bypass internal development are missing some big opportunities. Being a participant (or, better, a faculty member) in an in-house program can help a senior manager in ways too easily overlooked. Among them:

- **You can learn what's really happening in the rest of the company.** Internal development often jumbles ranks and divisions into one classroom. An executive can quickly weigh glowing annual report copy against firsthand testimony about the plant floor or another division, perhaps one that supplies his or her operations with critical parts or services.
- **You can lobby others to support your business strategies.** Since the people attending are often "hands on" managers, the seminar context is an excellent chance for a senior exec to explain what his or her own business unit is trying to do — and how managers in a sister division can help achieve those strategies. Moreover, a few days spent with those from other corporate operations can educate you on resources inside the company you might not have known about.
- **You can spot "hot talent."** It's curious how many companies pass over their own "star" managers for promotions — then recruit stars from a different company. Sitting next to managers in training can be talent-scouting. Every corporate class generates its own candidates for "valedictorian."
- **You can campaign for changes in the corporate culture.** By now, most of us accept that every corporation has its own unique ways of doing business. The current corporate culture can often exasperate senior execs, especially when burning issues like cost containment are not part of the general mindset. Written directives don't change cultural norms, but you can ignite a lot of management candles if 30 managers from across the company start to align with your calls for needed change.
- **You can get a readout on your corporation's core competencies.** The 30 managers in an internal seminar may not be a demographically perfect sample of the management skills of the company, but, then again, they are a sample. Internal training, especially if it includes role-playing or simulations, can be an invaluable tool for sizing up other talents in marketing, negotiating, engineering, innovating, or whatever other areas the class agenda embraces.
- **You can demonstrate visible commitment to "growing" people.** As a participant or professor, whenever an executive commits time to internal training, it's a profound declaration. Being part of a corporate seminar not only says you're willing to stretch your mind to consider new business thinking, it also shows you're willing to coach others who might lack the talents that boosted your own career.
- **You can help shape managerial esprit de corps.** Every company today has its share of problems; every manager is at some level perplexed. In an internal workshop, managers at all levels start pulling the same oars. Spirited seminar discussions and debates can be one of the most important byproducts of internal training, provided there's a mix of managers focusing on current common company problems.

(Editor's Note: A version of this article first appeared in The Wall Street Journal.*)*

- Be flexible and responsive to senior management, and to the needs of your customers and your company's external customers as priorities change in the organization.
- Be attentive to information about organizational issues received formally as well as informally. Follow through and offer one-on-one consultation.
- Find credible champions in the organization who support training. Help them focus and fulfill their needs, then turn to them for help in promoting training to others in the company.
- Volunteer for additional activities, such as positions on special task forces or committees, in order to increase your exposure and influence, as well as your awareness of organizational issues.
- Get involved with managers at the planning level.
- Train on demand to meet specific line needs.
- Schedule courses at times that are least disruptive to operations.
- Develop your staff into internal consultants who can be perceived as product-knowledge experts.
- Be a good listener.
- Get a grasp of the big picture. Think systematically, not like a know-it-all with stand-alone solutions to complex problems.
- Perform what you preach.
- Take responsibility and accountability, regardless of whether it is expected or extended.
- Respect confidences.
- Be enthusiastic. Care about what you are doing and let it show.
- At times, serve senior management's perceived needs until you can determine their real needs.

Professional Skills
- Track the results of your training, including those items mentioned under communications (training hours, costs, attendance, post-training performance, etc.).
- Institute systems to estimate savings that result from improved job skills learned in training.
- Set specific and measurable goals for training courses.
- Set standards for performance following training.
- Audit the results of your training according to how well trainees meet established standards back on the job.
- Determine the costs of *not training*, in terms of turnover, poor performance, injuries.
- Develop trainers who can assume other positions in the organization (or develop pass-through trainers on temporary assignment in training) so they are better prepared for those other positions as a result of their stint in training. Use them as evidence of how beneficial it is to participate in the training effort.
- Maintain your professionalism, and stay on top of state-of-the-art training techniques and technology, as well as business issues.
- Pre-test trainees. If someone knows the material you are about to teach, send that person back to the job and encourage the manager to send the person to training for something really needed. The manager will appreciate the time and money saved by not keeping an employee tied up unnecessarily.
- Explore and invest in ways to improve or develop new-employee orientation training — not simply welcome-to-the-company-here-are-your-benefits-training, but training that will get people up to speed more quickly on their jobs. Money spent wisely on new employees can pay off in superior performance in a much shorter time.
- Make it a goal to send people back to their jobs better at what they do and excited about what they've learned. They'll tell others, and no advertising is more effective than word-of-mouth.

Notes:

Overcoming Management's Training Fears

The smart training director knows how to cope with the negative attitudes that box people in and sabotage training programs.

BY SALVATORE V. DIDATO

Tom Trainer convinced management his new program was his best yet. He received full support, including a budget substantial enough to make his program fail-safe. Or *almost* fail-safe.

Of the first group of 20 trainees, three were excused from the training sessions by their managers, and six more seemed to resent being there. Something was wrong. Top management certainly was in his corner. Middle management was cooperating by sending trainees. Who could possibly be against him?

Tom was being sandbagged by undercurrent attitudes, by hidden defenses he had failed to recognize. Management and trainees often view training programs as threats to their security. Sometimes they are openly defensive and refuse to participate in the program; more often, they are silently resistive. They are hesitant to speak out, so even though they appear to offer full support, there is hidden resistance that can sabotage a program.

Management Resistance

It's just plain dumb, one might think, for managers to resist training. After all, Management Guru Peter Drucker told an American Society of Training and Development (ASTD) convention that trainers and their field are our economy's "only hope to have a really productive future."

But put yourself in a manager's shoes. How would you like to lose your own assistant for a week to a training program? Here are several ways managers feel threatened when their employees are selected for training:

1. My reputation will suffer. While an employee is away being trained, the output of the manager's department will decline — in quantity or in quality — reflecting directly upon his own reputation. His fears may be especially strong in a highly competitive atmosphere, where rewards tend to be issued on the basis of output.

2. There will be more work for me. A valuable employee may be difficult to replace for the duration of the training program, so the manager may feel he will have to take over some of the trainee's responsibilities during that time, or give extra supervision to a novice who is filling in.

3. It's my job to train my own people. There can be considerable resentment on the part of the managers when employees are taken from their supervision and trained by somebody else. Perhaps the manager thinks he is not being appreciated for the time he spends training his employees or, worse still, that his training efforts are falling short of company goals.

4. There will be a drop in department morale. The manager may anticipate resentment on the part of employees who are not selected for training, either because they feel they are being passed over for promotion, or because they must take on extra work while a colleague is absent. Someone in the department may even quit.

5. I'll lose a good worker. A manager may feel that, with training, his employee will become dissatisfied with his present work and seek a better job — or be promoted to another department.

6. I'll be replaced. The most unsettling of all management fears is that an employee will learn new work techniques and surpass, or even replace, him.

Coping with the Defensive Manager

In any organization, resistance to new action plans arises when feelings of personal security are threatened. The resistance remains hidden out of fear of reprisal (real or imagined) and tends to be greatest when there is a high-fear/low-trust atmosphere within the organizational structure.

Most resistance gravitates around the "pride system." If a program is a threat to his pride, a manager is going to resist it. Do training programs enhance the prestige, the department output or personal effectiveness of the manager? Or do they result in extra burdens; lost man-hours, trained workers who leave for better jobs, or innuendoes that a manager has failed to give his own people adequate training?

Generally, if a manager has experienced success with department employees who have undergone training, his resistance to new programs will be minimal — or nonexistent. But, if training has undermined his department, he justifiably might want to undermine the training program. Still, there are ways to cope:

1. Alleviate fears about output and reputation. Determine how understaffed the manager really is. At the very least, show a genuine concern for his problem. If top management is really behind you, you might be able to persuade the powers that be to alleviate pressure on those department managers who have employees in training.

An effective approach is to involve department managers in rap groups to discuss their problems with their peers. If they realize that other managers are able to cope with departmental absences, they may better accept absences themselves.

If the managers are encouraged to talk openly about the training program and its objectives, instead of grumbling among themselves, they're able to become more enthusiastic about the program. They may even be able to devise a workable solution to the absentee problem, such as

TRAINEES, TOO, FEAR TRAINING

Trainees also have complex attitudes toward training, attitudes which may be difficult to ferret out. Among them are:

1. Previous training failures. A trainee may resist a program because of negative conditioning to learning situations in which he has become frustrated. He may fear failure, ridicule — or even the loss of his job. A trainee may perceive training as an indictment of his own inefficiency — especially in companies where training is used as a form of punishment.

2. Peer indictment. If training appears to be punishment — or the first step toward advancement — a trainee may be subjected to peer ridicule. Those who are not selected for training may attempt to bolster their own self-image in the face of disappointment by accusing the trainee of trying to be a "big shot" — or of "apple polishing" to get ahead.

3. Encroachment upon the status quo. A trainee may worry about working overtime to keep up with his responsibilities while in training. Or, he may believe that training is a waste of time and has little value for his advancement — especially if he feels he is being trained along with others below his level, or if past training programs have failed to stimulate him.

4. Fear of advancement. Some employees actually fear success and whether the Peter Principle applies to them. Training might lead to positions they cannot, or don't want to, handle — to positions above their perceived capabilities.

Favorable pre-training publicity and pre-training orientation are effective ways to encourage trainee enthusiasm. Hold rap groups with prospective trainees and their peers who have come through training and been helped by it. A group is usually strongly impressed by favorable testimonials of peers. — S.D.

---

approaching higher management as a group.

2. Get the manager involved. Anxiety is a reaction to the unknown. A manager may develop anxiety — and resistance — because he doesn't know what the program is to accomplish. Managers who are involved in the program and its objectives from its inception tend to be less anxious about it.

Managers can be approached individually or in groups. But be sure to appeal directly to each manager's needs. Define your role as an adjunct. You are adding a dimension to his department. You are working with him, but in no way are you attempting to take over as manager or on-the-job trainer.

Outline the material to be covered in the program and ask for advice. Sometimes the program can be improved with management input. In addition, the manager who believes he's helping to develop a program retains a sense of responsibility for the trainee's progress and, if he continues to feel responsible for his employee, will be less anxious about the employee replacing him.

3. Train the manager first. If the manager is not familiar with the subject matter to be covered in the training session, he may need refresher training himself. He's less likely to feel threatened if he believes he's as current in new techniques as the employee who's being trained.

If the program appears to be the brainchild of one manager, other managers may view it as a waste of time and/or money. Also, managers who get negative feedback and strong dissatisfaction from those below them might think training creates more problems than solutions.

There is nothing more effective than an ongoing publicity campaign for maintaining interest in and a positive attitude toward training. Favorable publicity reinforces group consensus at all levels within the structure. Monthly status memos, monthly in-house newsletters produced and distributed by your training or sales department, articles in the company newspaper and in local and trade press all can enhance the prestige of the program. A number of successful trainers enlist the support of the public relations department in publicizing training concepts throughout the company and to the general public.

It's also crucial to find sources of resentment before they reach top levels. Complaints can surface when middle managers meet together and find mutual support for their dissatisfactions. Giving managers and supervisors the opportunity to air their views in rap groups under your supervision lets you understand — and try to solve — problems before they reach top management. And before they can sabotage your training programs. That's being a sharp training director — assuming that negative attitudes exist even if they aren't apparent.

Fighting Resistance to Training

Understanding managers' unwillingness to make the most of training.

BY STEPHEN P. BECKER

At some point in your career you'll probably meet — or have to cope with — a department or division manager who doesn't want any part of training. Chances are he won't ridicule or attack you openly. It's far more likely that you and your staff will simply be ignored — phone calls will not be returned, memos will not be responded to, and appointments will be broken or postponed.

When you find your training department in this situation, don't give up. There are some definite strategies that you can adopt to overcome such resistance and initiate needed training. Each strategy or solution to a resistance problem is dependent on the cause of the resistance. Let's consider four of the common causes.

The first cause of resistance to the training department has roots in the situation where a department or division manager wants to train — but *without* the involvement of the training department. For some reason the manager believes he needs complete control over training. He wants to call all the shots without anyone looking over his shoulder. The fact that the manager knows little or nothing about training seems to make no difference. This sort of manager thinks he knows enough to call all the shots.

Suppose the manager delegates many training activities to somebody in his department who has experience in the content area. This frequently happens in sales departments. Rather than get any help or advice from the training department, the sales manager believes that the sales department can and should do its own training. This sort of manager figures all that has to be done is to take an experienced salesman and have him show the *inexperienced* individual how to do it for a day or two.

At this point I won't go into all the reasons why this kind of mental posture regarding training is absurd. The fact that such an attitude is ridiculous makes no difference. What does matter is that for many of us it has the "ring of truth." If you are faced with such resistance, one strategy you may employ is confrontation.

Remember, training is taking place (if you call that training). Somebody is performing the tasks that the organization has mandated to training. In a way, this is a direct challenge to you — by the manager involved. The situation requires that you confront it. If you don't, you lose control of training and that's not what you were hired to do.

Tell It Like It Is

One of the best confrontation techniques — it's guaranteed to put your opponent on the defensive — is honesty. Bring the issue out into the open. If you are widely supported by other managers, make sure they are aware of your problem. Let Mr. or Ms. Resistance, the problem manager, clearly know of your dissatisfaction with your relationship. Use facts and examples to describe the way you have been abused instead of used. Don't send this manager any more memos — you already know that's a waste of time. Make sure your boss know what's going on. He/she should know exactly how you feel and exactly what changes you expect to take place.

Now let's put the cherry on top. In addition to all of these activities, you should whack this manager who's resisting training with two or three proposals for training that are needed and can help the performance of his department. Again, make sure everybody in the world knows of the proposals. That way the manager will have to explain to many people in the organization why the training proposals are being refused. He won't be able to ignore just you anymore.

It's important that you initiate more than one proposal. Here's why: A manager can find lots of reasons why a specific proposal is no good. But it's more difficult to shoot down each of three or more proposals. This is especially true if it's known that you are more than willing to make some modifications. It is, after all, in your best interest to give a little in order to get a lot.

If it sounds as if I'm advocating that you go to war with this person, you're exactly right. Actually, the war is already in progress and it's directed against you. If you do nothing, you lose, and a chunk of training goes down the drain. Too many times in the past, training managers have not fought for the health of the training department and profession. It's time for that to change. Organizational infighting is a part of reality, and it's time for us trainers to be very realistic. Our profession is growing and improving every day. Each of us must fight to protect what we've developed.

Let's look now at the second cause of resistance: The manager just doesn't understand the value of training. He has never given formalized training much thought one way or another. This is a subtle kind of resistance, because the manger doesn't feel as if he is resisting. He has merely elected *not* take advantage of the training resource available.

The strategy here is easy to say, but hard to accomplish — you must get this manager to understand what is meant by the word training. Ask the manger to participate in or observe types of training that might be helpful to his department or division. This may take time, but it's worth it. Once you "sell" this manager, he will become one of the best users of training. So, expose this manager to outside training programs which you have pre-screened. To put it another way: Help him to experience a smorgasbord of exciting training technologies and concepts.

The third cause of resistance stems from the situation in which the manager believes he or she understands training, but still wants no part of it. This manager probably sponsored or purchased some training in the past and felt that there wasn't enough payoff relative to the time and cash he invested. Chances are that judgment is correct. Much of the training provided in-house, or available for purchase, tends to be too broad in scope or too vague in its objectives to produce measurable results.

What to do? Sell training based on a demonstration project or pilot experiment. Show the manager that the way you perform training is dramatically different from what he has been exposed to in the past. Your project should be clearly aimed at output-producing results. Objectives must be specific, and a measurement system must be built in from the start. The program must be short term (three or four months) so the feedback can be obtained quickly. Hopefully this program will have high leverage. That is, there will be high payback relative to the investment or cost.

The fourth type of resistance occurs where you have a weak, insecure or incompetent manager who wants low visibility. He doesn't want to be discovered. This manager will always be very polite, full of smiles, and happy to see you leave!

You're dealing here with a fake. You are not, however, primarily in the business of destroying poor managers. This is an emotional problem in that this manager spends a lot of energy being afraid of losing his or her position in the organization.

Your strategy here: Because this manager will never come to you, you must take the initiative. Get him to trust you not to give away his secret. Once he believes you're on *his* side, he'll probably give the green light to your training proposal. The big problem now is that the manager gets dependent on you and involves you in many management issues that have little to do with training. This saps your time and strength and should be avoided like quicksand. The trick is knowing when to pull back or get out of there. If you must stay, you'll have to be continually aware that you can end up performing as trainer *and* department manager.

As training manager, you must deal with resistance whenever it prevents you from providing training to a key part of your organization. If you find resistance in the less important departments or divisions, a good strategy would be to walk away from it. Fighting resistance takes all the energy you've got. If you are going to invest your efforts, put them where they truly can make a difference.

It's easy for us to get caught up in the mechanics of our jobs; that is, in performing the normal administrative aspects of being a training manager. In fact, we can develop so many programs that need our careful attention, we run out of time for anything else. It's very important to structure your administrative responsibilities so that you also have time for important developmental tasks. So, analyze important pockets of resistance; determine causes; plan strategies based on those causes; and successfully implement your strategies. That way you develop your training department's opportunities to deliver training that really counts.

Notes:

Gaining Power for Training

Corporate politics pose a dilemma in training's search for a leadership role.

BY BRIAN McDERMOTT

Too often, training executives get locked into parallel play in their organizations, going through the motions of being involved in matters of corporate-wide significance while actually keeping a safe distance from the real decision-making systems.

That message, delivered with specific and challenging ideas about how to gain political power and influence for a training function, unsettled many of the attendees a conference for training managers. It was a message that many training executives agreed forced them out of their comfort zones to examine what it requires for a training function to be taken seriously in an organization. It was a detoxification program for idealism and a source of apparent dissonance for those wanting to hold onto humanistic values while playing corporate politics.

In his presentation, *Training Dilemmas in the Development of Leaders*, Leonard Hirsch, president of the Institute for Strategic Management, stressed the potential that training executives have for influencing their businesses and the development of leaders by being leaders themselves. He warned, however, that being a leader requires politicking and that agreeing to be political means being willing to pay the consequences.

"You are now a symbol in everything you do. If you want leadership, you have to face the fact that a television camera is on you day and night; you have no private life anymore. There is a microphone always around your throat, so everything you say will be used and misused in ways that you and I haven't even considered. We're also going to have to talk about telling the truth and lying because it is a different proposition for leaders of large organizations than it is for most people. Different ground rules. And you will live and die by those ground rules."

In its most negative sense, Hirsch says, politics is the substitution of style for substance. In his definition, however, it is a mobilization, a campaign of getting to know one's self and then stating that image unequivocally through actions instead of words.

"Politics means getting people to change their minds. There are a lot of ways to do that; probably the least (effective) way is to change their minds rationally. Also, you've got to remember, once you stick your head above the horizon you deserve what you get. You become everybody's ideal self and you become everybody's despised self. People dismiss you and pay attention to the wrong issues.

Hirsch's key suggestions for becoming and developing leaders include:

• **Image.** Get rid of the Hush Puppies; it makes you look non-business like and that's what training directors are always saddled with. Personnel types are usually dismissed as too out of touch so they are never really invited into the leadership circle. Dress, groom and posture yourself to fit your company's image of the successful leader.

• **Motivation vs. Inspiration.** A motivated employee can complete your assignments thoroughly and with little or no guidance. Unmotivated employees can't. Get rid of those who can't and look for ways to inspire those who can.

• **Managing vs. Organizing.** Management is necessary, but if you want to lead an organization you have to organize differently. Predictability is a result of management; leadership is something different. In what ways can you be inconsistent, innovative and surprising to your own staff. For instance, rely less on expertise and more on loyalty. Expert staff members can be lured away by the promise of slightly more money, or even slightly more challenge; loyalists cannot and therefore will be at your side in good times and bad.

• **Collaboration vs. Conflict.** Trainers tend to want to collaborate, but leaders need to work with conflict, carefully selecting the battles that can be won. Give up the idea that conflict should be replaced by collaboration because collaboration is *best after a conflict*. Don't deny the reality of business creating winners and losers.

• **Truth vs. Appearance.** Appearance is more important than truth because what people believe to be true is what you must deal with.

• **Networks vs. Spies.** Maintain informal information networks, but understand, too, that as a leader you must have spies in the organization. And the best spies are the ones who don't know they are spies.

• **Planning.** Understand that you often need to plan via a series of carom shots because people and problems and other business matters will block your direct path. Plan simultaneously from rational and non-rational perspectives.

• **Communication — Direct vs. Indirect.** Many people tend to distrust direct communication, especially when it is too heavy. Use it, but supplement it with indirect communication that leaks out to the people you want to eventually reach.

"Most people believe communication is a transportation problem: I have the knowledge in my head and I have got to get it across the room into your head. Clearly, that is not the case. People resonate, they don't just transport. You have to understand what happens when you talk. And you have to understand what you look like when you walk into a room. You have to be clear about people's reactions to you because you've got to communicate against those reactions. You have to understand the connections in people's minds and be in charge of your image.

"You have to use yourself as a symbol. When you ask people to do something, it has to affect them emotionally, as well as intellectually. Too many of us spend our time making communication dispassionate, so we are met with equal dispassion."

Hirsch says, "It's important to understand that (leadership) is a campaign. If you want to be part of the leadership of an organization, you have to understand that in any campaign the winning number is 50 percent plus one." In all campaigns, he says, there are three kinds of voters to consider: the *firs*, the 40 percent who automatically favor you; the *agins*, the 40 percent who naturally resent you; and the persuadables.

"You have to ignore the firs and agins. The firs already support you. Touch them once in a while and get them to move. You are not going to get the agins to change their minds.

"As a matter of fact," Hirsch says, "most managers spend about 80 percent of their time with the firs. We like to talk with people who agree with us. Occasionally we go and have a good fight with the agins to prove to ourselves how intransigent they always were. And we spend five percent of our time with the persuadables. What I want to get you to understand is that you don't have to talk to the people who support you anyway, other than keeping in touch. All you've got to do with the opposition is find out what they are up to. And you've got to spend all of your time with the persuadables; management by walking around. Find out how you can help them. Talk about things in terms of their lives. Pay attention to their cultures — there are sub-cultures within organizations."

How to Play the Game

In light of Hirsch's critique of human resources development, training executives provided the following feedback from group discussions during the conference:

• Training directors need to be more opportunistic and more realistic about business. It might also be beneficial to do less intellectualizing and more work with people on the lines.

• Training directors can't expect to be taken seriously by coaching leaders until they themselves become practiced leaders.

• Metaphorically, everybody in business gets shot. Risk takers, looking above the horizon of what has been done, get it in the head. Ostriches, with their heads in the sand, get it in the butt. Training directors need to decide where they want to get it.

• Perhaps the biggest leadership issue for trainers is that they are not recognized as being part of their organizations' business. Playing corporate politics could help, but in many cases training people don't even know the rules of the game.

• The question is not whether to be involved in business politics, but how. Trainers are part of the political game whether they like it or not. The remaining questions are: How does training fit in? How can trainers choose the risks and conflicts that can be taken on and won? How can training professionals be political and yet maintain their humanistic values?

Balanced View of Business

Hirsch believes that values come as paired, not unitary principles. "The problem with most of us is we assume that humanism says, 'Making nice.' If you really want to look at humanism you have to look at the other side of it, the nether side. And that says, 'Whatever is human is not far from me. I've experienced that.' I am consistently trying to push us out of our envelope. We don't want to try something that hasn't been tried before and proven successful. That's what I am trying to get our profession to understand. We've got to consistently make experimentations outside the comfort zone that we all operate in because that is what will shake the corporation up. And then we become responsible for the future dream of the organization. We are the caretakers of the dream, and that is not a comfortable position.

"I think, therefore, one of the jobs of every generation is to strip the mask off of the previous generation, to understand what we mean by humanism, but to strip the mask away and say, 'Wait a minute, we can't be afraid of defining this (politics) and accepting it as evil until we have explored it, until we have pushed ourselves into it.'"

Hirsch says, "In most corporations everybody now has come finally to realize that the HRD function is the most critical function in an organization, and we are being seen differently. The door is open for us to exercise ourselves and the rest of the corporation. Somebody has finally listened.

"Some of you will walk in that door and get beaten up. You're going to be given the opportunity to lead the organization and you will fail, the same way that the accountants failed, the same way that the marketers failed, and the same way that the manufacturers failed.

"Some of us are going to head corporations with real values about real people, and we're going to fail. And in that failure will be the little glimmer of success, because if we tried it and then we failed, we'll be seen as real players.

"And then we may get accepted as part of a management team that runs the corporation because that is ultimately where we're headed. No one person can run a corporation. But you only get accepted after you have been knocked out."

Tools and Ideas to Help You Pick and Prepare Teams of Line Managers

With operations folk delivering more training these days, it's important they get the right skills practice before they hit the classroom.

BY DAVE ZIELINSKI

It's one thing to use line trainers to deliver select portions of your training curriculum. It's another thing altogether to hand over the majority of teaching duties to line workers with little or no stand-up presentation experience. But the latter is a tactic more training managers are using because of shrinking delivery resources, a shortage of on-staff subject-matter expertise, and growing demands to deliver a lot of training in short time frames.

Cris Ballinger, a computer trainer with ScrippsHealth in San Diego, is in that group. When ScrippsHealth, a network of hospitals, clinics, and home healthcare services, acquired another hospital, it converted its new-patient registration and billing systems to the ScrippsHealth system. That meant 350 people in the acquired company needed immediate training on new procedures.

As a computer specialist, Ballinger knew she didn't have enough subject-matter experience in insurance, authorization, and other key issues to credibly teach these skills — especially in addition to teaching people how to use the new software and system. So she put into action a plan she had wanted to try for years — one relying predominantly on operations folks to deliver almost all of the training.

One key to her success in this tenuous post-acquisition environment, where employees in the acquired company were not exactly embracing the change, was using trainers from the acquired company, Ballinger says. "We wanted these people to be trained by peers they already had a high level of trust and familiarity with," she says. "We did not want people delivering this training who didn't know the unique challenges of the people in the acquired hospital."

Choosing and Preparing the Right Line Trainers

Potential line instructors where nominated by senior managers, and interviewed by a "facility implementation" team looking for candidates with potential to develop good presentation skills, she says. Some 36 line trainers were chosen.

"The pool of subject-matter experts (SMEs)," she says, "turned out to be outspoken, assertive, and quite humorous, which was important."

Ballinger created a "trainer's kit" for these newbie trainers, consisting of slides, handouts, computer demos, job aids, 10-minute videotapes, and exercise worksheets. The kit items ensure key points are covered in each class. The standardized exercises for different work areas consist of actual work situations trainees face.

Integral to the kit is a detailed "task matrix" that helps line trainers choose which training materials and approaches are best for specific content. "We give them many options — including the option of having one of the training staff members operate a computer or a projector for them if needed," Ballinger says.

A Big Dose of Real-World Simulation

The trainers received a full day of hands-on practice and simulations, in addition to practicing on their own, before going live. "We put them all through the most difficult course first, and then asked them back for a full-day course on how to teach effectively," she says.

One section of that teaching course had new trainers squirming. "I gave everyone an 'important point' from a course to cover in a five-minute presentation to the rest of the class," she says. "I gave them three days to prepare. Most griped about it — but later they thanked me." Those who objected strenuously to the five-minute "test" were given an option: use the time instead to lead a discussion with the group on training tips and ideas.

During these trial presentations, other class members were asked to "act out" the role of students and the kinds of questions trainers feared most. "I usually didn't have to say a word to assist," Ballinger says, "because the group collectively came up with suggestions on ways to handle the troublemakers and tough questions."

Those not presenting were given a sheet containing only positive adjectives and asked to circle five (of 30 choices) to describe their peers' presentation styles. "We used only positives to make this a confidence booster for them; we wanted it to be a relatively safe environment," she says.

As the trainers went "live," they met (with Ballinger or a peer acting as facilitator) each week in support groups to share lessons learned, trade tips, explore mutual problems, and get a booster shot of confidence. "They are still meeting after implementation, because there are issues that arise during training that need addressing," Ballinger says.

For courses with many students, Ballinger or a training coworker offered to help out as a facilitator. "Some took us up on it, but most instead chose to team with another line instructor."

Certification Process Key to Training Results

Certifying trainees in new system procedures involved having them complete a set of exercises on the computer that simulated real-world practices. In the ScrippsHealth registration and billing system, for instance, whenever new patients are registered — or visitors arrive — corresponding numbers are assigned to them. So Ballinger set up what she calls an "interactive soap opera" — a hypothetical patient family where "Grandma" had suffered a heart attack, "Dad" had a workman's comp issue, or "Uncle" had a substance-abuse problem. In the certification exercise, trainees have to — using the new system procedures — register these family members, enter all their insurance information, and effectively bring them into and out of the hospital. They then turned in the numbers they generated for the exercises so trainers could go back and check to make sure they entered things correctly and follow up with additional training if needed, she says.

Each student had to turn in at least one of these successfully completed exercise worksheets to receive a production ID card, which in turn enabled them to access the new system. In other words, no certification via training, no system access.

"Some who hadn't taken the training called and complained about lack of access, but peer pressure essentially told these people that if they didn't get the training, the organization couldn't really support them on the job. It was nice this message came from operations peers, rather than from the training department," Ballinger says.

By the time the new system went live, some 97% of the required staff were certified to use the system, and 50% had completed more than one of the required exercise worksheets.

A 24-Hour Troubleshooting "Command Center"

An around-the-clock, "go-live command center" was created to help answer trainee questions as they began using the new systems with real patients. Staffed largely by vendor representatives (from the company supplying the software) and technical workers, the command center responded to any problems during the first week of conversion. Workers answered phones and often dispatched the line trainers and Ballinger to go out to work areas — wearing highly visible purple T-shirts — to help with problems.

"Overall, the training provided was probably not as 'spit shined' as if training professionals had delivered it, but we had superior content – plenty of real-world advice and tips — by virtue of having the experts teaching," Ballinger says.

Notes:

A Manager for All Seasons

If a training manager feels ineffective and overwhelmed, the problem may be role confusion. Case in point: the counselor vs. the disciplinarian.

BY NEIL A. STROUL

Is it just me, or has the idea of a *crisis in management* become a full-fledged axiom of the conventional wisdom? In contemporary American managers, has the self-help industry found a new class of casualties to console? I go to the local bookstore, and I swear that the number of books about how to manage compares favorably with the number on being your own best friend, overcoming depression and forgiving your parents.

Contemporary managers really are having a rough go of it, but I wonder if the avalanche of management books is helping or hindering. The models in most of these books are CEOs and entrepreneurs; so, it seems, are the intended readers.

High-level executives operate in a vastly different universe from the one inhabited by middle managers. "Management" does not mean the same thing for an executive and a middle manager; in particular, it emphasizes different roles. I think most line managers tend to dismiss most modern management books because the books don't address the needs and issues confronting them. What's more, many line managers wouldn't even read a management book. They don't think like "managers." Or rather, they don't particularly identify with the management role. The idea of management as a generic skill is peripheral to their frame of reference.

Many of the line managers I meet are torn between attending to the needs of their subordinates and responding to the priorities of their bosses. They often feel that they lack sufficient resources to do their jobs. They're more confused about new technologies than they care to admit. They spend too much time in meetings of questionable value. They're activity-driven. They can talk glibly about the future, but they remain prisoners of the past. They are unable or unwilling to recognize the extent to which they resist change. With the American economy in a tailspin and many organizations finding it difficult to compete at home and abroad, today's managers appear harried, confused and conflicted.

I believe that much of this conflict is actually due to *role confusion*. Current trends in corporate restructuring, for example, are confounding many managers. More often than not, middle managers are not strictly overseers of other people's activities but also individual contributors — worker bees. On the one hand, the leaner, meaner organization has pushed responsibility and discretion downward in such a way that the overseer role has expanded: Managers have a wider span of control and a broader level of responsibility. On the other hand, with fewer resources and higher demands, their role as individual contributors has expanded as well. Consequently, the feeling of being pulled in two directions simultaneously has been heightened. The old cliché about serving two masters and serving neither well holds true.

Role Theory

The word "managing" suggests a more unified enterprise than reality warrants. In truth, managing is a multifaceted collection of activities. One way to view managing is as an assortment of roles, not all of which are internally consistent and some of which may, in fact, compete with one another. This partially explains why we rely on such a medley of terms to describe managing: administration, supervision, management, leadership. These terms describe not just different activities, but different roles.

Role theory gives us a useful vantage point for understanding some of the difficulties associated with being an effective manager. It also can help us see how contemporary circumstances are aggravating the problem.

Role theory acknowledges that each of us recognizes the existence of a *self*, which we experience as the core of our subjective awareness. But it is primarily concerned with how that self is manifested in a variety of ways depending upon external conditions — particularly social conditions. Among other things, roles help define relationships.

Every day, each of us moves through a variety of roles, changing our behavior to suit our perception of the circumstances. I rely on one constellation of behaviors when I am with clients, another with my children and still another at a football game. If I engaged in the same role-bound behavior that I rely on with clients when I interact with my children, all of us would end up confused. Each of these is a role: consultant, father, one of the guys.

In social settings, we scan the environment for cues that help us define the situation. We then draw upon our past experience of similar situations in order to determine what constitutes appropriate behavior. These cues are referred to as demand characteristics. They represent our interpretation of the range of socially acceptable behavior. As our experiences accumulate, we recognize that certain kinds of situations are similar, and we organize our behavior into roles. When we are thrust into novel situations, part of the challenge involves selecting a suitable role from our pre-existing repertoire. People newly promoted into management know this feeling all too well: How should I act?

Our best guide is personal experience. When we become managers, we use managers we have known as models, or we acquire models through reading, training courses and so on. But what happens when we assume a role that breaks new ground, one for which our previous experience is of little or no value?

The Manager's Dilemma

In the course of a workday, managers navigate several roles. Often, however, managers fail to recognize some of the demand characteristics that exist in certain situations. They fail to shift gears and adopt a new role that would be more effective. This phenomenon is sometimes written off to management *style*, which is a way of suggesting that some managers use a one-size-fits-all approach: They rely exclusively on a democratic or autocratic style, regardless of the situation.

Sometimes, incompatible roles are forced on managers through no fault of their own. Take performance appraisals, for instance. We want the appraisal to function as a feedback mechanism for employee development, so we insist that the manager adopt a counselor role. But we also want the appraisal to serve as a control mechanism, which demands that the manager play a judgmental role as well. The two roles are inherently incompatible, but many performance review systems continue to require managers to wear both hats during the course of a single appraisal interview.

Most managers, like most people in general, are selective about which roles they embrace. They prefer to remain in a "comfort zone" that defines a limited number of roles. They can be quite rigid about the management roles they are willing to play, or they may be unaware of different roles they need to fulfill.

Where change is rampant and uncertainty prevails, the distinctions between various roles become blurred. The demand characteristics may become incomprehensible. In such situations, individuals retreat to the perceived safety of old, familiar roles — the lowest common denominator, if you will. By way of analogy, in sailing, if weather conditions make navigating difficult, a sound strategy is to head for the closest, safest harbor.

What do today's confused middle managers consider to be their safe harbor? Like anyone else in an ambiguous situation, they're likely to defer to an authority figure — someone who may possess inside information and can guide them. Translation: When in doubt, make the boss happy.

Naturally, anyone who operates in an organization must be concerned with the judgment and desires of those higher up the pyramid. But with so much uncertainty at present, I worry that too many mid-level managers overemphasize their own subordinate roles. If managers become preoccupied with trying to fathom the often-murky expectations of their bosses, their focus moves away from managing others toward managing themselves — their worker selves, that is. Consequently, they become less effective in the management role.

Let's look at one area in which role confusion creates problems: the manager as counselor.

> "When a subordinate's performance deteriorates, the manager's major concern will be, 'Does this make me look bad?'"

Developmental Counseling

Counseling is a critical role for managers, and one which most of them recognize and accept as valid. To isolate counseling as a specific role, however, it's important to distinguish it from coaching. Many people use the terms interchangeably, but I define them as follows: Coaching describes a developmental process for working with people who possess basic skills and, in general, meet the expectations for their jobs. The intent of coaching is to help people achieve the highest level of mastery of which they are capable. Counseling, on the other hand, refers to a developmental process for an individual who is performing below expectations. The intent of counseling is to help people resolve performance problems that are preventing success. In other words, counseling is always a problem-solving process, not a "stretching" exercise for a good performer.

The term counseling also warrants some hairsplitting. We can identify at least three variations, the first of which has little to do with management. This is, of course, the sort of counseling, generally restricted to professional therapists, that deals with major mental or emotional problems. Managers are well-advised to avoid trying to act as amateur therapists.

Another kind of counseling is primarily *disciplinary:* A manager invokes her formal authority because an employee has violated an organizational policy — one having to do with, say, attendance or security.

Disciplinary counseling must be distinguished from *developmental* counseling: Developmental counseling occurs when the individual is failing to meet the expectations of the job, and the manager intervenes to help the person create a strategy for resolving the problem.

Development is synonymous with learning, and it's a naturally occurring process. Plenty of people continue to grow and develop regardless of what their managers do or don't do. If the manager decides to become involved, however, he can affect the *rate* and the *direction* of an individual's development. For example, a manager's influence may lead an employee to enter management early in her career or to remain in a technical position indefinitely.

When managers do become involved, it's important to recognize that development is relationship-based. To a large extent, it is *how* a manager manages the relationship that determines whether developmental goals will be achieved.

Here's where role confusion enters the picture. If a manager defines her role primarily in terms of pleasing her own bosses, then she is likely to confuse developmental counseling with disciplinary counseling. When a subordinate's performance deteriorates, the manager's major concern will be, "Does this make me look bad?" Consequently, in the best tradition of things that travel downhill, the manager will come at the problem from a blaming or controlling perspective: "You're making me look bad!" or, "Clean up this mess or else!"

What could have been a developmental opportunity has just become a disciplinary crisis. The manager has failed to manage the relationship in a way that helps the individual resolve his own difficulties. If managers want to encourage growth and development, they must separate their discipline-enforcer role from the role of developmental counselor.

Counseling for Success

Consider Mike Adkins and Karen Williams. Mike is the manager of a software engineering team for a computer company. Karen is the newest member of his staff. Mike is worried about Karen. Her projects seem to be behind schedule, scuttlebutt has it that she doesn't interact with customers very well, and she wasn't at her workstation the last two times Mike was walking about. He thinks she may need some counseling. What should he do?

Before Mike even attempts to slip into the role of counselor, he needs to gather some objective evidence. Is there, in fact, a problem? If so, how serious is it? If Karen isn't meeting certain expectations, is she even aware that those expectations exist?

Suppose Mike discovers that in fact only one customer was upset with Karen, and that this was an uncharacteristic incident. Also, it appears merely coincidental that she wasn't at her workstation when Mike happened to walk by. The missed deadlines, on the other hand, seem to represent an emerging pattern.

Time to put on the counselor's hat? Not yet. It's entirely possible that the situation may require only a "feedback" meeting with Karen, rather than a counseling session. Mike calls her into his office and explains that he has just learned she's been missing deadlines. Is she aware of this? What can she tell him about it?

If Karen acknowledges the problem but offers a reasonable explanation — one that suggests the problem is now contained — Mike can essentially drop the matter. He has merely sent the implicit message that he is conscientious.

If she simply didn't know about the deadlines, or didn't realize they were high-priority items, now she does — and she probably can start meeting them.

About half the time, a simple feedback meeting is all it takes to cure a performance problem. By separating ordinary feedback from counseling — by preventing role confusion, that is — a manager can give employees ample opportunity to resolve problems on their own.

But suppose that instead of acknowledging the deadline problem, Karen denies or minimizes it, forcing Mike to present the evidence he has gathered. Or suppose she agrees there's a problem, but confesses that she's stymied. *Now* it's time for Mike to adopt the role of counselor. But how?

If Mike is confused about his role, Karen will be confused about the purpose of the counseling session. When managers adopt a disciplinary role in dealing with performance problems, the emotional tone of the face-to-face discussion changes dramatically and obscures the purpose. Placing blame becomes as significant as solving the problem. Nobody likes to be blamed. If Karen is "accused," she will focus on blaming someone else or finding explanations that evade personal responsibility. Developmental counseling is intended to help employees uncover the sources of the problem and identify potential remedies.

And how does this role actually work? To conduct an effective counseling session, managers should first investigate the problem — complete a front-end analysis, if you will — to develop a clearer understanding of its nature. Far too often, managers prematurely conclude that employees are either unmotivated, incompetent or possess a "bad attitude."

In fact, the various causes of performance problems make up a hierarchy of sorts. Imagine a pyramid. At the top are causes that are more concrete and lend themselves readily to solutions. Toward the bottom are broader, more ambiguous causes that require greater ingenuity to resolve. Starting at the top and moving downward, we find:

Lack of direction. Does the employee understand the job requirements? Does he get enough feedback to judge his own performance accurately?

Most managers' biggest problem is the failure to distinguish between disciplinary and developmental counseling.

Lack of competence. Does the person have the basic capabilities and training necessary to do the job?

Poor work design. Are there workflow or structural problems that prevent the employee from getting the job done? Does she have the right tools and resources? Are deadlines realistic?

Poor job design. Does the individual "fit" the job? Is there anything about the job or the way the person is managed that creates disincentives? For instance, is good performance punished in some way or bad performance rewarded?

Emotional distress: Was the employee recently passed over for a promotion? Is there an illness in the family? A financial setback? A drug or alcohol problem?

This kind of front-end analysis helps the manager prepare for the counseling role. If nothing else, it at least gives him an "angle" to start with. But the manager who approaches the counseling role from a *disciplinary* perspective instead of a developmental one will inevitably fail to conduct this analysis. He'll just jump in and start dishing out blame.

At the actual counseling session, the manager should follow a definite agenda, one that looks something like this:

1. Establish a climate that emphasizes problem solving rather than blaming.

2. Explain the purpose of the meeting and the topics you intend to cover.

3. Review the tasks and standards of the job to ensure that the employee understands your expectations.

4. Express concern about the performance problem. The person must understand that this is a valid problem with serious consequences, one that must be resolved.

5. Listen responsively. Get the employee's point of view. Collect new information about the problem.

6. Invite solutions. Maybe the employee can come up with a good one. Also, once back on the job, she'll have more commitment to an idea of her own than to an idea of yours.

7. Collaborate to solve the problem. Chances are, the employee doesn't have a great solution in mind. You'll both have to look for one. Try to frame the hunt as a partnership.

8. Make commitments. Clarify each party's responsibilities and action plans in solving the problem.

In the best of all worlds, only one counseling session would be needed to diagnose the causes of the problem and to find valid remedies. But reality is rarely so benign. Even with good intentions on the part of both parties, this endeavor may require several meetings. As long as a manager senses that the employee is negotiating in good faith and is working toward resolving the situation, counseling should be continued. If, over time, there is no progress, the employee will have to be reassigned or fired.

I have talked to a great many managers about what they do to develop people, about what works and what doesn't work. Again and again, I hear stories that suggest role confusion abounds in the way managers enact their role as counselors. Most often, they fail to distinguish between disciplinary and developmental counseling. When they confuse the two, they neglect to investigate possible causes of a performance problem, and they inadvertently employ a blaming strategy rather than a problem-solving strategy. Blaming prevents relationship building, which is the most significant variable in producing favorable outcomes in counseling.

By making these distinctions and demonstrating the key issues in developmental counseling, we can help managers reduce their confusion and more successfully fulfill their counseling role.

Notes:

CHAPTER 3

TRACKING BUSINESS TRENDS AND ISSUES

Watching the Fads for Ideas That Won't Fade

Training executives skeptically scan for ideas based on sound business sense.

BY BRIAN McDERMOTT

Training executives are continually challenged to wade through the hype and hoopla of the latest business fads and fashions — the newest paths to excellence, the slickest systems for developing manager/entrepreneurs, the truest techniques for making leaders from followers. The trick is to know how to choose and use what works *and* not get caught with too many zoot-suited training programs hanging in the closet.

Often, some training directors say, it's difficult to be objective and well informed about the latest greatest cures for all that ails corporate America. But, it is essential, especially when new buzzwords get mass media exposure. Trainers then face increased pressure and temptation from at least two sources: line managers with a heightened sense of their production or service problems, and senior-level executives who sometimes latch evangelistically onto new ideas. And trainers also must contend with their reflexes to always search for new ways to reach adult learners.

Internal Consulting

Harriet Harral, director of training and staff development for the city of Jacksonville, FL, considers it one of her primary responsibilities to act as an internal consultant to other managers who, without guidance, might be swept away by fads or miss something of value.

"In general, it's likely that training people should be more aware of the new business trends. There should be a certain amount of skepticism involved in looking at anything new. And if you do training you should probably have a lot more experience to draw on for making judgments about what is a fad and what has lasting value. For instance, if the training department is supposed to be an expert on management needs, training should lead the charge with a new trend when it is appropriate."

Harral's basic criteria for separating the faddish from the classic is to determine if a new program or idea fits with her views of what training should entail. One program she has used successfully is Ken Blanchard's and Paul Hersey's *One-Minute Manager*. "Its principles fit with what I see as basic management practices. It's packaged well and it has served as a good introductory idea for our people."

Harral also has used Blanchard's *Situational Leadership II*, which she says is consistent with her academic background emphasis on communication and leadership styles. Both Blanchard programs, she says, fall into the category of things-that-are-new-that-aren't-really-new.

"Some fads have foundations that are not freakish. I don't put down an idea just because it isn't really new, just repackaged. I'm always trying to find vehicles to help things make sense to people. I think that's a necessary trait in training managers. In all areas of adult education you have to keep asking, 'How do people learn, when, why?' It may be the rephrasing of an old idea that sparks a new way of helping a group of people make sense of something."

Harral says she has not been burned buying into a fad that proved a flop. She is somewhat concerned, however, about the opportunities she may have missed by not trying some things. "Part of my role is also to be willing to take some risks."

Eliminating risk

Robert Henderson, director of training for *The Boston Globe*, says he looks skeptically at anything new and works to reduce risk in investing his company's training dollars.

"You have to be aware of the things you hear all the time and ask, 'What are the definitions?' I read articles about different trends and still come away many times with a fuzzy feeling about exactly what it is people are talking about. And there is a new term every year — corporate culture, leadership. They change the name of the same old concepts. But that might appeal to a particular organization.

"In our organization, innovation is the new word. You can sell anything if you say it is innovative. So the [fad] can be useful [in selling training to managers]. There is one big caution, though. People will sell you some very expensive experiences. If someone with influence in an organization is interested in something, you might end up owning a program and have no use for it at all. Recently, I had a vendor try to sell us a program on innovation that was no more than a slide show. It didn't tell me anything I didn't know. And it was quite expensive."

In selecting new programs or adopting new ideas, Henderson says, "I don't like to take risks. I want to be confident about what I'm getting. I'm the buyer and I'm very demanding. For example, a vendor must be willing to let me sit in on a program that the company is presenting for someone else. I'm not going to buy without that opportunity. And I really take umbrage when they want me to pay to sit in.

"If a vendor really believes in a product, he will be willing to meet any demands that I, as a buyer, should ask. A good majority of those demands should be reasonable. If a vendor is not willing, I would certainly steer away."

When looking at something new, Henderson suggests asking these simple questions: Does this make sense for my organization? Does it fit? Is it going to help anyone do things better or differently? Is there any real benefit? The answers, he says, depend partly on intuition and partly on knowledge of your organization, which is best gained by talking with other company people.

Henderson also suggests asking if there is legitimate research behind a particular program. "For every one legitimate vendor with a good product there are 1,000 snake-oil salesmen. No exaggeration intended. I am amazed at the number of people in this business who make exaggerated claims and have nothing to back them up. Ninety-nine percent of the vendors want you to buy something on faith because they say it is great. Those who have done research are proud. They offer information and they bend over backwards to get the results to you."

It is also helpful, Henderson says, to compare new programs and ideas to others you have used successfully. "I have to be willing to do the evaluation, make the phone calls, look at the product, ask the tough questions, be skeptical. Vendors are asking me to put up my company's money. I can't afford to be frivolous; that's what they pay me for.

"It's the same as buying an automobile. If you buy a lemon you spend all your time trying to hide it."

Thomas Druffel also relies on research to keep a safe distance from passing fads. Druffel, supervisor of education and training and library services for Beatrice U.S. Food Corp., says, "We sometimes have people ask for specific training *right now*, with an urgency that we should drop everything else to respond to them. We try to give a fair appraisal to their needs, determine whether we can meet their needs internally based on our own expertise, other projects and other factors. If we can't, then we look outside to see what may be available to satisfy those needs.

"Basically, we do as much research as possible in the shortest amount of time reasonable. When we select a program we let the first group act as guinea pigs."

Built on Business Sense

Dick Holman is manager of customer service, education and documentation for Prime Computer Inc. He says, "We are not immune to training fads in the computer business. But what is a fad for technical training for the computer industry may not be a fad in another business. Interactive videodisc, for instance, is so expensive and time-consuming that it takes a very stable technology to make it worthwhile." Prime has used videodisc systems for basic electronics training, Holman says, because the same material is taught over and over at the same location. The majority of his training, however, is much too volatile to apply this fashionable new technology.

"I look at all the new ideas that come along and weigh the costs against the program's ability and the target population. Sometimes the fads work; sometimes they don't. We are open to new ideas, but we are finding the old basics are the mainstay of our training: audio-based, video-based and very detailed job aids. They give us the most bang for our buck without heavy up-front costs."

Customer Service Craze

Holman has bought into the current customer service/customer interaction craze. "We tried several commercial packages. The upper-level management types felt good about them because they used all the buzz words. But the people who had to sit there and actually take the training lost a lot. The target population walked away cold."

As a result, Prime developed an in-house customer relations program based on its own corporate culture, product lines and customer base.

"I think it's kind of a cop-out when you buy a packaged customer relations course. We saved a considerable amount of money doing it ourselves. We used field managers as instructors. We used our salespeople to talk about customer expectations. But even more important than the savings, the results were positive. Our people got more out of it than they did from the clinical approach with all the buzz words."

Holman says he paid for one-time presentations of the commercial programs Prime tested. "I think that's important on anything we do. It's not as expensive to spend a dollar trying out three or four approaches as to spend a dollar getting locked into one. There are a lot of good programs out there. It's just a matter of finding something that matches your company.

"The thing I like to do is to find the person in our company who is most successful at what we want to develop training for. I identify the management aspects that make that person so successful, then try to find programs that match those aspects. Whatever the subject, I ask, 'What makes this person click? Can I match the training up to our own success stories?'

"I think that almost any fad you talk about is just a takeoff of common business sense. Really, I don't consider anything a fad. Everything has a use. A lot of people just tend to forget the common sense that brought them to where they are, they need a new buzz word to remind them what made them successes."

Weathering Change: Enough Already!

In search of the magic formula that will turn them into world-class competitors, companies frantically introduce one change effort after another. Employees have had enough.

BY BOB FILIPCZAK

Dear Employees:

For the last decade, we have been trying to change our organization.

Because we are frightened for our economic future, we kept looking for — and finding — another program du jour. We've dragged you through quality circles, excellence, total-quality management, self-directed work teams, reengineering, and God knows what else. Desperate to find some way to improve our profitability, we switched from change to change almost as fast as we could read about them in business magazines.

All of this bounding from one panacea to the next gave birth to rampant bandwagonism. We forgot to consider each change carefully, implement it thoughtfully, and wait patiently for results. Instead, we just kept on changing while you progressed from skepticism to cynicism to downright intransigence because you realized that all of these changes were just creating the illusion of movement toward some ill-defined goal.

Now we've got a lot of burned-out workers and managers, tired of the change-of-the-month club and unlikely to listen to our next idea, no matter how good it might be. For our complicity in this dismal state of affairs, we are sincerely sorry.

The Management

You may never get a letter like this, but you probably deserve one. You've realized that change is no longer your best friend, and the next announcement about a corporate transformation is going to be an invitation for employees to throw rotting cantaloupe at the company's change agent. Front-line workers are dog tired of all the changes foisted on them by managers frantically searching for the magic formula that will pull the company out of the red and into the black.

And it's not just little stuff anymore. With the shredded remains of the old-style employment contract fluttering around us, our work lives have become our primary source of anxiety. We're scared, angry and confused. The search for something stable to anchor our careers is the subject of several recent books.

It wasn't always so. Some may remember when change was a thing to be embraced and welcomed, a thing that promised excitement and economic prosperity in return for its challenges. In the early '80s, when Rosabeth Moss Kanter wrote *The Change Masters* and Tom Peters and Bob Waterman hit the best-seller list with *In Search of Excellence*, change meant progress.

Now the organizational-change bandwagon seems to have gotten out of control. And those who are riding it are scared. Advances in technology, the global marketplace, increasing competition, more demands from shareholders, mergers, acquisitions, and shifting government regulations are most often tagged the culprits that account for the lightning pace of change. These forces have been a catalyst for the panic-stricken cries of "More change!" from the leaders of our companies. It seems we've raised a kitten that's become a very hungry lion.

Before we go any further, let's get something straight: What exactly are we talking about? "Change" is a pretty vague term. Almost everything that happens to us during our lives can fit under its umbrella. But when we talk about change in the context of our work lives, we can narrow it down a bit. When management uses the term change, it usually means: 1) What we are doing now isn't working so we have to do something different; 2) Our present structure and culture are too bureaucratic, hierarchical and inflexible, so we have to restructure, reorganize or reengineer; or 3) Your position has been eliminated.

Change is a slippery term because it's often used to describe both very specific things and big general issues. When one person uses "change" to describe his company's move toward empowerment and another person uses it to describe a marketing adjustment her company has made in response to competition from Singapore, things get a little fuzzy.

For the most part, though, change is the term we use to describe the fact that we are facing too many demands coming at us too quickly from too many people to do things differently. If, for example, your department is trying to comply with the precepts of total-quality management at the same time you're revising the compensation system and moving toward self-directed work teams, you're liable to just lump the whole mess into one big ball and call it change. That may be as good a definition as any: Change is the umbrella under which we put all the things that we have to do differently in the future.

In organizations, change often is created by external forces that the company can't control: the aforementioned shareholder demands, mergers, global competition and advancing technology. These external forces create internal initiatives that attempt either to capitalize on or minimize the effect of the external change. If one of your competitors starts taking customers away from you, for example, you may have to restructure your sales force to compete better in those markets and drop your prices to regain your customers.

Companies do not always make changes for such clearly justifiable reasons, however. An executive may fall in love with a new idea — say reengineering, for example — and then go looking for reasons to justify it. At that point it's time to fire up your B.S. detector. Can you see a direct relationship between the change the executives are initiating and the reasons they give for it? If they say the company is facing new competition from Singapore, and, consequently, everyone in the company must become part of a self-directed work team, some employees may have the courage to ask, "Huh? How's that again?"

Daryl Conner is the founder and CEO of ODR Inc., an Atlanta research and consulting firm, and author of the book *Managing at the Speed of Change*. He says organizations often launch changes with poor justification. "Anything less than a business imperative is nothing but high-priced entertainment," says Conner.

Bandwagon Change

So what does a badly aligned change look like? It's not pretty. Just ask Gary Ransom, a senior vice president with The Forum Corp., a Boston consulting company. He recalls a client in the computer industry that essentially reengineered itself out of business. A year and a half ago, says Ransom, the company had hardware and software products that were the biggest sellers in its particular market. Then it decided to reengineer — because someone got the idea that reengineering was a good thing to do. In the process, it cut its customer-service department by half. When the company completed its change effort six months later, it discovered it didn't have any customers left. It took both its eyes off the ball by cutting back on customer service and ignoring its business so that it could follow the newest business craze. The company is now in Chapter 11.

The past decade has been rife with badly conceived and poorly executed changes. The consensus among the experts we talked to is that change has become a dirty word because so many initiatives have been driven by the wrong reasons, they have been replaced too quickly by the next bandwagon, and they have been foisted on a work force that is increasingly cynical about the intelligence behind these efforts.

Management guru Tom Peters bluntly diagnoses the problem: "Americans have always been suckers for snake-oil salesmen." Our No. 1 strength, and our greatest weakness, he says, is our tendency to jump on every new idea that comes along.

Recent research by the consulting firm Kepner-Tregoe of Princeton, NJ, found that 42 percent of the North American companies surveyed engaged in 11 or more change initiatives in the past five years. The survey report highlights the differences between executives' perceptions of these changes and workers' views about the changes they were supposed to embrace. In essence, the report describes a "change frenzy" that is creating cynical, demoralized employees and — if you ask the workers — failing to produce much of anything.

"Front-line workers are dog tired of all the changes being foisted on them by managers frantically searching for the next magic formula."

That description of the contemporary workplace rings true to Jon Lobe, an adjunct assistant professor at Loyola College in Baltimore and an independent consultant. "You get programmed to death," he says. In his previous job with Bell Atlantic, Lobe said he was trained in six different corporate systems, including TQM, in eight years. When TQM was introduced, another program, called Bell Atlantic Way — also aimed at revising the corporate culture — was still being implemented throughout the company. During another change initiative involving reengineering, Lobe reengineered himself out of a job and decided it was time for a new career.

"If there was ever a myth that we need to dispel, it's this craziness of change for change's sake," says consultant Conner. He proudly estimates that in the past year he has killed between 10 and 12 TQM projects and even more reengineering programs by convincing CEOs that their companies weren't ready to handle them yet. "Spare me from any client that is naive about reengineering," exclaims Conner.

The Illusion of Change

There are bad reasons to initiate a change in your organization — and change for change's sake is one of the worst — but there are also problems with implementation. Even if the engine driving a change initiative is sound, the execution plan is often defective. Consequently, companies create only the illusion of change, says T. Quinn Spitzer Jr., president of Kepner-Tregoe. "There's a tremendous difference between change and the illusion of change, and we've become master illusionists. We haven't been particularly effective at creating [productive] change."

Most companies fail to account for the human element in change projects, Spitzer says. Changing people is messy and takes a long time. On the other hand, systemic change is easier to see, faster to execute, and neatly fits into an analytical model. A flowchart documenting an improved process, or a nice big organization chart depicting a flattened hierarchy is comforting, Spitzer says, because "it creates a sense of certainty that I don't have in my normal business world." That desire for order helps explain the popularity of mechanistic models like total-quality management and reengineering.

Margaret Wheatley, author of *Leadership and the New Science* and principal of Kellner-Rogers & Wheatley, a consulting firm in Provo, UT, argues that we should toss out mechanistic change models in favor of those that envision the organization as a living system. If you "switch your metaphor to one of dynamic processes — which is what happens when you think of organizations as living systems — then change becomes a very different phenomenon," says Wheatley. Change becomes an environment you create to sustain life, she contends, not something you avoid or struggle your way through. More on that later.

A different problem crops up when companies mistake chaos for change. By throwing out many of the processes and procedures of the "old" hierarchical company in the name of creating a nonbureaucratic, empowered organization, companies can generate a lot of activity. This activity may look like progress, but it is really organizational chaos — which continues until employees figure out the new rules for doing their jobs.

Gervase Bush is an associate professor of organization development at Simon Fraser University in Burnaby, British Columbia, and a reluctant consultant to companies that say they want to change. He says he regularly witnesses chaos dressed up as change in organizations that decide they're going to empower employees. Typically, he says, senior managers "empower" workers by telling them to do their work the best way they know how, and to figure out new ways to be productive in a flattened organization where the old rules no longer apply.

What happens? Workers give up processes that worked quite well and expend three times as much effort inventing new ways to do the work. With normal channels for getting approval gone, front-line workers spend more time finding the people who can approve decisions and negotiating with others about decisions they now are empowered to make.

The problem in this scenario, according to Bush, is lack of leadership. As he sees it, corporate hierarchies and established processes are a substitute, albeit an inferior one, for leadership. Too often, he says, leaders get rid of the structure and then abdicate their responsibilities, all in the name of empowerment. Then, 12 months later, when employees are finally settling into new processes to get the work done, senior managers move on to the next management fad.

Embrace This!

Many companies follow a sure-fire method for creating resistance to change: They try to force it down employees' throats. Often, the CEO calls a companywide meeting and informs the congregation of the new path the company has decided to follow. "When senior management justifies a change...like that and then walks away thinking it's done its job, [it has] really missed the boat," says William Bridges, author of numerous books on change, including *Managing Transitions*, and president of Bridges Associates in Mill Valley, CA. "The people who are really being whacked by the change are still saying, 'Why did they do this to us?'"

And having change "done" to you is not a very pleasant experience. "Who wants to be a victim?" asks Bill Young, vice president for Aetna's Health Business, the division of Aetna that includes the insurance and health-care businesses, in Hartford, CT. "If change is managed in a way that people feel that they're just being jerked around, or if they don't have confidence in their management...I don't think anybody ought to be surprised by some skepticism or cynicism."

So ramming change down people's throats doesn't work. Big news. What does? It's pretty simple: Up-front involvement, along with plenty of communication and information.

Robert Jacobs, author of the book *Real-Time Strategic Change* and a partner in Dannemiller Tyson Associates of Ann Arbor, MI, is a vocal advocate of employee participation and involvement in corporate change initiatives. He recommends that *everyone* who will be affected by a major change should be called into a three-day meeting to decide what kind of change should take place and how it should be implemented. This critical

THOSE RESISTANT (FILL IN THE BLANK)

That whining noise that accompanies most corporate change efforts is the sound of managers complaining about employees who resist the great new productivity-improvement system that management wants to implement.

But if you want to locate resisters, you might do better looking up in the ranks instead of down.

Gervase Bush, an associate professor of organization development at Simon Fraser University in Burnaby, British Columbia, says he used to consult with companies that wanted to convert to TQM or reorganize their workers into empowered teams or whatever. But when push came to shove, Bush says, the truly resistant employees were often the managers who hired him in the first place.

When the leaders discovered that they were the major source of dysfunction in the company, all efforts to change suddenly got stonewalled, says Bush. Frustrated by the intransigence of executives who said they wanted to renovate the company until the finger of change pointed at them, Bush gave up change consulting with companies for years. Now, he says, he does it only when he finds a company with executives who seem sincerely ready to change. Nevertheless, he admits, some slippery executives still fool him; they seem sincere until the fat hits the frying pan.

Management guru Tom Peters says he hears similar complaints about resistant employees in his seminars. "Whenever I hear a middle manager say, 'My God, they don't want change,' my response is to say, 'I certainly agree that there's somebody who doesn't want change but I'm not sure that you've made your diagnosis exactly correctly.'"

Another peculiarity about employee resistance involves the popular quasi-truism that "people naturally resist change." Margaret Wheatley, author of *Leadership and the New Science*, says that as long as employees are involved with the proposed change, they are not naturally resistant and can even be a source of energy to keep the change going.

Furthermore, Wheatley argues, the notion that people can only handle so much change is a myth. We have yet to discover what, if any, limits there are to humans' ability to adapt, she says. Peters agrees, saying that if you watch people encounter truly horrific changes — hurricanes, earthquakes, wars — you discover that "the human being is shockingly adaptive."

Others insist there is an upper limit to the amount of change people can assimilate (see "Just Say 'No?'" on page 91).

If employees are resisting your latest attempt to create a totally customer-focused organization, there's probably a good reason. If you've been launching one change after another at them, their resistance may stem from cynicism. Jumping on bandwagons every six months, as some executives are wont to do, makes employees wonder if their leaders are thinking clearly. As Bush puts it, "When tops look down, in hierarchical systems, what they see is incompetence and resistance. When bottoms look up, in hierarchical systems, what they see is self-interest and self-padding." — B.F.

mass of employees, as Jacobs calls it, obviates the need for individuals to return to work after the meeting and "sell" their co-workers on the new strategy.

"Just a second," you're thinking. "We have over 1,000 employees. How can we get them all into the same meeting?" Yet that is exactly what Jacobs and his associates do — even if it means renting the local football stadium. They regularly deal with groups of 500 and have handled groups up to 2,200.

This method creates a "common database of information" for everyone in the company, Jacobs maintains. All perspectives are represented at the meeting and most of the information that might be needed is available.

The meeting relies on a structured agenda to move the assembly through discussion and decision-making to action planning. Employees tell stories that chronicle their frustrations with the company, as well as contributions they are proud of. Customers are brought in to describe how their needs are or aren't being served. At the end of the third day, the company emerges with a new strategic direction, forged by all the involved parties, and some details about how to implement it.

How do you get 500 people to agree on a plan to do anything? Though it sounds counterintuitive, Jacobs claims that adding more people to the decision-making process needn't lower the quality of the decisions. Just the opposite can occur, he says. The process gets its power from the common database of information, and decisions are guided by an alignment that everyone in the group helped to create.

A "real-time strategic change meeting" is designed to set up a dynamic that appears to be gaining adherents. Open-space meetings and future search conferences (the subject of *Discovering Common Ground*, co-authored by Marvin Weisbord) employ a similar philosophy: Both gather large numbers of people into meetings and try to use their collective wisdom to solve problems.

Loss of control is one of the things people dislike most about change, says consultant Conner. Humans so love control, he says, that they will choose dysfunction over ambiguity. The only way to get people to release their death-grip on control is to convince them that the price for holding onto the status quo is too high, that changing is the only way to survive as a viable business.

That implies a dialogue, and the most obvious way to begin it is just to ask employees up front what they think of a change the company is contemplating. This can uncover a lot of hidden facts that may either advance or retard the change effort. A frank exchange among front-line workers and executives is vital, says Bill Pottgen, senior adviser for the quality education and training department for Alcoa Aluminum Co. of America in Pittsburgh. "Anybody who goes into this, as a leader, saying they have all the answers is nuts because they don't," says Pottgen.

> **Leaders get rid of the structure and then abdicate their responsibility, all in the name of empowerment.**

Information As Nourishment

While you're talking over the proposed change with employees, give them as much information as possible. Information keeps organizations alive, says Wheatley, and most of them can give more information to their workers without endangering the companies' competitive position.

Enlightened executives, she says, will make a commitment to "put information out there without knowing who needs it or why they might need it. It will just be available. And then [employees] will organize around it." One CEO told Wheatley that information in his company had been transformed from currency (what you traded for power) into a source of nourishment for the employees.

T. J. and Sandar Larkin, directors of Larkin Communication Consulting in New York and authors of the book *Communicating Change*, also emphasize the need for timely information. Don't wait until you're sure of your facts before giving employees information, they advise; ballpark estimates are better than nothing. If there is an information void, employees will fill it with rumors that tend to be worst-case scenarios.

"I find that no matter how bad the change is — and many of the changes we've seen are really bad — they're always better than what the rumors are. You really are reporting good news most of the time," says T. J. Larkin. If, for example, the company plans to get rid of 10,000 employees, rumors will inflate the number to 30,000 if you don't fill the information gap.

Information vacuums leave employees wondering "what the bastards are up to," says Claude Lineberry, a senior partner with Vanguard International Alliance, a consulting firm in Conifer, CO. In this environment, he adds, "Your embedded organizational well-poisoners can really have a field day."

Change Translation

If informing employees of ongoing changes is important, it's equally important to make sure the information is in a form that's meaningful to them and their jobs. In other words, telling them the restructuring will increase shareholder value is probably not going to mean a lot to them. In fact, senior executives rarely communicate meaningfully with those on the front lines, contends Bridges. "Senior managers, by and large, are so far removed from the world of the individual worker that they just talk gibberish," he says.

So workers often come away from informational meetings about the latest change shaking their heads and wondering what they've been told. In their book, *Communicating Change*, the Larkins use a familiar example — announcing a downsizing — to demonstrate what's important to line workers. Most CEOs spend inordinate amounts of time explaining why a cut is occurring, mostly trying to justify the decision and protect themselves from criticism. The workers listening to this news, however, have some very precise concerns: Who is going to be cut? What criteria will be used to decide who gets laid off? What does the severance package include? The "why" of a downsizing is way down on the list of employees' concerns. One sentence about why the downsizing is necessary is probably sufficient, says T. J. Larkin.

Larkin and Larkin have three hard-and-fast rules about how to communicate a credible message throughout an organization:

1. Information going to front-line

workers should come from their direct supervisors, not CEOs or senior officers.

2. Communication should be face-to-face. Put away the video cameras, turn off the satellite dish, and shred the company newsletter. Employees are going to listen only if a real live person tells them this news.

3. Don't communicate values; communicate performance. That means people have to be told how each local work area needs to do its tasks differently. If you want employees to focus on quality, show them what quality looks like in terms of how they do their jobs.

Rita den Otter's experience as organizational and staff-development consultant for the Greater Victoria Hospital Society in British Columbia, bears out what the Larkins profess. Her organization oversees a group of hospitals. One of the older ones had to be closed down. Though it was a painful experience that involved layoffs, the overall closing was less troublesome than she thought it would be. "When people on moving day are smiling, you kind of go, 'Wow, we did something right here,'" says den Otter.

At one point, however, a vice president came to talk to a group of employees. Her speech was followed by a talk from den Otter, and by remarks from the workers' direct supervisor. All the messages were essentially the same, but workers responded to the vice president's message with: "We don't ever want to see her again. What she said was bullshit. What you and the manager said made sense."

Consultant Bush sums up this sentiment when he observes, "The higher up you go, the less truth-telling is going on."

A Culture of Change

Peter Senge coined the term "the learning organization" in his book *The Fifth Discipline*. By that he means an organization in which all employees are continually learning and updating their skills in response to changes in the world around them. Senge's model company essentially is one that has incorporated change into its culture.

When change becomes part of a corporate culture, the entire organization may persist in a fluid state. In 1946 psychologist Kurt Lewin described the process of change as unfreezing-moving-refreezing; in a culture of change it looks as if the refreezing part may be left out of the equation. In Peters' book, *The Tom Peters' Seminar*, he calls for continuous revolution. "Blow the whole... thing up and start from the ground up and rebuild," he said in an interview with *TRAINING Magazine*.

Peters is no longer content with exhorting companies to change the way they do business. Economic realities such as the end of job security call for a kind of flexibility and adaptability that most of us haven't even imagined yet, he insists. "There's a real possibility of making all this sound like the most scary stuff in the world. But it's just another way of living," says Peters.

In fact, he opines that an environment of continual revolution could be

---

JUST SAY 'NO?'

Contrary to advice that we should embrace change, there is a point at which we should just say "no," or at least, "enough for now."

So says consultant Daryl Conner, author of the book *Managing at the Speed of Change*. Conner uses the metaphor of a sponge to describe the effect of too many sweeping changes. People and organizations, he argues, can handle only so much, just like a sponge can hold only so much water.

When a CEO wants to launch a new "valuing diversity" program in an organization that's been downsized, restructured, teamed and TQMed, the sponge is already too full. "Unless you squeeze something out of the sponge," says Conner, "my recommendation is you don't proceed with this thing. You're not only not going to get what you say you want, you're going to teach people not to listen to you."

Rita den Otter, an organizational and staff-development consultant for the Greater Victoria Hospital Society in British Columbia, says she regularly runs into change overload and adjusts her programs to compensate. When her department was getting ready to roll out a new management-development program, for example, managers told her that they couldn't handle anything more at that point. Rather than filling classrooms with burned-out, resistant trainees, she postponed the course. Currently, she's delaying a course on coaching skills for managers because she senses that supervisors are involved in too many other changes.

Conner says top executives often ignore his counsel against pouring more water on an already saturated sponge. Behind closed doors, he says, executives admit he may be right about the organization's ability to withstand another change, but insist they have to do it anyway for "political reasons." Conner describes his reaction: "Let me get this straight. It would be politically incorrect to not have diversity training, but it's not politically incorrect to do it and fail?"

One of the most important questions to ask about a contemplated change is whether it fits with the company's mission or strategic direction. If it conflicts, it's time to reconsider.

Gary Ransom, a senior vice president for The Forum Corp., a Boston-based consulting company, recalls one situation in which a front-line worker had the courage to ask a tough question. While top executives were touring the plant, the worker overheard a discussion about a change that was going to be instituted in his work area. He stopped the tour and addressed the CEO: "Excuse me, sir, could you help me understand what's the value-added to the customer of this change?" At first the CEO was taken aback, says Ransom, but later he realized that question wasn't asked enough by anyone in the organization, himself included.

"The single most prevalent problem that we're seeing today among senior officers is they're engaged in much more change than they have any hope of being able to address," says Conner. Winning organizations, he adds, focus on business imperatives, the short list of changes they must accomplish to survive. — B.F.

a boon to workers. "The average independent contractor whom I come into contact with — whether they are making $8 an hour or $80 an hour — I would not say is more stressed out than the average poor, sad-sack bureaucrat who is spending the day passing papers around and kissing asses."

Others agree that success in the new economic environment means doing more than just "managing change." Wheatley says it's futile to discuss change as something to be managed. "This isn't a question of 'Has there been too much change? How do we stop it?' That's not the question. It's 'How do we work in this world which is so dynamic and changing all the time?'"

It's when people start talking about creating a culture of change that the concept of managing change is abused. "As long as we're talking about change management, we're doomed to failure," says consultant Lineberry. "Managing change would imply coping with something undesirable." The winners in the future economy will be those who (dare we say it?) embrace change as a competitive advantage and use it to meet customer demands faster than their marketplace rivals.

In their book *Corporate Culture and Performance,* John Kotter and James Heskett define a company with an "adaptive culture" as one that has managers who listen to customers and who value employees. These elements, the authors contend, allow companies to adapt to external economic forces faster than companies with managers less focused on their constituents. In almost every case — at least among the companies Kotter and Heskett examined — adaptive companies outperformed nonadaptive companies in terms of net income growth, return on investment, and increased stock price.

> "Senior managers are so far removed from the world of the worker that they just talk gibberish."

The Tough Part

The paradox of change is that it's ridiculously easy to initiate, but very difficult to guide so that it accomplishes what you had in mind in the first place.

How to change? Companies are still working on that. Alcoa's Pottgen uses the word "complexity" to describe his attempts to come to grips with change. His company is currently piloting a training program designed to help move people toward a culture of continuous change. The course has been shortened considerably, but it still lasts a full week. The training involves ropes courses, experiential learning, case studies, and a variety of other techniques. Each day features a different theme: vision, values, sustaining a renewal, big organizational change and deployment.

Who will change? "It takes people with commitment and smarts and energy and openness and honesty and all that kind of stuff to just dig in," adds Aetna's Young. "There isn't a magic formula."

In the past 10 years we've seen how easy it is to initiate a sweeping change — and how easy it is to do it wrong. In the aftermath of our attempts to jump-start changes in our organizations, we've left a string of failures and cynical employees who will either ignore or sabotage "faint-hearted" change efforts.

Most companies have at least a general grip on the "what" of change: They want to be customer-focused, quality-conscious, empowered, profit-making businesses. The "why" is accounted for by global competition, customer demands, and other external forces. That brings us to the actual "how" of change, and the trail gets tougher from here on. Conner sums it up when he says, "You've got people out there who still are convinced that they're just one videotape away from tranquility, that all they've got to do is get reengineering right and then life is going to slow down. Well, it's not going to."

Notes:

7 Keys to Successful Change

Change resistance? Piffle.
People will change their behavior when it suits them.
They just won't do it to suit you.

BY CLAY CARR

"Most change fails," the speaker declared, "because employees resist it — for almost no good reasons."

In a more honest world, somebody would have stood up and accused him of the most blatant kind of excuse-making. But the speaker was addressing a group of "change agents" — mostly corporate trainers and consultants — so of course everyone just nodded gravely. Change agents are very fond of repeating to one another the old saw that "people resist change."

Suppose we look beneath that facile generalization for a moment and see what we find:

• Individuals vary widely in their openness to and enthusiasm for "change." Most people initiate changes in their own lives, though with varying degrees of frequency. Some experience considerable anxiety before deciding to learn to square dance; others begin entirely new careers with a minimum of stress.

• Generally speaking, the person most comfortable with any particular change is the one proposing it. If we looked at employees' lives as a whole, instead of just at their reaction to the initiative *we're* pushing, we might have considerable difficulty finding this widespread and generalized resistance to change.

• We can find, and find quickly, that people resist *being* changed — especially when the change appears to have a payoff primarily for someone else. A great deal of organizational change takes this form; someone, somewhere decides that someone else would be better off if he changed. When you are the chang*ee* rather than the chang*er*, this feels a lot like coercion. Very few people like being coerced into anything.

• Regardless of individuals' attitudes toward change in the abstract, people generally do find that change produces anxiety. This is true whether the change is self-originated or imposed by some outside agent. Even if a person freely chooses to make a change (to a more interesting job, say), she moves from competence to incompetence and from stability to confusion. If the change is significant at all, she may worry that she will never really be competent again; she may be anxious that nothing will be as settled and comfortable as it was before. When the change is severe, the individual may feel lost in the middle of a chaotic situation, lacking the competence required to deal with it.

Given these rather obvious observations, and given the tendency of many organizations to indulge in flavor-of-the-month faddism, it doesn't take a rocket scientist to conclude that most employees will not run barefoot through the rain in celebration of the latest organizational-improvement scheme announced from on high. Instead, they generally hunker down, keep a low profile, and wait for the current mania to subside.

Key Questions

In short, it's true that change is often difficult. But working people have perfectly legitimate reasons for refusing to leap gleefully onto any bandwagon that happens to rumble by. It is fatuous to dismiss this reluctance as some universal, unreasoning aversion to change.

Instead, those of us who make a living by trying to change organizations — more precisely, by trying to get other people to change their behavior — need to be realistic about ourselves and our work. We need to understand the factors that matter in change and what impact they have on the people we expect to change. These factors are legion, and some of them vary significantly from situation to situation. A change to a new computer system, for instance, is not the same thing, and does not present all of the same problems, as a change to self-managing work teams.

However, there are seven key factors that play a role in any change effort, whether it involves technology, management policies, process reengineering or whatever. We can best think of the factors as questions that need to be asked by proponents of any significant change in a workplace. By understanding the questions and answering them carefully, we can markedly improve the odds that innovations will succeed.

Here are those seven questions. The first three concern the individuals who are supposed to change; the next three address organizational issues; the last one affects everything.

STEP 1.
Is this change a burden or a challenge?

Ultimately, each player in an organization will decide the answer for himself. But the way the change effort is designed and presented will heavily influence that decision. Here is the key:

A change with a clear payoff for those who must do the changing will feel like a challenge. If it lacks such a payoff it will feel like a burden.

This has absolutely nothing to do with the payoff that the proponents foresee, or with how strongly they believe that the change will be "good for" the changees. The road to business hell is paved with the remains of innovative programs whose advocates *knew* they were the salvation of their companies. (At the moment, for instance, this roadway reportedly includes roughly two of every three total-quality-management programs ever launched.)

Does the individual see how a proposal will help her solve a real work problem? If so, she will find the change a challenge. Will the proposal allow her to get her work done faster, more easily, more enjoyably? Will she make more money? Those payoffs will energize her. In other words, she will ask the famous WIIFM question: What's in it for me? The more attractive and convincing the answer, the more apt she will be to change.

Inconveniently, there is no single, all-purpose answer to the question of what would make work more challenging and less burdensome. Clerks need different answers from managers, engineers need different answers from trainers and so on. The payoff of a change is calculated by each individual affected.

STEP 2.
Is the change clear, worthwhile and real?

If an organization presents a proposed change so that its benefits appear unclear, trivial or highly unlikely to materialize, the change almost certainly will be seen as a burden to be avoided. On the other hand, when the change promises clear, worthwhile and believable benefits, it will look desirable.

What will things be like after the change? Many organizations can describe the new situation relatively clearly and portray it as worthwhile. But few can make it real to those who must change — real in the sense that people can vividly visualize the goal toward which they're moving. How to make it real? Word pictures help, as do videos depicting the new state of affairs. If the change involves, say, self-managing teams (SMTs), then visits to an organization that has already converted to a team-based system can help even more. Face-to-face meetings with members of a successful SMT will promote the change as no amount of motivational speeches ever could.

STEP 3.
Will the benefits of the change begin to appear quickly?

A common theme in modern management thought holds that "real" changes take years to occur and demand much sweat, strain and suffering in the meantime. This plays really well in executive suites and best-selling business books, but it generally flops in the office cubicles and on the factory floor. The longer it takes for the hard work of change to bear fruit, the more difficult it is to maintain the concentration and enthusiasm required to bring it about. To put it another way, the longer a change takes, the hazier its payoff will appear and the more it will seem a burden.

This doesn't mean that only quick changes can be successful. It does suggest, however, that extensive and lengthy changes are often best introduced by using pilot projects or other limited applications so that people can begin to see positive results quickly. For instance, an organization attempting to organize workers into teams will usually be most successful by starting with a few, highly motivated teams that can produce quick accomplishments rather than with a blanket

> "The perceived payoff of a change has nothing to do with the payoff that the proponents foresee, or with how strongly they believe that the change will be 'good for' the changees."

attempt to create teams everywhere. It also helps if organizations avoid shotgun-style training programs that aim at everyone simultaneously and instead provide more narrowly targeted training to particular groups just in time for its use. However an organization attacks the problem, the time between the first discomfort caused by the change and its first benefits should be as short as possible.

STEP 4.
Is the change limited to one function or a few closely related functions?

The first three questions dealt with the effects of change on individuals. These next three address its impact on entire organizational units. Nothing is more dear to the units of a traditional organization than preserving their functional integrity. When a change seems to threaten that integrity — as when two departments are asked to revamp their historical missions and ways of doing things in the name of "cooperation" — things can get dicey in a hurry.

While limiting the number of individuals involved may help where this factor is concerned, numbers alone don't create the problem. A change may involve dozens, hundreds, even thousands of players, but still occur within a single function (as when a large data-input operation is reorganized). But let a change on a much smaller scale involve two different functions, such as engineering and accounting, and the stakes immediately escalate.

Why should this be the case? Any given change will likely affect different functions in different ways — not all of them good. The more functions that must cooperate to produce a change, the greater the probability that at least one function will see itself as a loser in the change and work to sabotage it.

Even if no function actively opposes the change, those that see little gain from it may passively withhold the resources required to make it successful. If coordination among different functions is required for success (and it almost always is in TQM programs, reengineering, team-based problem-solving initiatives, et al.), this foot-dragging can be enough to delay or even doom the change.

Change agents can draw a simple lesson from this: At least in the initial stages, limit the number of functions affected by the change. Since many efforts at organizational improvement these days are designed specifically to change relationships among functions, limiting the functions involved is often easier said than done. But something can usually be accomplished. For instance, when an organization sets out to create multifunctional teams, one or a very few teams can be established at first — staffed with those most agreeable to the idea. Or teams can be formed with members from only two or three functions, with additional functions added later. However it's done, limiting the number of functions whose cooperation is required in the change will significantly improve the odds of success.

STEP 5.
What will be the impact on existing power and status relationships?

Power and status in organizations are often linked to departments or functions (as when production managers have more status than customer-service managers, for example), but they're never quite the same thing. Functions often remain the same over time, while power and status may be relatively fluid. For example, comptrollers who made the rules for organizations a decade ago may find themselves eclipsed by marketers in today's environment. Or the reverse may happen, with a comptroller remaining the real power in the company despite its formal adoption of a customer-centered mission, vision and so on.

Many organizational players work assiduously to accumulate power and status. Even those with other goals normally appreciate having power and status. And those who have it unfailingly work to maintain it. If a change directly attacks the power and status of any function or group, those who profit from the established situation will almost certainly oppose it, overtly or covertly. A great many change proposals *do* intend to diminish some group's power or status — which sets the stage for conflict from the beginning.

This conflict is not necessarily visible, however. Change agents often mistake the lack of overt opposition for support — particularly when managers go through the motions of supporting the change. It costs very little to have one's staff trained in the methods of the moment, make appropriate speeches of support, and pin up the right posters.

Only when time passes and nothing significant has changed does the real picture begin to come into focus. (In fact, the opposition may never surface, because the change effort may have died the death of a thousand cuts in the meantime. This permits those who covertly opposed the change to bemoan its failure and point out how vigorously they had supported it.)

The more that a proposed change conforms to the existing power and status structure, the less likely it is to be opposed by entrenched powers.

But what if the whole point is to change this structure — as in process reengineering, where existing departmental "silos" are supposed to give way to a whole new structure based more directly on the fundamental processes that serve customers? One possibility, requiring great skill and patience, is to introduce a change that only over time affects the existing structure. For example, the organization might begin reengineering on a small scale and count on the logic of it to drive the reorganization throughout the company.

Empowering changes such as self-managing teams may begin with only a small impact on the organization at large. As they become institutionalized, however, they often create pressure for greater involvement in other parts of the organization. This may lead to a major confrontation — but by then the forces of change may be strong enough to win the battle.

Just keep the basic point in mind: The more that you propose to change existing power and status relationships, the more difficult the change will be. And the more you can do to accommodate the change to these relationships (without rendering the change invalid or irrelevant), the greater its chance of success.

STEP 6.
Will the change fit the existing organizational culture?

We hear regularly about cultural change and other forms of sweeping, "transformational" change — revolutions like the ones at Motorola and Xerox. Such dramatic re-creation has a definite panache about it, although the enormous sense of accomplishment one would expect to feel when it's successful may be a chimera; both Motorola and Xerox seem to have found that once the initial changes are made they generate a need for continuing change. In other words, transformational change once begun may never end.

> "People are much more likely to get involved or to go along with something if they believe it is really going to happen."

But transformational changes fail far more often than they succeed. Even when they're successful, the cost to the organization is always high and the payoff may be considerably less than expected. Furthermore, major changes almost always succeed only because the organization is facing a major crisis. (General Electric is the only large company that comes to mind that has made transformational changes without the goad of an external crisis.)

Is the survival of your organization at stake? If not, then the better the change you propose fits the values of the existing culture, the better its chances of success. Even sweeping changes can be based on core values of the organization.

For example, many companies have struggled for the past several years with the conflict between "quality" defined as technical excellence and "quality" defined as customer satisfaction. When a firm has taken great pride in its ability to build technically superior products, the idea of building a lesser, cheaper product in the name of satisfying the customer may feel like selling out. (This has a functional component, too, since the attempt to focus on customer satisfaction instead of technical excellence often devolves into a battle between engineering and marketing. The situation also has clear implications about status and power.) The more that customer satisfaction can be presented — and any changes actually implemented — as an extension of the tradition of technical excellence, the smoother the transition will be.

It is extremely difficult to change an organization's core values or its basic culture. Never propose to change the culture one whit more than necessary to achieve the goals of a project.

STEP 7.
Is the change certain to happen?

We hear interminably that any kind of significant change must be supported by top management. A considerable amount of research data confirms this. In fact, top-management support counts for more than any other variable in the change equation. This support matters for a very specific reason: People are much more likely to get involved or to go along with something if they believe it is really going to happen.

If the CEO clearly supports the change — not by making one speech or signing a memo but by putting considerable personal time and energy into it — then the change almost certainly will happen. If the support comes from a lower management level, the change still may have the ring of certainty about it — but only if the managers pushing it have the independence and the clout to ensure its success.

Remember that any significant change requires effort, is disruptive, and takes time away from the daily job. In this context, what happens if the fate of an initiative is uncertain?

Even someone who strongly supports the change may conclude it's not worth putting his neck on the block for. And those who *don't* support the change? They'll simply hunker down and wait for this particular ill wind to blow by.

The point is simple: If you want something to change, line up enough organizational horsepower to ensure that it will — before you start the change.

Parting Lessons

Change is hard, and none of the above advice will make it easy. But understanding and asking those questions can help in three important ways.

First, if we take the factors seriously, we can avoid premature and stillborn attempts at change. For many people in the training business, change is exciting. Provided the change is intended to foster a more empowering or "humanistic" work environment, it takes little effort to sell us on the benefits. We become true believers quickly. Once we take a proposed change and analyze it against the seven factors, however, reality intrudes. The factors thus serve as guidelines that can keep us from rushing into things prematurely.

Second, we can use the factors to "sell" a proposed change. They provide a systematic structure that helps our audience evaluate what we propose. These factors are intuitively persuasive to most individuals experienced in organizations.

Finally, and most important, we can use these factors to ensure that a change creates no more resistance than absolutely necessary. We *can* influence whether a change is seen as challenging rather than burdensome; whether it is clear, worthwhile and real; whether it will start to demonstrate a payoff quickly. We can choose to limit the number of functions it will affect initially and thus minimize its threat to the existing power and status structures. We can identify the ways in which it reinforces, rather than opposes, the culture of the organization. And we can either ensure that there is sufficient horsepower behind an initiative, or else wait for a better time to launch it, or even find a more relevant initiative.

And that, as they say, ain't chopped liver.

Notes:

You're On Your Own: Training, Employability, and the New Employment Contract

From corporate stooge to free thinker is a big jump. But maybe it's one we all should be prepared for, because the rules of employment are changing.

BY BOB FILIPCZAK

Picture it as a scene from the movie "The Paper Chase." The severe Professor Kingsfield faces off with the young, optimistic, first-year law student Hart during a class. The discussion is about contract law:

Kingsfield: *"Suppose, class, that an employer terminates an employee who assembles rotary telephones. The employee has worked for the company for 20 years and has always received exemplary performance reviews. He has participated in many company-sponsored events and even taken pay cuts when the company hit troubling economic times. What, exactly, should this employee expect from the company? Mr. Hart?"*

Hart: *"The company should take care of the employee by, maybe, finding some other job he can do."*

Kingsfield: *"But what precisely does the company owe the employee, Mr. Hart? Remember that no written or verbal contract was ever established."*

Hart: *"But wasn't there an implicit agreement that hard work and loyalty would result in compensation and job security?"*

Kingsfield: *"And how would one enforce such an agreement, Mr. Hart?"*

Hart: *"But couldn't the company retrain him for other work or help him find a job in another company?"*

Kingsfield: *"It could. But we aren't discussing coulds and shoulds in this class, Mr. Hart. Without a verbal or written contract, what exactly does the company owe this employee?"*

Hart: (Frustrated pause.) *"Severance pay?"*

Kingsfield: *"Very good, Mr. Hart. You may sit down."*

So maybe the idea that the traditional employment contract is dead is not exactly *news* anymore. But the fallout from the end of job security as we knew it still poisons the downsized atmosphere of factory floors and office cubicles throughout corporate America.

And even as the fumes linger, companies are scrambling to re-establish a relationship with traumatized employees — a relationship conducive to building a highly productive, creative, empowered, quality work force. Whether the "betrayal" of the old trust is real or perceived, that trust has been broken. Something has to take its place.

Everyone from Harvard professor Rosabeth Moss Kanter to Labor Secretary Robert Reich to General Electric Co. chief Jack Welch has been saying that "employability" must replace the idea of employment security. By this they mean that employees' skills should be continually enhanced and updated so that when companies are restructured and layoffs occur, people can find new jobs somewhere, either inside the company or with another firm. And when we start talking about continuous upskilling, of course, formal training usually becomes a big part of the discussion.

Will training replace job security as the cornerstone of the new employment contract? Instead of promising long-term employment, will the company's new role be to take care of employees by providing some menu of training and educational programs designed to keep them forever employable — somewhere? Not really. Most current thinking holds that acquiring the kind of training that would make a person a valuable commodity in the job market is primarily the responsibility of the individual.

In other words, now, more than ever, you're on your own — in terms of job security, career development, and just about everything else.

Can't This Marriage Be Saved?

According to many consultants and authors, the challenge is not to replace traditional job security with something closely resembling it. Rather, we must move away (indeed, we are moving away) from a dependent relationship between employer and employee toward a more collaborative arrangement.

We all know from pop psychology that "dependence" is a bad thing in relationships, so it's no accident that many of the people talking about altering the basic "employment contract" are using concepts you might encounter in a marriage counseling session.

And is that so off-base? We routinely speak of being "married" to a job, referring to a person who spends too much time and emotional capital at work. In the past, says Dave Berlo, founder of The Berlo Programs, a St. Louis consulting firm, companies encouraged employee dependence — that is, dependence on the company for wages, for pensions, for job security, and a host of other things. This dependence fostered "loyalty," which essentially meant that people focused their energies on their jobs instead of looking for work elsewhere, and they didn't jump ship at the first sign of choppy water.

Berlo insists, however, that there are three kinds of employees: slaves, indentured servants and free people. We must move away from encouraging slave and indentured labor to helping people become more free, less dependent and more self-reliant, he says.

Cliff Hakim, a career consultant

based in Cambridge, MA, and author of the book *We Are All Self-Employed*, agrees that companies have to, dare we say it, break the cycle of dependency. He compares the "paternalistic" norm of the past to an adult-child relationship: The company was assumed to know what was best for employees, and they accepted its dictates in exchange for security. Since that security is no longer available, it's time for the relationship to be reworked. "Job security is being redefined, and the redefinition is: Individuals need to take more responsibility for their...career mobility," says Hakim.

The goal, according to this line of reasoning, is for every employee to move away from this dependent marriage with the employer to a more self-reliant model in which both parties are equal. The company needs the person as much as the person needs the job — but both recognize that the need is only temporary. This represents a profound change, not least in a psychological sense, says Dave Noer, vice president of training and education at the Center for Creative Leadership in Greensboro, NC, and author of *Healing the Wounds: Overcoming the Trauma of Layoffs and Revitalizing Downsized Organizations*. Too often, Noer says, "we force people to put a lot of their social and emotional eggs in the organizational basket." In a world where the organization may cut you loose at any moment, "What happens if who you are is where you work?"

The Employable Worker

So what does this new worker look like once he has broken the bonds of dependency and taken charge of his own career and training? Essentially, the newly freed employee begins a journey that will end with the customer. And the customer, the entity paying for the skills the employee has acquired, could be your company.

The independent employee who, as Berlo puts it, needs *a* job but not particularly *this* job, is always looking out for No. 1. She pays a lot of attention to her skills, to her résumé, and to the job market both inside and outside the company. Continuous training is part of the equation, but independent workers don't wait around for the company or the human resources department to tell them what kind of training they should get.

Sean Gawne, a technical trainer at the Southern California Edison nuclear plant at San Clemente, CA, says more employees indeed are starting to take charge of their own training. "They come to training wanting a different output than in the past," Gawne says. "They want to become a more employable product. They are starting to see themselves more as human resources." He says that this new orientation changes the way he does his job because now he has to market his courses directly to those who get the training, not to their managers. Consequently, he's got a whole different customer base.

> "Now he has to market his courses directly to those who get the training, not to their managers."

Companies that encourage their people to see themselves as "self-employed" urge workers to look beyond the narrow confines of their current jobs. That often means studying the company to see if any other jobs might interest them in the future and then pursuing the skills necessary for those jobs.

According to Claudia Davis, director of education at Hewlett-Packard in Palo Alto, CA, many of the company's sites have career centers where employees can research jobs that interest them — or take assessments to help them discover potential interests.

Both Hewlett-Packard, the Palo Alto, CA, computer maker, and Intel Corp., the Santa Clara, CA, manufacturer of computer chips, also post all internal job openings on an on-line computer system so people can find information about other opportunities in the company.

Consultant Hakim urges employees to consider their organizations part of the marketplace: The company isn't just a place to do your work; it's a place to shop for other opportunities where your skills might be applicable. Debbie Hicks, a manager of organizational development at Harvard Community Health Plan, a healthcare provider in Brookline, MA, adds that "self-employed" people need to market *themselves*, not only to find jobs, but to foster the mind-set that keeps them focused on developing new skills. "You're only as good as the skill sets you bring" to a job, says Hicks.

Berlo takes that thought a step further and gives it a hard twist. The people most worried about job security, he says, are those who are making more money than the market says their skills are worth. As he puts it, "The only reason you've got job insecurity is that you believe you're being overpaid." If your compensation is in line with what the job market will pay, Berlo argues, you can take your skills anywhere without losing income.

Understanding the demands of the marketplace inevitably brings the self-employed worker to the top of the food chain: the customer. Someone who has broken free of her dependence on a particular company will start looking at the world differently, and she will see that there are customers out there seeking her skills. "You're your own employer," Hakim says. "That company you work with — not for — is your customer." Noer tells of one executive he met who expressed the self-employed attitude perfectly by saying, "The best thing I can do is find a customer and work for a customer."

Exactly how this perceptual shift will change the basic employer-employee relationship is far from clear. In theory, however, it's part of a bigger cycle of attitudinal change. By taking their careers and future employment potential into their own hands, employees act in their own best interests. That starts a kind of chain reaction, wherein the employee starts looking at his skills as something for sale. If he has something for sale, he must seek a place to sell it. That takes him to the job market. The job market is full of customers, and if this skilled employee has done his homework, he knows what these customers want and how he can give it to them.

True, that sounds very much like the process familiarly known as "looking for a job." And true, the search may lead the employee full circle to realize that his current employer is his best potential customer. But the payoff for the company/customer (again in theory) is a more responsive employee.

If your vendors and independent contractors don't treat you any better, or work any harder, than your employees do, this all may strike you as a moot point — a mere semantic game. On the other hand, perhaps the idea of transforming your organization from employer to customer in the minds of your current workers sounds intriguing. And if you want to dispel the entitlement mentality in your work force, developing more independent employees is a step in that direction.

Robert Waterman, author of *What America Does Right*, says that independent employees are good for a company because they tend to tell it like it is. He recalls co-workers he admired at his previous employers. "The people who were best for the system — even though sometimes irritatingly honest with us — were the people who could leave," he says. Because these people knew they could go anywhere with their skills, Waterman explains, they could afford to ask tough questions and ruffle feathers in the interest of making a project successful.

Where does the concept of loyalty to a company fit into this new way of thinking? Frank Hoffmann, director of learning and development at Rosenbluth Travel in Philadelphia, says that loyalty still exists, it just doesn't inspire the career-long commitment it once did. Hoffmann says the feeling at Rosenbluth is, "We're delighted to have you while you're here, and expect a commitment while you're here."

Robert Johansen, co-author of the book *Upsizing the Individual in the Downsized Organization*, says that, for the time being, companies will have to manage people who are less loyal. But, he adds, loyalty will come back into fashion once the terms of the employment contract have been renegotiated.

The Company's Responsibility

If each employee has to take charge of his career and make sure his skills continue to match the demands of the market, what about the company? If we are talking about agreements between equals in this new relationship, do corporations have any responsibilities at all besides delivering a paycheck?

Yes, say most advocates of the non-dependency scenario. The consensus is that individuals need to own their own employability, but companies must support them in their efforts. Hoffmann suggests that an essential first step is executive support for individual career development. You have to give people permission, and that most precious commodity, time, to work on their careers or nothing is going to happen. At Rosenbluth, that means permission for workers to "shadow" other employees and watch them do their jobs. Rosenbluth employees can also join a cross-functional team and find out what other departments are up to. "There's nothing worse than giving people accountability for something and then not giving them the resources for it," says Hoffmann.

Harvard Community Health Plan supported its employees' career development by doing a rigorous analysis of the competencies involved in most company jobs. This means employees now can find out exactly what skills are needed for any job that interests them. Add that to top management support for lateral moves, and you get a "career lattice" instead of a career ladder, says Hicks.

In her six years with the company, Hicks has only moved "up" once, and she concedes that in traditional terms her career might not look very impressive. In terms of competencies, however, she has acquired an array of different skills because she's been able to move laterally through different departments in the organization. In light of the diminishing opportunities for advancement at most companies today, the career lattice notion may begin to appeal to a lot of people.

> **"The people who were best for the system — even though sometimes irritatingly honest with us — were the people who could leave."**

The idea of supporting people's employability comes easiest to organizations that have a history of valuing continual learning. At Hewlett-Packard, for instance, a commitment to lifelong learning has been part of the corporate culture for more than 30 years, according to Davis. In the preamble to the corporate objectives composed in 1961, cofounder David Packard wrote, "...in an era of increasing change, continuous learning must be undertaken by all from top to bottom in the organization."

In Hewlett-Packard's competitive, high-tech market, this environment of continual learning is integral to work, not just some nice platitude, Davis says. The skills of some H-P engineers have a half-life of only 18 months, meaning that half of their knowledge becomes obsolete in the space of less than two years.

Another way companies can foster an environment of employability, similar to the career lattice, is through "inplacement." Inplacement is a commitment to find as many internal jobs as possible for employees whose positions are eliminated. One of the most progressive companies in this area is Intel, which recently was cited in a benchmarking exercise conducted by the University of Michigan as the American company best at redeploying its work force. According to Intel's corporate redeployment manager, Marile Robinson, the company has set up a whole structure, including budgets, to facilitate redeployment throughout the organization.

This commitment to inplacement, which started in 1990, has been fine-tuned over the years, says Robinson. Currently, someone whose job is going to vanish has four months to do research, take some career assessments, receive computer-based training, and look for opportunities within the company. Funds are allotted for relocation, training and, if there isn't a job within the company, outplacement. Employees can also become part of a redeployment pool where they can be "called up" when jobs become available, says Robinson.

Training Them To Leave?

One of the touchiest concerns about this whole employability strategy was brought up by someone who declined to be interviewed for this article. She didn't want to be part of a story that was telling employers to help workers acquire skills so they could go work for some other company — including, perhaps, the competition.

The possibility of training workers only to see competitors steal them away has always been a concern in the business world, though companies don't like to talk about it. But if all this rhetoric about employability and breaking away from dependence on the company is to be anything but a bag of gas, the issue has to be faced.

Waterman and Noer argue that, ideally, it's a good idea to train employees so they can leave your company. In this way, they say, you completely sever the umbilical cord that encourages unhealthy dependence. But realistically, as Hewlett-Packard's Davis points out, "We don't want to lose people because the knowledge goes right out the door."

That concern doesn't stop Hewlett-Packard from training people in highly portable skills, however. And H-P has always had one of the lowest turnover rates in the electronics industry, says Davis.

That brings up a paradox that Waterman describes like this: "I think [companies] should be training people so they can leave. And I think the very fact that they do so probably means most people won't leave."

The paradox runs both ways. If an employee takes charge of her own employability by keeping her skills updated and varied so she can work for anyone, she de facto builds more job security with her current employer — assuming the company values highly skilled, motivated employees. By the same token, if a company provides a lot of training and learning opportunities, it is more likely to retain workers because it creates an interesting and challenging environment. As Davis puts it, "What is going to entice them away? Money? Maybe you can buy them for a short term, but what keeps people excited is growing and learning."

Thus, in theory, increasing an individual's employability outside the company simultaneously increases his job security and his desire to stay with his current employer. Berlo suggests that the ideal corporate environment would be one in which everyone in the organization is there, not because they have to be, but because they believe it's the best game in town. As far as Berlo is concerned, any CEO who says he can't afford to train his employees because the competition might steal them away is admitting that people wouldn't work for his company if they had any other choice.

Skills for the Future

It's all very well to tell people to upgrade their skills continually and to be lifelong learners, but what is it, exactly, that individuals should go learn?

Understandably, pundits hesitate to make predictions about the demands of future job markets, mostly because, 1) being wrong tends to make people angry if they've trained themselves for a career that suddenly becomes obsolete and, 2) nobody, including experts and futurists, has anything but a vague idea what the future might look like.

Still, there are skill sets that seem somewhat immune from obsolescence, at least in the foreseeable future. Waterman suggests that acquiring almost any skill that makes you more adept with computers and information technology is probably a good idea. Aside from that, he suggests an equal mix of technical skills and softer skills (teamwork, listening skills, etc.) as the key to being part of what he calls the career-resilient work force.

> "We don't want to lose people, because their knowledge goes right out the door."

As far as employability is concerned, one rapidly growing trend in the computer industry seems to be providing at least a little direction: formal certification in particular software or hardware skills. If a company like Novell Inc., the Provo, UT-based network software developer, certifies you as a network engineer, you may increase both your present job security and your employability in general.

Novell was one of the first companies to adopt a standard certification process, and its certificates have come to be accepted in both the computer industry and industries that use computers (which means almost everyone). In other words, if you are a CNE (certified NetWare engineer), many potential employers will accept that you have the skills to set up and handle their computer networks. The same goes for certification by firms like Microsoft, Lotus, and other computer companies.

Skill certification has been tried in other industries — and the federal government has pursued the idea of skills standards in many occupations since the Bush administration. But the idea appears to have caught fire in the computer industry. According to Rick Romine, Novell's director of strategic development, the company originally set out to establish certification for its vendors as a way to make sure its customers were getting the help they needed with the sometimes cryptic affairs of networked computers. Other computer companies began to examine and imitate Novell's standard. Romine now predicts that certification will become a trend in other industries, as companies look toward helping workers stay employable.

Novell surveyed managers from 400 companies that sent employees for certification. According to Romine, 70 percent said they would do it again. Ninety-five percent said the training improved performance. Almost a third (30 percent) said certification was recommended for employment; 23 percent said it was important for promotion. And even though this certification makes a person eminently employable at other companies, 91 percent of those certified said their employers paid for their training. Novell has certified 50,000 engineers at last count.

Romine predicts that certification will spread to other areas of the computer industry in the future. Workers would then be able to document, for instance, that they are certified in a certain kind of word processing software. This would establish that they can actually use most of the features rather than knowing only enough to use the word processor as a fancy typewriter.

Down In the Valley

Hewlett-Packard, Novell, Microsoft, Intel ... it's no accident that many of the companies mentioned here are in the computer business. Though not all are officially in Silicon Valley, there is a "valley" mentality in the computer industry that seems to foster employability and self-employment. Certainly, the industry serves as a bellwether of the new-style employment contract that many envision for the working world at large.

Movement between computer companies becomes a way of life for many in Silicon Valley, where, as Berlo puts it, you can change companies six different times without selling your house. Author Johansen describes the culture as one in which corporate loyalty is defined as loyalty to your Rolodex: Keeping yourself networked with the people you worked with in the past is the surest way to guarantee continued employment. Increasingly, says Johansen, loyalty in the computer industry is something employees feel only for the people they work with, the teams they work on, and the projects they help complete.

If the Silicon Valley mentality is going to provide a model of the new employment contract, will we all be free-wheeling independent contractors in the future? The smart money says there will always be a place in corporations for a core of full-time, permanent workers who will be the guardians of the corporate culture and the keepers of the collective knowledge. For one thing, suggests Waterman, some long-term employees will be necessary if the company wants to execute any kind of longer-term strategy. "One of the hardest things to do in strategy is get the damn thing implemented," he says. "And the people who do the best job of that are people who are going to be around for awhile."

Nevertheless, even core employees can benefit from adopting a philosophy of employability. After all, today's core employee can become tomorrow's independent contractor faster than any of us like to think. Beyond that, some say the employability model will lead to more interesting, fulfilling work wherever individuals end up. But more than anything else, employability is about people taking control of their own careers.

Notes:

Do-It-Yourself Career Development

Who is responsible for an employee's career development? At British Petroleum Exploration, employees are expected to take charge of their own.

BY ROBERT TUCKER
AND MILAN MORAVEC

Gerry was unhappy with the progress of his career at British Petroleum Exploration (BPX). "I've been here almost three years and I'm no further along than I was when I started," he complained. "Not only haven't I been promoted, but management hasn't given me any career planning, training or development. And I'm not a bad performer! What is this company doing to help its employees move ahead?"

The response from the human resource counselor was blunt: "What are you doing to help yourself?"

A year or two ago, that response would have been shocking and inappropriate. BPX, the arm of British Petroleum that finds and develops oil and gas reserves, was a typical paternalistic bureaucracy with power concentrated at the top. Employees at lower levels believed — with justification — that they had no real influence, so they seldom seized the initiative to better themselves or the company.

Under a new leadership regime, however, BPX is striving to transform itself into a lean and flexible tiger. That means flattening the organization, replacing hierarchy with networking and empowering the staff.

"Employees have expected managers to 'give' them a new set of static, predetermined duties and a grade increase when either the organizational need arises or management feels the employee is ready to make a move," says one BPX executive. Under a new human resource initiative, however, all that is changing. Empowered employees, BPX reasons, take charge of their own careers. Of course, they need a few "tools" to do so.

One of the tools BPX now provides is a personal development planning program that employees can use to improve their skills, performance and job satisfaction. The net effect: They become more marketable, inside and outside the company. The program is strictly voluntary; employees can still choose to wait until someone notices they deserve a promotion. But those with more drive are rewarded with recognition, support and faster career progress.

Self-Guidance

At the core of personal development planning at BPX is a guidebook that leads the individual through four phases: assessment, goal-setting, development planning and implementation. An interdisciplinary team of BPX staffers from around the world tailored the guidebook for the company's needs.

The first step is to assess current skills. In this exercise, the employee refers to a list of skills that fall into two broad categories: core technical skills pertaining to the oil business and nontechnical skills — communication, planning, business awareness and decision-making, for example — that are transferable to many BPX jobs. The person then documents his or her own accomplishments related to these skills.

Skills are only part of the assessment picture, however. The exercises also ask employees to identify their interests and values. The idea here is that people who hold jobs they consider satisfying in terms of challenge, intellectual stimulation or recognition will be more productive and motivated to achieve.

Once employees have determined which skills, interests and values they have and which need to be developed, they are encouraged to ask for perceptions from others: supervisors, peers, subordinates, family, friends. Feedback such as "You're forgetting your presentation skills" or "What about your interest in international travel?" often leads people to revise their original assessments.

In the next phase, employees establish goals for their current jobs and for future positions. They may decide to improve their performance in a present job, take on new responsibilities, do something (attend a training course, for example) to enhance their core skills or volunteer for lateral moves. During the third phase, employees turn this blueprint into a real structure by specifying development and improvement actions, target dates for completion and resources required.

Throughout these three phases, employees work with their supervisors to make sure their goals are realistic. In the final phase, employees and supervisors must agree on assessments, goals and action plans. Again, the employee and supervisor do a "reality check": How can the employee reach this goal within BPX? If interests and values do not mesh with the current job, what other jobs are available — inside or outside BPX? What job qualifications does the employee need to meet? Which new skills could be practiced and demonstrated through work assignments in the current job? What about special training? On-the-job coaching? A lateral move within BPX or the parent company, British Petroleum?

The process does not end when the employee and supervisor agree on a course of action. Personal development plans must be updated as employees grow in skills and knowledge, as they complete items on their action plans or as business needs change.

A Matched Set of Tools

The personal development document is more than a career plan. Because it focuses on interests and values as well as skills, it also can be used as a life plan. If an assessment suggests that Gerry would be happier and more productive as a consulting engineer for a small firm than he is as a BPX engineer, he can begin planning his career change. Since BPX is downsizing and reorganizing, the company gives its blessing to anyone who uses personal development planning to find a better fit inside or outside the company.

Obviously, however, any scheme in which the employee and the supervisor are expected to speak candidly about the employee's plan to leave the company presupposes a climate of extraordinary trust. Employees must not fear that their careers will be jeopardized if they talk about seeking work outside the company and then elect to remain. The guidebook actually encourages them to consider all types of career opportunities — within BPX, within British Petroleum and elsewhere. BPX managers would rather have a frank discussion about employees' career needs — and have an opportunity to influence their decisions — than be surprised by a two-week notice. And it is in supervisors' interests to play it straight. They know that if they violate someone's trust just once, they henceforth will hear only what employees think they want to hear.

People can also use their plans to market themselves inside the company. They can approach their current supervisors, or potential ones, and propose themselves for new jobs and work assignments, pointing to specific capabilities and interests identified on the plan. By stimulating discussion about what they want and what they can offer the company, employees gain visibility and support for their development goals.

Expectations

If personal development planning were a stand-alone program, it would probably raise expectations that could not be met. At BPX, however, it is just one tool designed to be used in conjunction with others.

For example, BPX has developed "skills matrices" that describe in great detail the skills, behaviors and training required for each step in the career plan of a manager or a non-manager in every "job family." These skills matrices, which describe both non-technical and technical skill requirements, form the database for each phase of personal development planning.

Another item in the BPX toolbox is an upward feedback system. Employees rate their supervisors' people-management skills and then join them in discussions about how to improve communication. Skills matrices provide information to stimulate the discussions. Results from these upward-rating sessions are fed into the managers' personal development plans.

BPX gives its blessing to anyone who uses personal development planning to find a better fit inside or outside the company.

While this program aims to help employees develop their own careers, managers are not let off the hook. On the contrary, supervisors are required to attend workshops on how to assist their subordinates in personal development planning. They are expected to make time and other resources available for the process, to give employees open and honest feedback, to help find and evaluate information, and to open up development opportunities. Senior BPX management vows to supply information about specific business decisions and the likely outcomes of those decisions.

Managers continue to make decisions about job placement and promotion. No one moves up the career ladder (or sideways) until he or she has demonstrated mastery of current responsibilities. Supervisors who want to attract the best talent at BPX try to acquire a reputation for being the best at developing people who report to them. Working with employees on development plans gives managers more insight into their subordinates' skills and how those abilities mesh with business plans. In the process, hidden talent often surfaces.

Benefits

Unanimously, employees have found both the process and the materials valuable. Follow-up surveys indicate that employees do believe BPX is committed to personal development planning. They understand that the company provides genuine opportunities to develop, but there are no guarantees. Performance and individual responsibility for career development are the keys to success.

The company benefits by empowering employees. They've learned to ask, "What's the gap between the skills I have and the skills the business requires — now and in the future?" "What do I need to learn and demonstrate?" They are constantly challenged to acquire the new skills BPX needs to maintain leadership in an industry characterized by rapid, global changes in technology, markets and finance.

The dialogue between supervisors and subordinates reinforces the climate of open, two-way communication that BPX hopes to create. The program gives high visibility to the type of employee BPX wants to attract and encourage — entrepreneurial, committed, skilled and ready to demonstrate initiative. It sends the message that mere longevity in a given job does not determine readiness to advance.

Finally, a better fit between employees and jobs makes for better use of human resources. Personal development planning enlists both employees and their managers in the search for congruence among individual goals, skills, motivations and business goals.

Why I Despair for the HR Profession

A search for a new human resources director becomes a terrifying journey into the heart of darkness.

BY ALAN WEISS

I am a consultant by trade. I've worked closely with training and human resources professionals throughout my career. Some of my best friends are HR professionals, all right? Let's get that straight here at the start.

For years I've preached to people outside the field that the human resources profession has matured, that the department formerly known as "personnel" is no longer a dumping ground for marginal employees who can't be trusted with jobs that are actually important. HR people are often my clients, and surely we all must respect our clients. If we don't, how can we respect what we do ourselves?

That's why my recent experience helping a client to hire a human resources director was such a chilling one.

Although I'm not a recruiter, every so often a client asks me to help fill a position. Since I'm on retainer to the client anyway, I tend to know the operation and the key people pretty well, I understand why the incumbent didn't work out and so on.

Several months ago, I was asked to find a HR director for a division of a well-known corporation considered one of the finest in the world in terms of its working environment as well as the quality of its products and services. The position carries a base salary of $95,000, with short- and long-term incentives that can bring total compensation to more than $125,000 per year. The benefit package is superb.

Here is the one-time ad we placed in two regional editions of *The Wall Street Journal*. As the text suggests, this is not only a high-level position, but one concerned at least as much with human resources *development* (training and performance issues) as with classic personnel matters such as compensation and benefits:

DIRECTOR OF HUMAN RESOURCES

Major division of one of the most respected and successful companies in America is seeking a professional's professional to lead its human resources effort. The position reports to the president and is part of the management committee.

We are seeking dynamic leadership for our small team of professionals which must provide innovative application of all aspects of human resource expertise to our business goals. The director is an integral part of the senior management team and is, therefore, involved in all phases of the business.

The successful candidate will have:
• A track record of success leading a human resources group in a major organization.
• Impeccable references and credentials, which will be carefully checked.
• An undergraduate degree and, preferably, a postgraduate degree.
• A comprehensive and thorough knowledge of all aspects of human resource administration and application, including recruiting, compensation, benefits, training, organization development, EAPs, diversity, team building and internal consulting. Excellent interpersonal and presentation skills are a must.
• Experience working as a partner with senior management.

Limited travel is required. We offer a competitive salary, incentive and benefit package. Please submit a detailed résumé and salary history. *Submissions without this information will not be considered.*

Within 30 days we received 1,085 responses. Of those, 38 candidates were selected for interviews. Nine of the 38 were recommended to the client for a second interview, and the client granted that second interview to five of the nine. Finally, the organization hired a very capable director of HR. The story ended happily.

So why this lingering sense of dread?

The Horror...The Horror...

I was stunned by the way so many candidates handled themselves, both in writing and in person. Right off the bat, for instance, 312 of the respondents (29 percent) included no salary history whatsoever, despite our clear warning in the ad.

If we said we wouldn't consider candidates who failed to submit salary data, what accounts for these omissions? Is it that they simply didn't believe the ad (skepticism)? Did they imagine their credentials were so superb that we would ignore *their* ignoring of our requirements (arrogance)? Or were they simply not paying much attention (sloth)?

In an effort to give excellent-looking candidates the benefit of the doubt, I called 15 people whose résumés otherwise met our criteria. I asked them directly why they didn't include a salary history, and if they would provide one over the phone. Nine told me they chose not to for one reason or another. The other six said they hadn't noticed our requirement or had forgotten it.

You might conclude that the nine probably were canny negotiators with excellent reasons for refusing to reveal their present salaries on their résumés. But if that were the case, why did every last one of them give me salary information over the phone — without even making any attempt to verify my identity? My favorite response was from a superbly qualified vice president from a premier company in California: "I saw the requirement, but I didn't feel comfortable sending in my salary details without meeting you. Here's what I made last year..."

In addition to the salary shy, two types of submissions were rejected out of hand. First, the sloppy ones: We received 86 résumés — every one from a current or former director or vice president of human resources — that were poor copies, contained sloppy erasures, had handwritten corrections or were entirely handwritten.

Then there were the mystery candidates. Twenty-five people sent résumés that didn't reveal their former employers but simply listed positions such as "HR director for a major financial services company." This, of course, is a major obfuscation. Even if one is sensitive about revealing a current employer, what's the point in hiding the prior four?

More strangeness: Somewhere out there, I concluded, is a sinister outplacement firm whose "Résumé 101" course teaches layoff victims to dazzle prospective new employers with a distinctive format: On one side of a piece of paper, list "your requirements," meaning the ones the employer stated in the ad; on the other side, match these requirements with a list of "my accomplishments." If you're ever tempted to do that, here's some free advice: Don't. It's unimaginative. And it's annoying.

Finally, an odd little factoid that I'll leave for the reader to interpret: We received 22 résumés from attorneys, every one of whose cover letters insisted that they would make excellent human resources directors. These were *not* candidates with HR experience who happened to have law degrees (there were quite a few of those). They apparently were full-time practicing attorneys who wrote to us on their letterhead: "Judy Jones, Attorney-At-Law."

The Interviews

The 38 candidates who looked best on paper were scheduled for interviews in first-class hotels in two different cities. That's when the real nightmare began.

I carefully explained to every candidate, in advance, that travel expenses for this first round of interviewing were not reimbursable. One out-of-town applicant showed up for the interview and demanded that his plane fare and his $250-a-night hotel room be reimbursed. He declared that this was "standard practice" and denied that I had said anything to the contrary. This was after he was an hour late for the day's final appointment, which meant I had to take him to dinner and pick up the check. (I reimbursed his airfare as a gesture of good will. He said he hoped our misunderstanding wouldn't influence his candidacy, and that he wanted to go to the next round. It did, and he didn't.)

After 20 minutes of conversation, another candidate told me that he was really only there to network; he wanted to know what other jobs I was recruiting for. I told him I wasn't a recruiter, and that this was the only job. "Oh," he said. "Well, that certainly puts a different spin on things." He informed me — as I cut the interview short — that I conducted too much of a "New York" interview. "We don't use that style in this city," he explained. I told him I didn't care what was done in this city, I only cared about what was done in my client's organization. He said, "Well, maybe that's important, too...."

While accepting the interview over the phone, one candidate had seemed strangely sarcastic. But I gave him the benefit of the doubt. At the interview he declared that he was suffering from food poisoning and might have to vomit in my bathroom. (His phrasing of this possibility was considerably more vivid than that.) Throughout the interview, however, his manner was not so much sick as cynical. When I finally asked him why, he denied displaying any such attitude. He wrote a week later to mention that it wasn't food poisoning after all, and he might have exposed me to a "noxious virus."

> **"I was stunned by the way so many candidates handled themselves, both in writing and in person."**

One candidate informed me that I had asked questions too rapidly. He would have preferred a more leisurely pace. The conditions I had established did not allow him to show himself at his best. I asked him what he would do in a company in which the conditions I had established prevailed. "I guess I'd adjust somehow," he said.

In the space of 15 minutes, another candidate described his internal consulting work with the phrases, "You know how Germans can be," "Europeans have a hard time with American thinking," "that Argentine," and "You have to make allowances for these people." I made no allowances for him.

On his résumé, one candidate listed BA, MA, MBA and JD degrees, the last from Notre Dame. I asked why he'd felt he needed a law degree on top of the others and how he'd managed to acquire one in two years. He answered that he didn't have the degree; it must be a "misprint" on the résumé. Well then, had he ever *attended* the law school at Notre Dame? He replied that he took six hours of courses. Did I think the résumé was misleading, he asked innocently?

I told all 38 candidates in advance that they would have an opportunity during the interview to ask whatever they liked about the position, the company, the culture and so on. Fewer than half had any articulate or insightful questions about the job for which they were applying.

Every candidate except the guy I had to feed showed up for the appointment on time. Everyone was professionally dressed and well-groomed. If punctuality and dressing for success were the only qualifications for an HR director, this would have been an impressive group.

As it was, nine candidates were superb. Two were the finest I've ever seen. One was hired by the client.

Pop Quiz

Before the interviews began, I created a short quiz — I thought of it as a "calibration device" — mostly to help me understand what my expectations should be regarding candidates' general knowledge of the field. I asked all 38 candidates the following six questions during the interview. The responses did not figure into my evaluation, although I couldn't help but be impressed by those who knew all six answers.

1. Who was Frederick Winslow Taylor?
2. What is NAFTA?
3. Who popularized the term "self-actualization" as a key aspect of his work?
4. Who was B.F. Skinner?
5. What is ROI, ROE and ROA?
6. Who is _____?

(Here I inserted the name of my client's CEO, a person about as well-known as, say, John Sculley of Apple Computer.)

Answers appear at the end of this article, in the event you'd like to try the quiz yourself.

Though it was purely subjective, I thought that a well-informed human resources director should be able to identify these people and things. Only four of the 38 candidates knew all six answers. This surprised me a little, but it wasn't especially daunting. I didn't "grade" the unscientific test, and two of the four who got perfect scores were not among my final nine recommendations.

The shocker, however, was that of the remaining 34 people who couldn't answer all the questions, only four asked me how they had done or wanted to know which ones they had missed. (If a candidate missed any of the questions, I simply said nothing and moved on with the interview, unless asked.) That means 30 people had no idea how they did on a test in a job interview — though most had no response or a wild guess for at least one of the questions — yet weren't curious about the answers.

Gloom

Now, admittedly, this was no scientific study and my candidates constituted no scientific sample of the HR field. Still, the process left me with some rather dreary conclusions:

• High-level human resources people, who presumably serve as exemplars of interpersonal communication, are not, by and large, very effective communicators.

• Many rely far too heavily on outplacement "formulas," both when preparing résumés and when responding to an interviewer. These formulas smother the individual uniqueness that makes candidates attractive.

• Many seem to suffer from a belief (whether through arrogance or plain simplemindedness I still can't decide) that they have no need to adapt to circumstances; they simply expect other people to adapt to *them*. This includes other people with $125,000-a-year jobs to offer.

• Candidates enter the search process in a defensive mode, trying to conceal weaknesses and ready to parry tough questions. It's rare to find them in a poised and assertive mode, drawing the interviewer's attention to their abilities.

• The top incumbents in HR and HRD are mostly people who have been in the profession for 20 years with few job excursions to line areas. Most of those who submitted résumés began their careers in the bowels of the personnel ship and climbed a single ladder steadily until they reached the bridge. The pattern held true of the 401 women (37 percent of all applicants) who answered our advertisement, as much as for the white-male majority.

This magazine has a set of writers guidelines that it sends to prospective authors. The guide includes a line that has always intrigued me: "TRAINING isn't just about training. It's about human performance." The performances I witnessed, both in writing and in person, from people presumably responsible for *molding* performance within their organizations, were desultory. Sure, we were able to find a few excellent candidates through the process. But I fear for the profession when I witness such overwhelming mediocrity.

Twenty years ago I might have rationalized the whole thing, thinking, *That's why these people are looking for work*. But that argument doesn't hold water in the age of corporate downsizing. Some of the best candidates I saw were out of work, and some of the worst held influential jobs. I was left wondering, finally, if the human resources field may have become too specialized, insulated and arrogant for its own good.

ANSWERS:

1. Frederick Winslow Taylor is considered the "father of scientific management." Early in this century, he pioneered time-and-motion studies and the exploration of human productivity. His classic work is *Scientific Management*.

2. NAFTA stands for the much-debated North American Free Trade Agreement.

3. Abraham Maslow placed "self-actualization" at the highest level of his "hierarchy of needs."

4. B.F. Skinner was probably the most famous and influential of all behavioral psychologists. He wrote *Beyond Freedom and Dignity* and devised the "Skinner box."

5. ROI is return on investment, ROE return on equity, and ROA return on assets. One candidate told me that "nobody uses ROA anymore." I told him my client used it as a key index. "Oh," he said.

6. CEO of the client's company.

Notes:

From Paternalism to Stewardship

It's not the job of human resources to take care of employees and ensure morale.
At least not according to a management philosophy called 'stewardship.'

BY PETER BLOCK

In Stewardship: Choosing Service Over Self-Interest, *Peter Block proposes a radical shift in the way we're accustomed to leading, managing and working in our organizations. His label for this shift is "stewardship," which he defines as "an organizational philosophy whereby employees serve the larger organization by operating in service of, rather than in control of, those around them. Stated simply, it is accountability without control or compliance." Block, author of* The Empowered Manager *and partner in Designed Learning, a consulting firm in Plainfield, NJ, maps out the changes stewardship will require throughout the organization. This chapter, adapted from the book, focuses on the implications of applying the stewardship philosophy to the human-resources function.*

In most organizations, the traditional role of line management is patriarchal. Whether spoken out loud or muttered sotto voce, the message to employees in such a company is this: "We own you." To balance this overbearing bent, human-resources departments in these organizations have been put in charge of paternalism. Their statement to employees is this: "Don't worry so much about the fact that they own you, because we will take care of you." In essence, the human-resources function has evolved into a caretaking and enabling function whose assignment is to take responsibility for the morale and emotional well-being of employees.

This combination of good-cop/bad-cop messages creates the golden handcuffs that make living in a workplace of dominance and dependency so tolerable. As subordinates, we yield sovereignty with the expectation that our leaders will care for us in a reasonable and compassionate way. As leaders in this traditional organization, we think that if we have protective and caring human-resources policies, we have ruled with grace and kindness. This type of leadership does not question its own desire for dominance; it asks only that the dominance be implemented humanely.

In most organizations, human-resource policies and the human-resource function are used to deliver on this promise of protection and satisfaction. The problem is that caretaking and protection feed the company's self-interest and undermine employees' responsibility.

There is another way, which I call stewardship. Choosing stewardship means a fundamental rethinking of our human-resource policies and the role of the human-resource function. Stated simply, it is a move from parent to partner in how we hire, fire, pay, appraise, train, promote, transfer, provide benefits and improve the organization.

In most organizations, the HR department's muscle comes from its approval authority. In other words, if you want to do training or adjust your pay system, add a new job or a new level, hire someone or redo any people-related process, you must first go to the HR people for their formal or informal approval. The fact that your HR department may be wholly supportive of the plan does not change the parent-child nature of the relationship.

Adopting a stewardship model for the human-resources department means getting it out of the policy-selling, policy-implementing business. No more personnel policies centrally defined and implemented across the board. No more approval authority residing in a staff function. HR can live a stewardship philosophy by defining the core work team as its primary client, rather than top management. Better for HR to provide the tools, skills and processes for people close to the work to develop their own personnel practices. Let a plant, a department or a sales region design its own hiring, pay, appraisal and training practices. If there is a genuine need for consistency across units, let the affected units work it out among themselves.

Human resources has special expertise in the people area and in the realm of creating culture, so let them teach that expertise, and let go the role of creator and compliance officer. The teaching role is much better aligned with partnership and distributing ownership and responsibility.

In some cases, staff people rightly claim that the line organization does not want to create its own personnel practices. Line managers like being able to send people to HR when problems occur because they have someone else outside the intimacy of their own family group to hold responsible for unpopular decisions.

All this may be true. But blame cannot rest solely with line managers. Any staff group like HR usually has a choice about the nature of the services it offers. Top management may have commanded HR to act like a police department, but in most cases, HR itself has sought a more muscular role, feeling that policing powers would enhance its contribution.

As with most staff functions, HR has considered top management its primary customer. When HR groups define their role as implementing top management's strategic intentions, they become agents of top management. The HR executive becomes the counselor to the top executive. There is no problem with this per se, since everyone needs an adviser. It becomes a problem when attention to the top becomes a primary focus and a statement of purpose.

HR executives' frequent dialogues with higher-ranking executives on how to handle "those people," patronizing as it is, will continue if HR executives think their most critical relationship is with the top of the house. This is HR's collusion with patriarchy.

As soon as HR defines its purpose as supporting partnership among those in the line organization, however, it stops being the agent of the top, and begins to work with top executives to find ways to better support core workers. In stewardship, core workers are the customers of top management.

There are two aspects of the HR function that are worth exploring to make these ideas more concrete. One is the way the function is structured and works with its customers. The other is the set of beliefs underlying human-resource policies and practices.

The Structure

As part of its legacy of defining and implementing policy, HR is organized according to professional specialty. There are separate sections on compensation, executive compensation, management development, skills training, recruiting, benefits, affirmative action, organization development, total-quality management, labor or industrial relations, and employee relations. Organizing this way makes it easier to train people, to control the operation and to focus energy; it also encourages in-depth, specialized knowledge.

The main limitation of a functional structure is that it does not react well to the customer's need for quick and whole-system solutions. The functions in HR are so interrelated that you cannot really solve a problem in one area without touching many of the others. When a supervisor comes to the compensation person and says, "I need an exception to keep one of my best people," it is most likely a symptom of another problem. The underlying problem could be a recruiting issue: Perhaps a promise was made upon hiring that was unfulfillable. It could be a problem with how a team is working together, which would involve the organizational-development group. Or this request for exceptional pay treatment could involve a performance-appraisal or career-development problem.

A functional organization has trouble bringing to bear five different viewpoints on a customer problem. If human resources intends to be a model of a customer-oriented service function, it must structure itself around customers. Most likely, that means creating teams whose members learn all of the disciplines of human resources.

How HR is structured affects how it makes the transition from a policing and conscience role to one of service to a customer who has a choice of suppliers. Helping a line department redesign practices can be a job for just one or two internal HR consultants, rather than five or six experts consulting with the group on each of their specialties. The HR person becomes a facilitator or a helper, rather than the all-knowing expert. Organizing teams of staff people with good consulting skills around customer groups provides structural support to a service and stewardship orientation.

> **In many cases, HR has sought a more muscular role, feeling that policing powers would enhance its contribution.**

The Set of Beliefs

It's not just the structure of the HR group that needs to change; the actual substance of HR practices also needs to be reconsidered. Here is a brief helicopter survey of how conventional personnel practices embody patriarchy, caretaking and compliance, as well as some thoughts on the stewardship option.

• *Performance appraisals.* These are instruments for social control. They are annual discussions, avoided more often than held, in which one adult identifies for another adult three improvement areas he should work on during the next year. Performance appraisals can be softened by calling them development discussions or letting the subordinate choose the improvement areas. They can be held frequently to take the sting out of the one big annual assessment. None of this changes the basic transaction: bosses evaluating subordinates, with the outcome determining the amount of pay.

It doesn't matter even if the boss conducts the appraisal in as loving a way as possible. Most supervisors have been trained in listening skills, making good eye contact, asking open-ended questions, checking for agreement, making support statements, and identifying strengths as well as weaknesses. All of this helps; none of it heals. The transaction has an element of sovereignty to it that will not go away. Even if the intent of the appraisal is learning, it is not going to happen when the context of the dialogue is evaluation and judgment.

Besides not being conducive to learning, performance appraisals are a mistake from the standpoint of accountability. We should be appraised by those to whom we are accountable. If there must be an appraisal process, let people be appraised by their customers/suppliers. This means bosses will be appraised by their subordinates.

When we have people appraised by their bosses, what we are creating is trained followership. If we want stewardship, we must turn the model around. One way of doing this is to let all employees be responsible for their own annual appraisals. This gives them a choice about whether they want to use this method to learn, it gives them choice over the people they learn from, and it puts the responsibility for learning where it belongs — with each individual.

Self-directed appraisal will work only if we unhinge the learning process from the pay system. If you must rate people to pay them, then have a brief encounter in which you tell each person where she stands and ask if she has any questions. Don't call it a learning experience. Call it a meeting, not a performance appraisal or a developmental experience. No learning can occur when employees are being told by powerful people how much they are loved and how much pay they are going to get as a symbol of that love.

The appraisal process is a tough one to let go. I was talking about all this with a group of school superintendents, one of whom said he did 200 teacher evaluations each year. He had developed a rating scale of effective teaching behaviors, and he showed us numbers to demonstrate that each year teachers were improving on his scale as a result of his evaluations. He also was confident the teachers appreciated his evaluations.

The point that superintendent missed is the dependency that his practice creates. Here is a superintendent taking responsibility for teacher improvement, measuring dimensions he alone has chosen, and deciding when and where the teachers' learning should take place. At the end of it all, he feels useful when the teachers tell him they appreciate being watched.

It is so deeply ingrained in us to expect an evaluation from people we report to and to give an evaluation to those who report to us that we feel a little lost when it does not happen. This is the child in us, equating people's opinion of us with their protection. If I please them, they will provide for me. Conversely, the parent in us believes that the way we show concern for those we manage is by evaluating them and helping them grow.

The desire for feedback and learning should come out of conversations with our customers and peers. However deep and human the longing for praise from powerful people, it should be kept out of the means used to govern.

If you are a boss and your people want to know where they stand, tell them; just do not formalize it, document it and file it. If at some point you have to fire someone, you will have time to create the documentation. It is so rare that we fire people that there's no point in dragging everyone through the knothole of appraisals to be legally safe for the 1 percent or 2 percent we eventually fire.

Remember that with the stewardship model, what we seek in each HR practice we design is a way to answer a business requirement — in this case, learning how to improve — with each person taking responsibility for meeting the requirement.

• *Hiring.* This one is fairly simple. The intent of community is to have all of us committed to one another's success. We commit ourselves to those we have chosen. If bosses choose subordinates, as tradition dictates, then it is the boss who is committed to make that choice work. Team members may choose to support a new member, as they most often do, but peers are not accountable to one another unless they have in some way selected one another. The solution: Have teams hire new members. If consensus is too hard to achieve, give each member of the team veto power, so at least no one will have to live with someone she objects to. Treat the boss as a full member of the team; bosses should not have to live with team members they do not want, either.

• *Career advancement.* Our practices in career development are the seedbed of institutionalized caretaking. In our recruiting efforts, at the point of hire and often on an annual basis, we promise people we will take responsibility for their careers. The purpose of a career-development discussion is to help people think about where they are headed, and determine what training and work experiences they need to get there. In sophisticated organizations, bosses emphasize that it's the employee's job to define his own future. Bosses can help employees clarify their values, and identify their strengths and desires.

No matter how human and helpful the dialogue, its structure and implied promise make it a vehicle of parenting. The elements of this type of workplace parenting are:
• The boss calls the meeting.
• The focus is exclusively on the subordinate.
• The boss has private information about the subordinate's future that is rarely shared. And for good reason. If the boss discusses a future move, it had better be a done deal. Organizations pay dearly for creating expectations within employees that can't be fulfilled.
• Some elements of the discussion are mandated. For instance, the boss and the subordinate must talk about the employee's future. You even hear some employees complain because

> "Each executive training session conducted in an exclusive resort reinforces patriarchy."

they have not had their career-development discussion. Is there any doubt about who is the child and who is the parent?

Leaders in these traditional organizations take a proprietary interest in the future and fulfillment of those being led. One of the hallmarks of autocratic leaders is the pride they take in providing for the well-being of those who have been loyal to them. When people become our possessions, we feel responsible for them, just as we do for our children. This caretaking inevitably has an element of control to it. The career-development process is one of the key elements at work through which the vow of caretaking in exchange for compliance gets consummated.

Partners care about each other's plans and future, but take no responsibility for making it happen for the other person. Stewardship honors people's career aspirations but keeps responsibility for a career within the individual. There is no need to institutionalize the process of helping people with their future. The way to decrease someone's dependency on us is to emphasize that his future is in his own hands.

If an employee wants a discussion about her future, let her ask for it. And employees are not limited to asking their bosses; they should ask anyone they think can give them good information. If they want to write down their aspirations and have the HR department keep the list in its personnel files, that can certainly be done.

Management may want to do its own planning of personnel moves to make sure good people are ready for key jobs when they are needed. Succession planning makes sense. However, management does this for its own sake, not for the sake of the employee. Managers should not give employees the impression that a human-resource planning system is designed to provide a structured career path with the employee's interests primarily in mind. The reason is that when we tell people we will provide careers for them, we can deliver on the promise only for about the top 10 percent of them. The rest are essentially on their own.

Consequently, it's better to keep career development completely in the hands of the individual. We ought to support people in their aspirations whenever possible. But there should be no annual discussions, no formal procedures and no hiring sealed with a promise. There should be no recruiting brochures showing employees with two years of service making presentations to attentive executives in paneled offices. These practices conspire to make an unfulfillable promise in addition to feeding the self-interest of people who would join an organization for the sake of a fast-track career, rather than to be part of an entrepreneurial experiment. We ought to pay well and promote as best we can; we just should not promise it.

Reforming Management Development and Training

Another area of human resources that needs attention is how we go about training and development. If our intent is to invest in the skills and capabilities of people in a way that keeps ownership and responsibility in their hands, the strategy hinges on who chooses the training and what form it takes. Therefore:

• *Stop reinforcing the class system.* We frequently deliver training events according to the organizational level of the participants. Many organizations have a person in charge of executive development, another in charge of middle-manager development, a supervisory-training person, a skills-training person, and an organization-development person.

Needless to say, the executive-development training is done in a quite different style from the supervisory and skills training. For executive training, the cost of the instructor is high, the learning space is elegant, and the meals are delectable. In contrast, for supervisory training, the instructor costs little, the learning space is utilitarian, and the group is on its own for lunch.

All this is done to align the training event with the status expectations of the students. It has little to do with their learning requirements. Consequently, each executive session conducted in an exclusive resort reinforces patriarchy. Each two-hour-a-week session, taught after hours on employees' own time, reinforces patriarchy from the other perspective. The solution is not to send everyone to the resort or to the basement; just send them to the same space.

• *Mix levels in the classroom.* Composition is another training question. When we segregate participants by job level, we perpetuate their isolation from each other. There may be some genuine differences in the training requirements between levels, but not to the extent that we must always separate them. Plus, what better place for people to cross the boundaries that separate levels than in a learning environment?

In the training business I am part of, we still get calls from people who like our course content, but ask whether we will have any vice presidents in an upcoming class, because a certain executive insists on attending courses with other executives with "similar problems." Makes sense on the surface, but it is code for the class system.

When constructing any training on quality, changing culture, fostering high-performing and self-managing teams, set the rule that each class needs three or four levels in it. Make classes for separate levels the exception. As for the structure of the management-development unit, let a team of training people serve the training needs of all levels. This breaks down the elitism within the staff functions as well.

Human-resource practices do not affect the culture of an organization; they *are* the culture.

• *Permit choice in learning.* The third training-and-development strategy that would support stewardship is to give people real choice in the matter of their own learning, especially at the lower levels. It is a principle of stewardship that people need to choose the services they receive. People at the lower levels of most organizations are nominated for training or simply sent to it; they do not really choose it.

Typically, managers are informed of training opportunities by a training department, and they then fit the person or the team to the course. This means that the manager's choice is limited to the menu offered by the training function, and the core worker's and supervisor's only choice is to say yes or no to what is offered. Saying that we do not force people to go, that we only "nominate" them, is fancy footwork. Even when high-quality training is offered, and participants learn, the intention of supporting ownership and responsibility is undermined.

The matter of choice also brings into question the use of across-the-board, common learning experiences. The usual argument is that having everybody go through the same course gives them a common language and common tools, which eases a culture-change effort. Most of the time this wish is not fulfilled. Everyone likes the program, but few own the outcome. One division of AT&T sent all employees through a five-day training program every year for four years. Each year the program changed, each year the ratings were high, each year business was conducted much as the year before. So much training for so many people, with so little impact on people's fundamental experience at work. It was a high-control, caretaking system at the start and still is today.

If you want to create a common language, hold a meeting. Even a long meeting. Make clear your intentions for the business. Then let teams or small units decide on their training and their own paths.

• *Train teams.* We know that personal skills and management training for individuals produce little change in organizations. It becomes difficult for an employee to sustain new behaviors in an old environment. Yet we still send individuals to training programs. If our intent is to create community, and teams are a vehicle for doing that, we should offer training that is attended primarily by teams. No team, no training. Or at least we could say that unless three people from a unit attend a program, no one should come. Technical training may be an exception, but the general rule should be to offer training to work groups.

When we offer training to people one at a time, we are supporting individualism and missing an opportunity to be a force for political reform. Even the stance of saying that our management-development strategy is to train teams is a political stance in and of itself.

You can look at every practice in the realm of human resources and easily imagine what the application of stewardship would look like. The above are just some examples that touch everyone. Human-resource practices do not affect the culture of an institution; they *are* the culture. And most of our common practices reflect our legacy of consistency and control. When we seek great leaders, we will create great followers. Human resources along with financial practices are the primary messengers for communicating the kind of relationship an institution wishes to have with its members and, through them, with its customers. Whatever the name of your change effort — total quality, self-management, entrepreneurial government, school-based education — nothing will get institutionalized until practices in these arenas are redesigned.

Critical Mass: Putting Whole-Systems Thinking Into Practice

What if you held a meeting and *everybody* came? Some companies are doing precisely that, gathering large groups of people together to hash out past problems, current realities or a future vision.

BY BOB FILIPCZAK

The more people in a meeting, the less that gets done. That may not be a cardinal rule of business, but it's close. The idea of pulling together a great big group to accomplish a task wars with that inner voice that tells us smaller is better. Our '90s team sensibilities insist that groups of more than eight or nine people are unlikely to do any real work.

Isn't this why the business giants of yesteryear are downsizing, decentralizing, and trying to find the energy that smaller, more nimble organizations have harnessed? All compass needles seem to be pointing us toward smaller companies, smaller divisions and, especially, smaller work units.

That's why it's hard to explain a new movement coming out of the world of organizational development (OD), one in which very large groups are brought together to work on a problem. These interventions wear many different labels, but one consistent factor is the size of the groups involved. Typically, participants number between 50 and 150, but there may be as many as 5,000 employees involved.

Because these large-group meetings go by so many different names, we'll call them "critical mass events." There are umpteen variations on the theme, but in general, critical mass events are used to move organizations, often large organizations, in a new direction quickly. If Rosabeth Moss Kanter's book *Teaching Giants to Dance* comes to mind, you're not far off.

No rigid formula determines the number of participants in these meetings, says Barbara Bunker, a faculty member of the department of psychology at the State University of New York at Buffalo and a student of the current groundswell of large-group interventions around the country. But she suggests that more than 10 percent of the people in the organization undergoing the change should be present. Ideally, most experts agree, everyone in the organization should be in the room.

If getting that many people together sounds difficult, try this out: Many of these critical mass events don't just last hours, they last days. Three days seems to be a common stint. If your company prefers to keep information confidential, this is not the kind of gathering you will want to sponsor. Many of the meetings include customers, suppliers and community stakeholders.

Critical mass events aren't called to decide what kind of paper towels to put in company rest rooms or what color to paint the cafeteria. These meetings are about change with a capital "C," and organizations currently engaged in battle with the change monster are beginning to see large-group intervention as an effective weapon. Companies like U.S. West, Ford, Levi Strauss and Boeing have used critical mass methods to attack a variety of challenges. In the case of Ford, the company needed to open a new plant quickly. For U.S. West, the task was to establish strategic priorities. As for Boeing, the next time you get aboard a new 777 jetliner, you'll be riding in one of the outcomes of this large-group strategy.

The technique is used most often to do things such as change business strategies, develop a mission or vision about where the company is headed in the next century, or foster a more participative environment — simple stuff like that. In some cases, critical mass events are used as ways to kick off other popular initiatives like committing to total quality management, starting self-directed work teams, or reengineering the organization.

STS Grows Up

Critical mass interventions grew out of the field of organizational development, evolving from OD practices born in the 1950s. These current iterations started with Fred Emery, Eric Trist, the Tavistock Institute, and a bunch of coal miners in England. Trist's discoveries about self-directed work among these coal miners became the genesis of a theory called socio-technical systems (STS).

As William Passmore, professor of organizational behavior at Case Western Reserve University in Cleveland, explains it, the STS approach to organizational development means analyzing your company on at least three different levels. First you look at the outside forces acting on the business — customers, market forces, the community, competition and change. Then you observe the technical systems — the processes the company uses to make and deliver a product. Finally you analyze the human side of the business — rewards, motivation, training systems, and the relationships among people.

Once you've gathered all this data, explains Passmore, you get what OD people call a "whole systems" view of the organization.

This whole-systems approach led to traditional OD "interventions." For many years, the "right" way to bring about change in organizations was to assemble a design committee, a vertical slice of representatives from all areas of the company, that would collect data about the organization's "whole system." This design committee would gather the information, analyze it, and recommend ways the company could become more effective.

According to the current critical mass proponents, two problems were inherent in this traditional approach:

It tended to be slow, and the design committee became insulated. The data-gathering and analysis often took the better part of a year to accomplish. During this period, people on the design committee, though they contacted many different groups throughout the organization, often were consumed by the process itself. Then, at the end of the year, with all the recommendations in hand, the design committee faced the daunting task of selling them to the rest of the company. Not surprisingly, committee members often burned out on the whole process long before any of the recommended changes had a chance to cascade throughout the organization.

The drawbacks of the design-committee intervention started STS people thinking in a new direction: Get the

THE TRIPLE 7: A MODEL FOR LARGE-GROUP MEETINGS

One of the most remarkable examples of large-group intervention is embodied in Boeing's newest airliner, the 777.

Most applications of the critical mass idea are events — meetings that kick-start significant changes in an organization. Boeing, however, applied these same methods to a way of working: Large groups used the techniques learned in the initial events as a way to manage meetings. Some of the meetings involved 500 to 5,000 participants. The effort lasted four years and was the single largest product-development project in the United States in this decade, says Don Krebs, director of organization development for Boeing Commercial at its headquarters in Seattle.

Krebs, the primary consultant on the project, adapted for Boeing's needs what he had learned about large-scale meetings from Kathleen Dannemiller, president emeritus of Dannemiller Tyson Associates, an Ann Arbor, MI, consulting firm. He had significant support from Phil Condit, who was in charge of the Triple-7 project until he was promoted to his current position as president of Boeing. "I'm delighted with what was accomplished," says Condit. "It was very definitely a learning experience. We were learning as we went." He admits candidly that he and Krebs invented much of the process they used on the fly (no pun intended).

Condit had been the chief designer on Boeing's 757 project, and he wanted to try something new with the Triple-7 project, explains Krebs. "He wanted to get everybody on board, get them involved in the process throughout the design-and-build cycle, get feedback on how we were doing, and build a different kind of community."

A tall order? Yes, but one that meshed with the strengths of critical mass events. The method was well-suited to Boeing's needs because many of the Triple-7 working groups were large. A gathering of just the top managers in a team called the Oxbow Group, for example, included some 80 people.

The Oxbow Group met about every six weeks. Managers and directors from engineering, manufacturing, finance, personnel and tooling gathered to solve problems and talk out issues. Condit set the stage for every meeting by delivering a 20-minute "View From the Bridge" presentation, an overview of the progress of the project that included an update on competitors, customer orders, and significant outside events that might have an impact on Boeing's work.

Table groups then discussed the new information and asked clarifying questions of Condit. The first hour of the five-hour meeting was reserved for this information exchange, with a break built into the agenda so that participants could have informal discussions before they reassembled into the larger group. The rest of the meeting homed in on one or two issues, and possible solutions to the problem that had surfaced were batted among the table groups and the large group.

One stubborn question that came up during three different meetings was how to best organize the Design-Build Teams (DBTs). There were 220 of these DBTs, with 20 to 60 people on each team. The Oxbow Group wrestled with the question of who would lead these teams: Someone from manufacturing or someone from engineering? The group eventually arrived at the only solution that made sense, says Krebs: The teams would have co-leaders, one from each discipline. And, because everyone who needed to agree to this solution was in the room, the Oxbow Group could make the decision at the meeting.

After a year of these meetings, says Krebs, he and the group decided that formal action planning at the end of each meeting, a veritable staple of critical mass events, wasn't necessary. The combination of Boeing's can-do culture and the five-year deadline on the Triple 7 made action planning superfluous. Once a decision was made in the meeting, says Krebs, "these guys knew how to take the ideas and put them in place." Getting a bunch of manufacturing and engineering professionals to act on a decision has never been a problem at Boeing, he says.

An indication of how critical mass events can speed up a process: When the whole Boeing organization went through a quality-improvement program, Triple-7 employees completed the program in just two days of meetings. Every other group at Boeing required four days.

Large-group work wasn't the only innovation that brought the 777 to fruition. Condit also used concurrent engineering principles, which call for a mix of everyone who will be involved with a product to have a hand in the design right up front. For the first time at Boeing, all the design work was done on 3-D mock-ups using computer-aided design (CAD) software; no paper drawings were produced.

Every group that joined the project attended a large-scale meeting, an orientation to this new way of working. Each session was led by a vice president of the company, which was also a change from the norm. In the past, says Krebs, people could work for Boeing for 20 or 30 years without ever talking to a vice president.

After successfully using critical mass methods to design and build the Triple 7, Condit says he would like to see the rest of Boeing begin to apply them as well. He wants to keep improving the process and use it to break down more functional barriers, share more information, and get customers more involved in product development. — B.F.

"whole system" in a room together and do a year's worth of work in an intense, three-day session. Working with large groups is not a concept that just recently fell off the truck, says Bob Rehm, a consultant in Boulder, CO, who has been involved with STS and critical mass events for many years. Fred Emery was doing large-group work in the late 1960s, says Rehm, using a technique called a search conference.

An Empowered Database

OK, suspend your disbelief for a minute. If you sit around thinking about organizationwide interventions, like a lot of OD professionals do, it makes a certain amount of sense to get a big group involved in a company's change. It's much easier to talk about whole systems when the whole system, or a significant part of it, is present.

So, what are the characteristics of critical mass events? That's a little hard to nail down because the methods are so diverse, and different interventions fit with different objectives. (For a short course on the many forms of critical mass events, see box page 116.)

For example, an "open-space" meeting has no agenda, no limit on participants, and no real guest list; at the other extreme, a future-search conference has agendas, exercises, and lots of up-front planning. The conference-model approach can be used for everything from visioning to designing a new organization; a work-redesign event might tackle only one aspect of a production problem. Some methods require table groups — groups of eight to 10 gathered around a circular table — while others have no tables at all. Some have limits on how many people can or should participate; other approaches may involve thousands of people in a single event.

The common denominators among all of these varieties of critical mass events are participation, information-sharing, finding common ground, developing action plans, and implementing change quickly.

Participation is key because it can change the dynamic of a whole organization. For years, companies have tried to empower workers with varying degrees of success. Critical mass events also attempt to get employees involved and empowered, but only as a side effect. The real objective is to change the organization for the better; getting everyone involved is a means to that end.

And that makes sense. If the decision to change a company is a mandate from the top, it usually generates resistance, cynicism or apathy among employees. If, however, front-line workers labor alongside executives and managers to build the new organization, buy-in is a likely byproduct. In critical mass events that rely on table groups, the tables tend to be mix-and-match collections. One group might consist of two managers from different divisions, an executive from a third division, and five employees from various areas.

The beauty of a critical mass event: Every viewpoint and area of expertise, from front-line worker to supplier to customer to executive to stockholder, is present.

For example, Mobil Oil's Gulf of Mexico operation recently held a large-group event in New Orleans that involved more than 400 employees. The objective was to discuss how to turn Mobil into a high-performance organization. At this meeting, roustabouts who work on oil rigs in the Gulf of Mexico sat in table groups with executives and managers. This was probably the first time these disparate individuals have been in the same room, much less discussed business concerns, says Marleah Rogers, employee-relations leader with Mobil's Gulf of Mexico operation in New Orleans. "We like to get [input from the] roustabouts on up because this is about all of us creating our future together," she says.

According to Robert Jacobs, a partner with Five Oceans Consulting in Ann Arbor, MI, and author of the book *Real-Time Strategic Change*, another important part of the critical mass equation is a common database of information. During these large-group meetings, you don't have to go outside the room to get the information you need to make a decision. Every viewpoint and area of expertise, from front-line worker to supplier to customer to executive to stockholder, is present.

Sometimes if it's impossible to get representatives of all the groups in the room, people role-play stakeholders. Bill Fitzgerald, vice president of organizational development and human resources for Comstock Michigan Fruit, a Rochester, NY, division of Curtis Burns Foods, tells of a meeting in which one individual played the role of a company bondholder (the company had recently sold bonds to help finance an acquisition). The faux bondholder got up and said, "I'm 32. I drive a Porsche. I have three goals right now: to make money, to make money, and to make money. I don't care about your jobs. I don't care about your families. I care about my 12½ percent. And you owe that to me twice a year on this date." That, says Fitzgerald, brought home the reality of the situation to the people in the room in a way that just explaining it couldn't.

It's not just information from the outside that is shared in a critical mass event. Because such a mixed bag of functions and levels are represented in table groups, some surprising conversations occur among people who never had reason to talk before. There's often quite a bit of laughter when front-line people report to the group what's actually going on with customers or on the shop floor, Passmore says. He's even seen a case in which managers and executives tried to convince front-line workers that they weren't actually seeing what they were seeing. There was a real sense, says Passmore, that "that can't possibly be happening here."

'And the Scales Fell From Their Eyes...'

Once this information exchange and participation gets started, a miracle happens. No, not really. But a certain energy is generated, although everyone who has led or participated in these meetings has a difficult time describing it.

Consultant Jacobs calls it alignment, the point at which people begin to see how the organization fits together as a whole system. In his book *Discovering Common Ground*, Marvin Weisbord describes this alignment as — you guessed it — common ground.

Sandra Janoff, co-director of SearchNet, a nonprofit group dedicated to furthering future-search methods, and partner in Future Search Associates, a consulting firm in Philadelphia, works closely with Weisbord on future-search conferences. These events are designed to help organizations collaborate at all levels to find an ideal future and then aim for that future. Janoff says she and Weisbord try to develop "a group that's able to hold on to its differences, work in spite of differences, and choose to go forward on similarities. That's the key shift that happens in our work."

The energy, as Janoff describes it, becomes transformative when the group decides to work beyond intractable issues toward a more ideal common future. Janoff says she's never facilitated a future-search conference in which the group failed to find this common ground. In one case, she and Weisbord were working with a group composed of managers, union members, union negotiators, internal customers, shop stewards and upper managers. The tension in the room was palpable. But after the group established what it *couldn't* talk about, Janoff says, it went forward and found some common ground.

Kathleen Dannemiller, president emeritus of Dannemiller Tyson Associates, a large-scale meeting consulting firm in Ann Arbor, MI, describes this alignment as "one brain, one heart." But, she adds, it's a very complex union of brain and heart that encompasses a wide array of individuals who have joined together for a common purpose.

That's all well and good, but what's to stop a critical mass event from turning into a warm, fuzzy, brainstorming session — one of those affairs where everyone leaves feeling as if they've just had a big oriental dinner, filled up temporarily but hungry again in two hours?

One of the most significant aspects of these large-group interventions is the final action plans built into all of the models. Action planning means that participants do more than just talk about change: They must commit to the change in concrete and practical ways.

Birgitt Bolton is the executive director of Wesley Urban Ministries, a large social service organization in Hamilton, Ontario. She facilitates open-space meetings both for Wesley and as a consultant to private companies. She recently held an open-space meeting on the issue of creating a

CRITICAL MASS MODELS

We could lump large-scale interventions under one big category and just leave it at that. But if you're contemplating a critical mass event for your organization, you might find it helpful to know the labels and the players involved. Here are the primary practitioners of the most popular variations on the theme:

• *Future-Search Conferences.* The goal in these meetings is to help the organization find an ideal future and aim for it. The event is typically scheduled for 16 hours over three days. The ideal size is 64 people (eight tables with eight participants at each). Marvin Weisbord and Sandra Janoff, partners in the consulting firm Future Search Associates in Philadelphia, are the recognized experts in this method. It closely resembles the search conference invented by Eric Trist and Fred Emery. Emery's wife, Merrelyn Emery, who is on the faculty of the Australian National University in Canberra, developed the methodology over the last 30 years and runs search conferences all over the world.

• *Conference Model.* This comprehensive system involves up to four separate two- or three-day events. It is used to accomplish a top-to-bottom redesign of an organization and includes a customer/supplier conference, a vision conference (sometimes using future-search methodology), a technical conference, and a design conference. Dick Axelrod, a partner in the Axelrod Group Inc., a consulting firm in Wilmette, IL, created this system. The method can be reconfigured to fit the needs of an organization, he says, so you don't necessarily have to go through the "whole treatment."

• *Large-Scale Interactive Process.* Kathleen Dannemiller, president emeritus of Dannemiller Tyson Associates, a consulting firm in Ann Arbor, MI, uses this method to implement organizationwide changes. This intervention, like many others, involves mix-and-match table groups of eight to 10 people and usually lasts three days. Dannemiller recommends using it with groups of up to 600 participants, although she has used it with much larger groups.

• *Real-Time Strategic Change.* This approach grew out of Dannemiller's work in large-group interventions and is likewise used to implement organizationwide change. It was developed by Robert "Jake" Jacobs, a partner with Five Oceans Consulting in Ann Arbor, MI, and author of the book *Real-Time Strategic Change*, who worked with Dannemiller's firm for many years. The event follows a similar trajectory as the Dannemiller intervention, but Jacob stresses that this is an approach to work, rather than just an event. The event, he says, is just the beginning of a process that changes the way an organization works.

• *Participative Work Redesign.* Another innovation from Fred Emery, this one emphasizes a democratic approach to job design. The people who do the work are in the best position to determine how it should be done, explains Robert Rehm, a consultant in Boulder, CO, who works with Fred and Merrelyn Emery. This too involves table groups of eight to 10, a three-day event, and is suitable for groups of 30 to 40 participants, rather than hundreds. It often follows a search conference; the vision for the future of the organization is established before this event occurs.

• *Open-Space Meetings.* This is the least structured event. Its creator, Harrison Owen, president of H. H. Owen and Co., a consulting company in Potomac, MD, calls it a technique for holding better meetings, not just large-group events. The group gathers, a blank page on the wall constitutes the agenda, and participants are encouraged to sponsor their own discussions by writing the title of their "session" on one of the many flip charts in the room. People then gravitate to the topic of their choice. The strengths of this method lie in the safety and openness of the space created for the discussion, says its creator. The bane of open space: someone who tries to control the meeting or take it to a predetermined outcome.

community health center. Participants included government ministers and the marginalized people who would be served by the center. Wesley already had the $750,000 grant to build the facility; it remained to work out the specifics.

When it came to action planning, the homeless people in the meeting "were willing to take responsibility for this health center, against what everyone has told me," says Bolton. The marginalized people on the steering committee, for example, will elect the board of governors for the health center and get the paperwork together so the center can be incorporated. As customers of the health center, the homeless determined that the standard package of medical care was inappropriate. Instead, explains Bolton, they decided the center should stress psychological care, emotional counseling, dentistry and foot care. At the end of three days, the group had appointed 21 people to a steering committee that would determine what kind of services the health center would provide.

If the event is just about brainstorming, the change process comes to a grinding halt, warns Bolton. "But when you have to ask yourself if you'll put your name on the bottom line and take responsibility," she says, the large-group meeting becomes meaningful.

Action planning is the beginning of real change in the organization, says consultant Jacobs. When people commit to new ways of working, they are already starting to work in a different way. For example, barriers that are broken down between departments at the event often stay down when people get back to work. Consequently, he argues, transferring what happened in the event back to the job is not so big a leap because a significant proportion of the organization has already touched, seen and participated in a new way of working. That makes transfer and buy-in all the easier.

The action planning that occurs in large-group meetings is not your typical end-of-the-training-session variety: Everyone who *can* make a decision is in the room; no one needs to wait for a decision "from above" to implement a plan. Moreover, if someone tries to stall the process by pleading that more information is needed, it is quite likely the holder of that information is also present. That's why it's important to get as many stakeholders as possible to attend the event.

Even board members should be included in a critical mass event. One source, who prefers anonymity, relates an incident that demonstrates why: At one organization, the board of directors was not as involved as it should have been, either in designing or participating in the large-group meeting. At the end of the event, after the action plans had been agreed to and the group had just given the executives a standing ovation, one of the board members stood to announce that "the iron boot of the board will be on the neck of the executives to make sure they carry this through."

The law of two feet governs open-space meetings: Anyone who is bored, not learning or not contributing is honor-bound to walk out of the discussion.

So the group had one brain, one heart, and one iron boot. The incident showed the manager who shared this story that the board really didn't get it. The director's threat didn't destroy the community spirit that had been built, but it certainly shattered the mood.

How Much Structure Is Enough?

While critical mass events have a basic philosophy in common, the various methods look dramatically different. The most obvious differences lie in the structure. Open-space meetings, for example, have very little structure, while Dannemiller's large-scale interactive process involves a lot of up-front work, including lists of who should attend, specific issues that will be dealt with, and a detailed agenda.

Regardless of the critical mass method to be employed, many consultants begin by choosing a task force of cross-functional employees to plan the event — just as they would for a traditional OD effort.

Instead of spending a year gathering information, these planning committees simply plan the event, making sure the right people will attend and setting up the agenda and activities. Often another team handles logistics, seeing to it that handouts, pens, flip charts, sound systems, microphones and meal orders are in place. This team's job is to ensure that the meeting remains distraction-free. Comstock's Fitzgerald contends that the logistics team is the backbone of the event; without good logistics, the meeting can easily get bogged down.

The planning committee should be a microcosm of the group that will attend the event, says Dannemiller. Dannemiller asserts that once she has a microcosm of any large group, she can plan a critical mass event that will work for the whole group, no matter how large. When Ford Motor Co. was planning to open its Mustang plant in 1993, it held a critical mass event for a group of 2,400 people in four separate ballrooms. Each ballroom had two facilitators, but it all occurred simultaneously, with Dannemiller coordinating the whole thing.

Still more structured is the conference model, created by Dick Axelrod, a partner in the Axelrod Group Inc., a consulting firm in Wilmette, IL. This conference model, a comprehensive large-scale intervention, consists of four separate events, which last from two to three days with a month between each event. The first conference is a vision quest, which focuses on creating an organization's direction for the future. Next is the customer/supplier conference, which examines the outside forces that will shape the direction of the company. The third conference is a technical meeting, which concentrates on the processes used to create the company's products or services. The final meeting is the design conference, in which the new organization is designed and action plans are developed. Each conference has a detailed agenda, group exercises, scheduled presentations, and discussion time for table groups. In some cases, there is a fifth implementation conference.

Even in a very structured event, however, there has to be some freedom to change direction. "We never have a completely open slate," says Axelrod, "[but] the outcome really has to be in question."

On the opposite end of the structure spectrum is the open-space meeting, invented by Harrison Owen, president of H. H. Owen and Co., a consulting company in Potomac, MD.

Open-space meetings have no up-front planning, no agenda, no tables, and only a few rules.

It is Owen's contention that organizations tend to be too structured and people try to control things too much. So his open-space events take the opposite tack: The large group is assembled in a room with a bunch of flip charts. Anyone who wants to talk about any aspect of the company can sponsor a discussion by writing the subject on a flip chart and gathering others who want to talk about it. Owen's meetings are governed by two sets of guidelines: the law of two feet and the four principles of open-space meetings.

The law of two feet simply states that anyone who is bored, not learning or not contributing to a particular discussion is honor-bound to use her two feet to walk out of the meeting or discussion. This law is designed to stress the voluntary nature of the event.

Owen's four principles are more Zen-like, but equally straightforward:

1. Whoever comes is the right person.
2. Whatever happens is the only thing that could have.
3. Whenever it starts is the right time.
4. When it's over, it's over.

Owen's primary caveat to anyone who wants to hold an open-space meeting: "It won't work if anyone thinks they are going to control the outcome."

The open-space model taps into the informal ways in which companies really operate, he says. "If we actually did business the way we say we do business," he contends, "we'd be out of business." Instead, open space recognizes that the employees who do the work often get the job done by circumventing the structure instead of following the formal dictates of management.

Still, Owen says, open-space meetings are not as chaotic as the press has portrayed them. A structure emerges as the meeting progresses; but rather than being imposed by those at the top of the organization, it comes from all the participants at the event. "When the space is safe and the direction is clear and the people are present, structure happens," says Owen.

Form Follows Function

Just as the structures of critical mass events vary, so do the objectives they are designed to accomplish. Axelrod's conference model, for example, is used to redesign every aspect of a company's operations. A future-search conference helps an organization's stakeholders create a shared future vision and strategic-action plans. Consultant Rehm uses participative work redesign, another method developed by Fred Emery, to help companies rebuild the processes that are either interfering with their success or hampering future effectiveness. Dannemiller uses her method to help execute popular business solutions like total quality management and reengineering. Owen says that open-space meetings can do all of the above and more.

> "I have three goals right now: to make money, to make money, and to make money. I don't care about your jobs. I don't care about your families. I care about my 12½ percent."

Professor Bunker and her compatriot, Billie Alban, president of Alban and Williams Ltd., a consulting firm in Brookfield, CT, have become proselytizers of large-group interventions. They travel the world explaining these techniques and which methods are most effective for the objectives the organizer has in mind.

Sometimes "none of the above" is the answer. Take, for example, the California government agency that decided to do a future-search conference to convince its suppliers to adopt ISO 9000 standards. The future-search method was not appropriate for the organization's objectives; the method is a way to collaborate about the future of an organization, not to sell suppliers an idea. To their credit, explains Alban, the consultants involved said so.

If you're considering a large-group intervention, pick your company's most important objectives as the focus, stress Alban and Bunker. The meetings are expensive to run. And keep in mind that if your corporate culture isn't participative, and likely never will be, a critical mass event will probably backfire. "Think about what the power structure of the organization is, and how much power management is genuinely willing to give away," says Bunker.

Leaders

It takes a special kind of facilitator to handle a group of 50 to 500 people. Most of the consultants and practitioners we spoke to stressed that the danger lies in over-facilitating, interfering with the small table groups when they don't really need help or direction. On the other hand, when 150 people start to head in a direction that won't yield positive results, it takes a strong facilitator to intercept them. At one of their workshops, Alban and Bunker asked their professional colleagues what characteristics were needed to say "no" to a group of 600 people. "They described it as chutzpah," says Bunker. "Or, in one case, one of our groups said, 'You've got to have ovaries.'"

Other necessary qualities for large-group facilitators include a good sense of humor, stage presence, comfort in the face of conflict, and an ability to interact with an audience. Janoff would add another skill: The facilitator must be able to manage the anxiety of a group faced with so much information. "We pay attention when groups are getting into fights rather than dealing with the task, when groups are doing anything but facing the issue," she says.

Owen sees his role as a facilitator of open-space meetings in more ethereal terms. In one case, he was doing a meeting with sugar workers in Latin America who, in previous weeks, had held the plant manager and shop steward at machete point. "My job under those circumstances is to kind of hold the space, and everybody else's job is to get the job done," says Owen. If he does it right, he explains, no one remembers who facilitated the meeting. In the case of the sugar workers, he says, all he did that was observable was sit beneath a tree and tip his sombrero from time to time.

Both Owen and Bolton say they prepare for an open-space meeting by meditating.

Courage and Commitment

While critical mass events have been around for 20 years, we are only now seeing significant numbers of companies and communities using them. We are still learning how they work. A lot of questions remain to be answered. For example, how do you create a safe environment for participants, but still use the anxious energy of the group to keep people from sitting on their hands? How do you balance the structure and chaos of the event so you get results without forcing your solutions down the throats of the participants? And once you get everyone in the room participating and taking responsibility, how do you deal with issues of workplace democracy and authority?

We do know that the decision to use a large-scale intervention requires a certain kind of leadership. "It is a very courageous thing for the leaders to do," Mobil's Rogers says. "You either do this really well and commit to radically changing your own behavior or you do damage to your organization. You'd better be committed going into it. There are no two ways about that."

Yet more and more leaders seem willing to make that commitment. Why? Perhaps because if critical mass interventions work their magic, say proponents, organizations see results immediately, not a year down the road. Rogers sums it up: "You are making decisions right there in the room. You're changing behaviors right there in the room. You're using your processes right there in the room. So people who are part of that experience will never be the same. And that's fundamental change."

For Further Reading

Discovering Common Ground, by Marvin Weisbord and 35 international co-authors, Berrett-Kohler Publishers, San Francisco, 1992.

Real-Time Strategic Change, by Robert Jacobs, Berrett-Kohler Publishers, San Francisco, 1994.

The Journal of Applied Behavioral Science, Special Issue, December 1992, Volume 28, No. 4, Sage Periodicals Press, Newbury Park, CA.

Large Group Interventions for Organizational Change: Concepts, Methods and Cases, compiled and edited by Tom Chase. "Readings" from a March 1995 meeting in Dallas sponsored by the OD Network. Contact: Tom Chase, OD Network, Northwood, NH.

Tales from Open Space, edited by Harrison Owen, Abbott Publishing, Potomac, MD, 1995.

Future Search, by Marvin Weisbord and Sandra Janoff, Berrett-Kohler Publishers, San Francisco, 1995.

Notes:

The Case for Using Personality Tests in Training

If your personality is fixed, why assess it in a training program designed to change behavior? Good question. Here's an answer.

BY JOHN J. HUDY, RONALD A. WARREN AND CHRISTOPHER W. GUEST

Personality assessment has become a popular way to kick off a management development program. The feedback from a "personality test" acts as a sort of needs analysis for the individual. The premise is that managers who glean insights into their own strengths and weaknesses will be more willing and able to make changes in their behavior — changes that will allow them to operate more effectively.

We know, of course, that managers' personalities affect the ways in which they approach their jobs. Human behavior is not only the result of rational analysis and choice, but also of deeply set personality traits and attitudes. Hence the idea that an effort to improve managerial performance depends upon increasing a person's awareness of how personality traits affect attitudes and behavior on the job.

Still, the use of personality assessments in management training programs remains controversial. At the heart of the controversy is a question that is both philosophical and practical: Why use feedback about personality — personal characteristics that are enduring and unchanging over time — when the goal of training is to change behavior?

Good question. Ready for an answer?

Ground Zero

What is personality? It would be easy to answer that question if everyone defined personality the same way, but they don't. Even among psychologists who study personality, "there is no absolute or generally agreed upon definition as to what personality is," wrote Lawrence Pervin of Rutgers University in his 1975 book *Personality: Theory, Assessment and Research*.

In a sense, the diversity of personality theories reflects the nature of the beast itself. Personality is not simply one thing: Most psychologists agree that it is multidimensional, composed of the unconscious, the subconscious, the conscious and, finally, behavior.

Some psychologists maintain that personality is unconscious and fixed, established by early childhood events or even by genetic makeup. This core personality is with you to stay, they argue; even long-term psychotherapy will not alter it significantly. Others contend that, while the core personality remains unchanged, certain related facets of your personality (including attitudes, interaction patterns and ways of looking at the world) are indeed changeable.

By contrast, consider the view of Gardner Lindzey of Stanford University. In *Theory of Personality* (1978), Lindzey defined personality as "the most outstanding or salient impressions a person creates in others." Richard Arvey of the University of Minnesota offered another definition in *Fairness in Selecting Employees* (1979): Personality is "a person's typical behavioral traits and characteristics."

A far cry from the "inner core" view, these two perspectives obviously suggest that personality is defined by your outward behavior — and even by the impression your behavior has on others. Like the image you see when you look in a mirror, behavior is an observable "reflection" of your personality. Thus, we contend it is legitimate and useful to focus on the intrinsic links between personality and behavior instead of trying to separate the two.

So let's lay aside the issue of personality constructs (the psychoanalytic "id," for example) that may exist on an unconscious or instinctual level. Let's consider instead some features that are conscious and more obviously related to behavior. The personality "trait" of authoritarianism is one example. You are (or at least could be) consciously aware of your own authoritarian attitudes, and these attitudes certainly are reflected in your behavior.

Traits, Attitudes and Behavior

Raymond Cattell is one of the pioneers of trait-based personality theory. In his 1965 book *The Scientific Analysis of Personality*, he described a trait as the pattern and regularity of behavior over time and in different situations.

"Trait" and "type" are often used to describe what people are like, the "structure" of their personalities. The concept of trait refers to the consistency of your response to a variety of situations. Terms that describe personality traits include rigidity, honesty, competitiveness, perfectionism and apprehensiveness.

There is an important and often-overlooked distinction between surface traits and source traits. Surface traits are expressed by behaviors that seem to go together, but do not necessarily have a common, causal root in the makeup of your personality. This becomes an issue in personality testing. An instrument that lists behaviors such as "smiles a lot" and "seems to be pleasant" appears to be measuring the source trait of amiability. But unless statistical analysis demonstrates that the instrument is reliable and valid, it may be measuring only surface traits.

How can you tell the difference between a surface trait and a source trait? You can't. But it's important to know that there *is* a difference if you are shopping for an assessment instrument.

The reason is that an instrument that measures surface traits often yields different results for the same person when it's taken at different times (today vs. next month) or in different situations (a new job). According to *Personality: Theory, Assessment and Research*, this instability occurs because a surface trait is often a mixture of several source traits. While surface traits are likely to appeal to the commonsense observer — they seem to make sense on the surface — source traits are more useful in accounting for behavior.

A source trait is expressed by several behaviors that together form a single dimension of personality. Unlike surface traits, source traits are quite stable across both time and situations. Thus, they reflect more of the true "core" or "source" aspects of personality. Source traits tap the real structural influences that underlie personality; they represent its "building blocks."

It's necessary to use the refined statistical procedures of factor analysis to measure source traits. So if you're selecting an instrument to assess various management traits for use in your organization, demand proof of its psychometric rigor (in the form of validation reports) from the publisher. A high-quality assessment tool will have ample evidence of reliable and valid measurement of source traits. Less carefully developed instruments often measure only surface traits, and will tend to rely solely upon testimonial and commonsense arguments to support themselves. The phrase *caveat emptor* applies strongly in the assessment and feedback arena.

> **The goal of many types of feedback instruments is to help you think before you act.**

By identifying source traits we can gain insights into the whys and hows of behavior. These are the traits that give rise to attitudes, which, in turn, indicate our readiness to act a certain way in a given situation. Attitudes are similar to the individual bricks that make up a house. Since we can measure your attitudes using statistical processes, we can create a picture of the "structure" of your personality and behavioral tendencies.

Assessment Tools

Many assessment tools, such as the Myers-Briggs Type Indicator, FIRO-B and Acumen, have been developed to assess a manager's "thinking style." In fact, the term "thinking style" has become a catchphrase to describe the hierarchical relationship among traits, attitudes and behavior.

Research conducted by Peter D. Gratzinger, Ronald Warren and Rob A. Cooke (included in *Measures of Leadership*, published by the Center for Creative Leadership in 1990) demonstrated that attitudes arising from traits such as approval, dependence, self-actualization and achievement-orientation play a key role in managerial effectiveness.

Why is it important to assess or "measure" attitudes? Simply because what gets measured gets done. If you want to change a manager's attitudes and behavior, measure them. Measurement gets our attention, helps define exactly what changes are required and can provide important data about how to make the change.

That's what self-assessment inventories are designed to do. Many measure traits by collecting information about attitudes — specific attitudes clearly related to important behavior patterns.

This brings us to the heart of the matter: Even though some of the attitudes that produce counterproductive behavior will resist change, the behavior itself can be modified through learning and personal insight.

Developing an Observing Ego

The "black box" model of human behavior can help us understand the role of assessment and feedback in the change process. According to this model, you receive stimuli from the environment, process them in your mind (the "black box"), and respond with behavior of some kind. Over time, you develop habitual ways of processing and responding. For example, some people are easily angered, some look quickly to others for structure and direction, and some try to dominate. These habits are both attitudinal and behavioral.

Many self-assessment inventories are intended to help you better understand the causes of your habitual responses to situations. Once you understand the impact your attitudes have on your behavior, you can choose alternative responses. Simply put, the goal of many types of feedback instruments is to help you think before you act.

Psychologists refer to this as developing an "observing ego." By ego, we mean the rational, reality-oriented part of the psyche that people use to live in and adapt to the world. By developing these self-observation skills, you develop a capacity to observe, monitor, evaluate and, therefore, modify your behavior.

> **The diversity of personality theories reflects the nature of the beast itself.**

For instance, consider managers who are aggressive, driven and impatient — the ones with so-called "Type A" personalities. For these managers, the goal of the assessment-and-feedback process would be to develop self-observation skills to monitor the effects of their controlling, impatient attitudes on their behavior. Even if they retain their driven attitudes — even if they still feel impatience and a need to dominate — they can choose to alter their behaviors. The key is quite simple: Think before you act and then behave in a more patient and cooperative manner.

In short, a self-assessment inventory will not change your attitudes. But it can help you develop an observing ego that checks your first, counterproductive impulse and prompts you to follow a more productive course of action.

Focus On Change

Self-assessment inventories, and the feedback that comes with them, can show you how your attitudes are affecting your ability to reach your goals. They can also show you how to use your strengths and compensate for your weaknesses.

Since your attitudes have been formed by a lifetime of accumulated experience, they will not be changed quickly or easily; behavior is much easier to modify. Nevertheless, changing an attitude is certainly possible. Feedback from co-workers or subordinates can play a key role here. When you compare others' perceptions of your thinking and management style with your own perceptions, you may be moved to change not only your behavior but some underlying attitudes as well.

Let's say as a result of self-assessment and group feedback, you've identified an attitude you would like to change. How do you proceed?

First, identify examples and situations in which this attitude-related behavior occurs. If you are extremely competitive, for example, what do you tend to do to compete with others? When do you do it? When and how does it undercut your effectiveness?

Next, acknowledge the value of thinking and behaving in new ways in those situations. Practice behaving in a different way in situations that evoke your old, competitive attitude. Pay attention to how others respond to you. Their responses to your changed behavior may lead you to develop a new attitude about the situation.

Why do personality tests show up so often in management-development programs? Because a manager's job is to achieve the organization's goals through the work of others. That means leading, influencing, directing, persuading, inspiring, coaching, demanding — and knowing when to just get out of the way. To do any of this effectively, managers need all the insight they can get into how they are perceived by others and how their attitudes affect their behavior.

Notes:

Mentoring: The Democratic Version

Used to be, a 'mentor' was someone older, wiser and more experienced than you. Someone with clout. Today, it ain't necessarily so.

BY ERIK GUNN

In a telephone company with a reputation for complacent conservatism, the new hire was a shot of adrenaline.

Actually, more like a spine-stiffening jolt. The employee, recruited from the cable television industry, was "totally market-driven — a very aggressive person who brought some really assertive characteristics," recalls Nancy Teutsch, a vice president for human resources at Ameritech, the Chicago-based five-state Baby Bell. The same hard-charging drive that had helped him get the job in the first place was almost his undoing.

"This person came in and almost instantly alienated people by talking about 'Bell-heads' and criticizing our old culture," Teutsch says. True, Ameritech itself was trying desperately to change many attributes of that culture, but the new hotshot broadcast his scorn "in such a way that it appeared he was criticizing his team members. People viewed that as so obnoxious they didn't hear the wisdom he was bringing about fast cycle time and market responsiveness."

Managers intervened and the man shaped up, Teutsch says. But the experience was typical of problems that led to a program at Ameritech for new hires, especially those from other industries. The telephone company teams newcomers with more seasoned types for 60 to 90 days. The relationship is aimed at helping newcomers ease into the company without squelching the ideas, attitudes or skills for which they were hired in the first place.

Ameritech doesn't call the program "mentoring." The official term for staffers who fill the mentor role is "reciprocal guide"; Teutsch uses the nickname "coaching buddy." But despite its short-term time frame, the reciprocal-guide program reflects much of what's happening in formal mentoring programs around the nation.

In what Tom Peters likes to call "the nanosecond '90s," corporate mentoring programs haven't gone away. But today's versions tend to be more tightly focused and shorter in duration. At the same time, many are more open, at least on paper, to a broader range of employees within a company. And while a wave of popularity for mentoring programs in the mid-1980s was sparked in part by efforts to improve the promotion and retention of women and minorities, today's programs often reflect a wider variety of corporate agendas. Even where the explicit aim is to improve a company's cultural diversity, the consensus is growing that white men, not just women and nonwhites, should be provided with mentors if they want.

They're Back

Formal mentoring programs blossomed in the decade after management theorist Rosabeth Moss Kanter concluded in 1977 that having a mentor was critical to career success. Employers wanting to improve the representation of women and minorities in the executive ranks created specialized mentoring programs to help achieve that goal. In 1993, more than one in five respondents to a joint survey for the Society for Human Resource Management and the publishing firm Commerce Clearing House said their workplaces had mentoring programs geared for minorities; twice as many rated such programs as necessary.

Affirmative action for women and minorities wasn't the only aim, of course. Many firms either established structured mentoring programs or simply encouraged managers to create informal mentoring relationships as an additional tool for succession-planning, making sure future leaders were constantly in the pipeline.

Now, after a few years of quiescence, mentoring programs are back. No source could cite numbers, but many observers see a definite resurgence of interest. "Every time I turn around people are talking about developing a mentoring program," says Marquette University management professor Belle Rose Ragins, who studies women's issues in business.

"Employers and organizations are not offering the kind of security and caretaking that they used to," adds Kathleen Kram, who teaches organizational behavior at the Boston University School of Management and consults with private companies on mentoring. Whether formal or informal, says Kram, "mentoring is seen as an alternative to that."

Indeed, far from being cast off as expensive frills in the endless rounds of corporate restructuring and downsizing of the early 1990s, some mentoring programs actually have been fueled by the changes. That's the case with Ameritech's "coaching buddy" program. Even as the company has been selectively hiring experienced managers and professionals from other industries, Ameritech has shed thousands of white-collar employees in the last several years to gird for emerging competition in local and long-distance telephone service.

The same is happening elsewhere. "As organizations downsize, the people who are kept in an organization tend to have deeper skills in a specific area," says Margo Murray, president of MMHA, an Oakland, CA, consulting firm, and author of the book *Beyond the Myths and Magic of Mentoring*. Downsizing companies may turn to mentors to teach additional skills to workers who remain, in hopes of creating a more flexible work force. "We're seeing more pairing for specific skills rather than pairing [in the sense of], 'I'll tuck you under my wing and take you along for the rest of your life,'" Murray says.

In addition, firms "are hiring external expertise at higher levels than they did before," Murray says. A bank, for instance, may turn to someone from the securities industry to manage a branch office as its financial products expand. The new manager needs coaching in the bank's culture, but also needs an opportunity to share knowledge that may be new to his banking colleagues. "We're creating more mentoring partnerships, so it's a two-way transfer of skills and experience," Murray adds.

This more democratic approach to mentoring appears increasingly popular. Traditionally, "the mentor is someone who provides wise counsel," says William Gray, who operates The Mentoring Institute Inc., a Vancouver, British Columbia, consulting firm. "There's still a place for that. But it is only half the concept of mentoring that we use. The other half is that the mentor acknowledges that today's protégés are better-educated and know more than the protégés of yesterday. They bring with them ideas, creativity, initiative, responsibility, a passion to do something. The mentor needs to empower protégés as well as to equip them with what the mentor already knows."

A Sense of Inclusion

In much the same spirit, companies are moving away from mentoring programs that focus only on minorities and women. "Organizations, in a variety of ways, are trying to figure out how to make mentoring more available to a wider group of employees," says Boston University's Kram.

Take General Electric Co. The Fairfield, CT-based conglomerate's mentoring program grew out of earlier efforts often tailored primarily for minorities and women at GE subsidiaries. And the goal of the program remains creating "an environment that is inclusive," says Gene Andrews, the parent company's manager of work force diversity.

"We are investing quite a bit in recruiting the best that we can," Andrews says. "We want people as they join this organization to as quickly as possible feel a real sense of inclusion so that there's no question that they're part of the team."

Orientation programs and a "buddy system" for new employees help, he continues, but if women and minorities get left out of the informal loop — sharing lunch or getting a drink after work with some of the older white men who continue to dominate the managerial ranks, for instance — then they feel excluded. Their growth is stifled, their productivity and innovation suffers, and in the long run they may go elsewhere, forcing the company to replace them at a cost of as much as $100,000 per person, Andrews estimates.

But the very value of inclusiveness quickly led GE to make its mentoring program available to everyone. One reason was to avoid backlash of the sort dogging affirmative action programs — the notion that a program exclusively for minorities and women constitutes a form of preferential treatment. But another seemingly contradictory concern was even more important: making sure everyone in the organization takes mentoring seriously. "If it's seen as a program just for women and minorities, in the eyes of the majority it loses its value," Andrews says.

Kram, who worked with GE in establishing its program, says that approach reflects a general movement in corporate America to go beyond narrowly drawn affirmative action goals to the more sweeping objective of managing diversity: "There's a shift in orientation from helping women and people of color to creating a culture that empowers all people of whatever background to succeed."

Moreover, not all white men have benefited from mentoring, either. When consultant Gray gives workshops, he asks everyone — including the men — if they can recall a time "when they needed mentoring and no one stepped forward to provide it," Gray says. "Almost every hand goes up."

Today GE, with 157,000 U.S. employees, boasts more than 1,000 pairs of mentors and protégés around the corporation. Mentoring is most heavily entrenched at the company's appliance-manufacturing unit in Louisville, KY. There GE has matched 300 pairs of mentors and protégés. Among them are 12-year GE veteran Doug King, 34, operations manager for laundry manufacturing, and Lance Harrington, 28, a process engineer who has been at the company for five years. King has mentored Harrington for more than two years, and also has had a mentor of his own.

"The mentoring is very informal," King says. "Sometimes we might see each other five times a week; other times, not for two months."

For Harrington, the program proved its value when he joined a team that was working on a problem involving the use of new plastic-molding equipment. What he lacked in experience Harrington made up for in enthusiasm, sparked by classes he was taking on the subject of injection molding plastic. Harrington's studies suggested to him a solution to the problem.

Persuading his more seasoned teammates proved difficult, however.

MENTORING DO'S AND DON'TS

Not everyone agrees on all the details, but companies with mentoring programs usually subscribe to similar rules. Among them:

• Do make a business case for a program, and get top management commitment for it.

• Don't limit the program to certain groups — minorities and women, for instance. Otherwise, you may stigmatize the beneficiaries and inspire backlash among the excluded.

• Tell mentors and protégés about what to expect from the relationship and what not to expect. If there are cross-cultural mentor-protégé pairs, train the partners as well in sensitivity to those issues.

• Don't portray the program as a guaranteed path to promotion — and communicate clearly to dispel that impression.

• Do clarify and communicate your selection criteria for mentors. And recognize that not every good employee has the right style to be a successful mentor.

Experts differ on how easy it ought to be for mentors and protégés in formal programs to opt out of "arranged marriages." In some companies, like General Electric Co., that's easy to do early on if the relationship isn't working. Others encourage protégés to stick with the partnership even if things get rocky, urging them to use the opportunity to learn from and get along with people different from themselves. — E.G.

He kept talking, but they weren't listening, King recalls. It turned out that Harrington's analysis was the correct one. The experience left Harrington feeling a bit like Wesley Crusher — the brilliant teenage ensign on television's "Star Trek: The Next Generation" who forever must overcome the patronizing skepticism of the adult crew. Harrington went to King for advice on "how I could have gotten those team members to listen to me quicker." He credits King with helping him develop a facilitator's style: drawing out everyone's ideas, then taking the group through them methodically. As a result, he says, "Now I'm one of the team."

CSX Transportation in Jacksonville, FL, a unit of CSX Corp., designed its mentoring program to include hourly, unionized employees, not just managers and professionals. Protégés are matched with more senior-level mentors, not necessarily from the same departments, for a period of one year. The railroad's mentoring program grew out of concerns in the late 1980s about the lack of advancement among women and minorities, though it has always been open to white males as well, says Derrick Smith, assistant vice president for minerals marketing at the rail carrier.

Up to now the opportunity to be assigned a mentor has been offered only to employees in nonoperating departments such as sales and marketing, finance and the like — about 20 percent of the company's 29,000 employees. (About 130 people have actually been paired up with mentors in five years.) This year CSX began a pilot project to introduce mentoring to its operations employees, the bulk of its work force.

Grass Roots

While some mentoring programs are highly structured, both GE and CSX keep theirs very informal. GE outlines some broad objectives to make sure each of its 12 member companies develops a mentoring program, but leaves many of the details up to individual business units. The CSX program is not administered by the company's human resources department, although department representatives join those from other areas in the team that runs it.

"This is an employee-driven, grass-roots effort, run by a committee of employees," says CSX's Smith. With this committee matching mentors and protégés, the program has more credibility, adds Doug Klippel, manager of organizational development at the corporation: "We aren't seen so much as a flavor-of-the-month from human resources."

By contrast, Douglas Aircraft Co. in Long Beach, CA, a unit of McDonnell Douglas Corp. of St. Louis, has a much more structured mentoring pro-

> "We don't put a gun to anybody's head. You're talking about people who are there because they want to be."

gram in which protégés are hand-picked based on their promotion potential. However, enrollment in the program is neither a guarantee nor a requirement for future promotion, says Susan Boyle, a senior human resources specialist at Douglas.

Boyle acknowledges that because the program is open only to a select few, it runs the risk of being resented as elitist. But side by side with the formal program is a corporate expectation that "every employee should have a mentor and be a mentor," Boyle says. Using guidelines laid out in a Douglas handbook that goes to all salaried employees, "every employee here can have a mentor if they want one," she adds.

If every employee, no matter how inexperienced, can also *be* a "mentor," the term obviously is used very loosely. This is the case with many of the informal, "democratic" relationships currently being described under the rubric of mentoring. They often are a far cry from what most people would still think of as the real thing.

Perhaps the most dramatic example of the new, more democratic approach to mentoring is group mentoring. Beverly Kaye, a Sherman Oaks, CA, consultant who has promoted mentoring groups with colleague Betsy Jacobson, sees a group approach as the logical extension of efforts to flatten hierarchies and encourage teamwork. "The group process says we can learn from each other as peers," Kaye says. "If it's one on one, you hear only the advice of the person on high."

In Kaye's scheme, a senior staffer still plays the role of mentor, but "the agenda is in the hands of the 'mentees,' not the mentor," she says. "The mentor comes in and responds to the kinds of things that the mentees want. It empowers the group to really think about what they want. It supports the notion of teams in organizations, and it supports the idea of diversity in action."

Compare that approach — or Douglas Aircraft's "everyone can be a mentor" campaign — with Douglas' formal mentoring effort for high-potential employees. The elite program is closely monitored, with written surveys of participants and a steering committee that revises the program periodically. Mentors and protégés also set goals and objectives for the protégé to meet during the yearlong period the relationship is to operate, and evaluate progress toward achieving them.

GE, meanwhile, relies mainly on focus groups of employees to gauge results and fine-tune its program. At CSX, where pairings last at least a year, the company evaluates its program by surveying participants halfway through and again two months after the 12-month period ends. Those surveys, says Klippel, are aimed at helping CSX "build a profile of what a successful relationship looks like."

Consultant Murray says that evaluation of mentoring programs has never been more important: "I really believe that in today's economic environment, unless you measure and show results, no new systems or programs stay in place." Murray's firm uses a test to measure improvement among protégés in skills such as time management, communication and decision-making.

Ideally, Murray says, a mentoring program is integrated into the organization's overall systems for grooming and developing its work force. "If an organization maintains it and supports it, it becomes a way of life."

Flameouts

But some programs don't last. At the Internal Revenue Service in Kansas City, MO, a mandatory mentoring program for new managers begun about five years ago has been phased out, says Phyllis Kitchen, an employee development specialist. With the advent of government reengineering a couple of years ago, our managerial ranks thinned," Kitchen says. "We don't have enough people to make it meaningful or workable right now."

And like many other human resources initiatives, some programs fade when their champions move on. That's what appears to have happened at the *Norfolk Virginian-Pilot* and *Ledger-Star* newspapers, where newsroom employees for a while were getting cross-training from colleagues in a short-term, one-on-one program. When Connie Sage, the newsroom editor in charge of staff development, moved into a corporate position with parent company Landmark Communications Inc., the program largely disappeared, Sage says.

Formal mentoring programs continue to face skepticism in some quarters, dismissed as little more than "arranged marriages." At Ameritech, the same company that has begun providing new hires with short-term "coaching buddies," Neal Kulick, another human resources vice president, remains wary of longer-term, more formalized arrangements. "I don't think you can prearrange matches between people that will sustain themselves over time," Kulick says.

But Kulick's own unit of the company doesn't rely entirely on chance to create mentoring relationships. Senior managers meet regularly to review the names of newly promoted and talented junior managers, and quietly assign themselves the job of getting to know them individually. "It's something we can do to accelerate the development of high-potential people," Kulick says. "We set up additional relationships to broaden people's knowledge of who the talent is. It's informal, there are no rules, and nobody's writing reports."

At the same time, he adds, the company is trying to create an atmosphere of self-reliance in which junior employees and senior ones alike form mentor-protégé relationships on their own. "When people come into the business, we explain to them that nothing's going to get handed to you," Kulick says. "We try to motivate the parties to be out there looking for matches, if you will, but [we don't] try to arrange them. Some people network well and some people don't."

Of course, it's for that very reason that advocates say formal mentoring programs are needed — to help those who don't excel at networking. And companies that have mentoring programs, along with the consultants who help establish them, say the idea can work. As for the "arranged marriage" criticism, "this is a voluntary thing," says CSX's Klippel. "We don't put a gun to anybody's head. You're talking about people who are there because they want to be, and people who want to be involved in these programs tend to make things work."

Notes: